The Form of the Unfinished

The Form of the Unfinished

*English Poetics
from Spenser to Pound*

BALACHANDRA RAJAN

Princeton University Press
Princeton, New Jersey

Published by Princeton University Press, 41 William Street,
Princeton, New Jersey 08540
In the United Kingdom: Princeton University Press, Guildford, Surrey

Library of Congress Cataloging in Publication Data will be
found on the last printed page of this book

ISBN 0-691-06637-X

Publication of this book has been aided by The Andrew W. Mellon
Fund of Princeton University Press

This book has been composed in Linotron Palatino

Clothbound editions of Princeton University Press books
are printed on acid-free paper, and binding materials are
chosen for strength and durability

Printed in the United States of America by Princeton University Press
Princeton, New Jersey

Contents

Acknowledgments

THIS BOOK BEGAN in an essay on Marvell which C. A. Patrides urged me into writing several years ago. I am grateful to him above others for his foresight and support and for the sense of direction his persuasions gave me. My thanks also go to Joseph Wittreich and to George Bornstein for their attentive and sympathetic reading of the manuscript on behalf of the publishers. I am particularly indebted to Joseph Wittreich for suggesting that I add an interchapter which, I believe, contributes materially to the cohesion of the book. Stuart Sperry very kindly read the Keats chapter, making suggestions I have attempted to incorporate and raising queries I have endeavoured to meet. Among my colleagues, I am grateful to Ross Woodman for reading and listening to parts of the book and for sharing my thoughts on Romanticism. A. C. Hamilton, Kent Hieatt, and Elizabeth Bieman encouraged me by their open-minded responsiveness to the distinctive view of *The Faerie Queene* which I advance in these pages. Tilottama Rajan brought to the reading of five chapters a receptive and vigilant understanding which has helped me to sharpen several discriminations. Chandra Rajan contributed not just her generous acceptance of the demands a wide-ranging book must make, but also her radiant translation of Rig Veda X, 129. Launa Fuller typed the manuscript with accuracy in the midst of many duties.

The writing of this book was greatly assisted by a sabbatical year granted by the University of Western Ontario and by a Leave Fellowship from the Social Sciences and Humanities Research Council of Canada.

ACKNOWLEDGMENTS

The chapter on Marvell first appeared in *Approaches to Marvell*, edited by C. A. Patrides and published in 1978 by Routledge and Kegan Paul. The chapter entitled "*Paradise Lost*: The Uncertain Epic" first appeared in *Composite Orders*, edited by R. S. Ide and Joseph A. Wittreich, Jr., and published in 1983 as *Milton Studies* XVIII by the University of Pittsburgh Press. An addition has been made to the original essay. Permission to reprint in both cases is gratefully acknowledged.

London, Ontario

The Form of the Unfinished

Introduction

THE UNFINISHED POEM is an important strand in the literary heritage. In fact three of the most notable long poems in that heritage—*The Faerie Queene, Don Juan,* and *The Cantos*—are unfinished. A fourth major long poem, *Paradise Lost,* achieves closure only by placing a completed structure of understanding around a deeply uncertain outcome. The strong affiliation which prevails between the unfinished and the history of the long poem in English is thus a matter of simple record. Yet no extended study of the unfinished seems to have been undertaken so far. This book seeks to initiate such a study.

Though five of the nine principal chapters in this book are about unfinished poems, the unfinished is not simply a matter of stopping short of a formal ending. As the most insistent form of resistance to closure, the unfinished must occupy a central position in a study such as this. But the remaining four chapters seem desirable as excursions into that environment of indeterminacy in which the unfinished assumes its formal prominence. The pervasiveness of this environment, the strength of the forces of non-closure in thought and language, will be evident, I hope, from these extensions of the central interest. Milton's powerfully logocentric poem is shown to be by no means impregnable to the forces of openness. Marvell is studied as a polished practitioner of the art of destabilization. Eliot, in his working out of the macro-poem, testifies to the ongoing self-supersession such a poem carries within its nature.

Within the poetry of indeterminacy the unfinished forms a dominant area where pervasive confrontations are thrown into relief by the poem's rejection or avoidance of closure. In delimiting this area it may be helpful to consider where the ruin stands in relation to it. Such a placing is made more desirable by Thomas McFarland's recent book *Romanticism and the Forms of Ruin*.[1] If the unfinished were simply a variant of the ruin this book might be largely a matter of extending McFarland's investigation into the Renaissance, into later Romanticism (McFarland's consideration is restricted to Wordsworth and Coleridge) and into the twentieth century. However, as will be shown, the unfinished is other than the ruin. The crucial facts about the ruin are that it was once finished and that contemplation of it is instigated by the discrepancy between the whole that was and the fragment that is. It is important not as itself, but by virtue of its position in the restorative effort which its vestigial existence appeals to the viewer to undertake. The relation of the part to the whole, the consciousness of loss, and the endeavour of retrieval which characterize our contemplation of survivals are thus singularly prominent in the way the ruin is viewed. It therefore needs to be emphasized that they are not singular to the nature of the ruin itself. In fact their foundation lies in a more inclusive form of circular seeking in which the aspiration is the union of *telos* and origin. In the earlier unfinished this form is a strong and indeed a controlling presence. But it is also a presence which can only be partially inscribed in the enterprises it regulates. The unfinished, at this stage in its development, is the poetics of this partial inscription.

The torso like the ruin implies a whole, leaving the completion of that whole to the viewer's imagination, but regulating that completion by the character of the nucleus. In announcing itself stylistically as a fragment (which any

[1] Thomas McFarland, *Romanticism and the Forms of Ruin: Wordsworth, Coleridge and the Modalities of Fragmentation*, Princeton, Princeton University Press, 1981.

4

fragment must do to be recognized as such) the torso seeks resumption of its membership in an entity which is not necessarily lost as with the ruin, but which may be withheld so that the viewer can participate in the restorative effort. Both the torso and the ruin invite completion. Their aesthetic appeal depends upon a consequential meditation aroused by the relationship between the whole and the part. This can be true even with a poem, such as *Ozymandias*, which treats the surviving trace not as vestigial, but as the reality outliving the original pretence.

Unlike the torso and the ruin, the unfinished should not invite completion. If it falls short of finality (as *The Faerie Queene* and *The Cantos* do) or resists it (as *The Triumph of Life* does), it should do so because of forces that have been demonstrated to be grounded in its nature and that forbid arrival at a closure even when (as in *The Faerie Queene*) the gestures accompanying closure are richly invoked.

The inquiry narrows when we recognize that the form of the unfinished is the form of the poem as it is and not some larger form in which the poem participates and to which we are persuaded to annex it. A poem that is properly unfinished should be less satisfactory if we were to pursue any of the conceivable ways of finishing it. Instead of speaking of its failure to achieve closure we should regard any prospective closure of it as an imminent admission of its failure.

It may be felt that to speak of the form of the unfinished is to acknowledge an addiction to paradox. If the phrase seems to repudiate itself it may be because of the conventions of criticism rather than because of the literature which that criticism addresses. The assumption that literary forms, like thought forms, ought to proceed to conclusions has been subject to increasing challenges but still has a strong hold on our minds. Current celebrations of openness have some distance to proceed before they eradicate ingrained reading habits, and it is not obviously desirable that they should simply replace the assumption of closure by its opposite. To achieve a just assessment of contesting energies, some change in receptivity may be needed. Barbara Herrnstein Smith is speaking of poets but she also speaks for many of us as readers when she observes that, up to the present, "anti-closure has been repeatedly seen as an impulse and not a reality."[2] The Romantic era bristles with unfinished poems, yet M. H. Abrams in his magisterial book seems to have little if anything to say on inconclusiveness, fragmentariness, incompleteness, indeterminacy, or the problem of the unfinished. Certainly none of these topics are listed in an index of over fifteen pages.[3] The point is made only to indicate the remarkable exclusions that are possible even with so comprehensive and judicious a work and to caution ourselves about the degree to which our findings may be controlled by the nature of our discourse. One of the frustrations of speaking about fragments is that the word itself submits to and is embed-

[2] *Poetic Closure*, University of Chicago Press, 1968, p. 261. In a later book, Smith suggests that "aperture" rather than closure could "indeed be seen as the subject of the present volume: not in the sense of openings but rather of unendings, interminables, indeterminacies." *On the Margins of Discourse*, Chicago, University of Chicago Press, 1978, p. ix. The main focus for the discussion of these possibilities is chapter VI, particularly pp. 144-45. A poem in its engagement with the reader displays "the infinitely open curve of a parabola" and forms "parables for an infinite number of propositions."

Smith does not pursue her suggestion in detail. In any case the study of non-closure here is more restrictive, confining itself to resistances within a poem insofar as the poem may be presumed to have borders. The word aperture is used conventionally in this book to signify an opening, with the shape of the œuvre controlled (particularly in Eliot) by the possibilities for continuation that are filtered through the opening.

Smith's earlier statement remains representative and influential. The further view that the events instigated by a poem beyond its boundaries are answerable to the manner in which the poem defines its boundaries is one to which this book evidently subscribes. These extraterritorial instigations can be notable in poets like Donne and Yeats in view of (and possibly because of) the firmness of their closures.

[3] *Natural Supernaturalism: Tradition and Revolution in Romantic Literature*, New York, W. W. Norton and Company, 1971.

ded in a concurrence of implicit propositions which treat it as secondary, residual, and derived, which endow it with identity only in relation to an authenticating wholeness, which grant it dissension and indeed the extreme dissension of rebellion, but which will not contemplate its revolutionary independence. "Unfinished" in this respect is a more malleable word than "fragment" since even in popular discourse the finished is not always the desirable, a fact to which more than one public figure will attest. Yet while recognizing the constraints of inherited discourse we do not necessarily advance our investigation by situating it within a counter-discourse of openness. A counter-discourse, it might be noted, is all that is possible. Historicity does not permit us innocence. It is not clear that the advocates of such a discourse will greet propositions about the form of the unfinished as anything more than defensive manoeuvres designed to safeguard the book against the text.

Once our Scylla and Charybdis have been identified, the vulnerable passage between them can be seen as charting a poetry of contestation between closural forces in a work and forces resisting closure that are equally grounded in the work's identity. It can further be suggested that tracing this passage through literary history enables us to identify models of the unfinished and to set them in relationships which are logical as well as historical. One makes this suggestion with caution and reluctance. The triumph of Proteus over Procrustes which Isabel MacCaffrey sees in the fourth book of *The Faerie Queene*[4] ought not to be reversed in a scholarly book, particularly when the phenomena being studied are the forces of resistance within a poem to incorporation in the poem's organizational field. Nevertheless it may be useful, before specific case studies are un-

[4] *Spenser's Allegory. The Anatomy of Imagination*, Princeton, Princeton University Press, 1976, pp. 330-31.

dertaken, to outline a field and to indicate the nature of some of the principal tenancies.

Contestation is most easily naturalized in literature through the confrontation of genres. Recognized genres establish codified expectations in the mind of the reader, who is then enabled to place the poem between rival possibilities and to read the poem according to his placing. Spenser's poem pits epic against romance and Virgilian purposiveness against Ariostan errancy. These oppositions can be further dichotomized as pattern versus flow, organization versus proliferation, spatial disposition versus sequential disclosure and, more modernistically, œuvre versus text. The poem, placed on the line of engagement of these two arrays, partakes of both without allowing itself to be annexed by either.

A strategy for deferral is needed if we are to make a virtue out of errancy and not simply charm the reader with digressiveness. Spenser's elegant solution is to begin the poem with a carefully over-conclusive opening encounter in which not simply Error but the entire brood of Error are destroyed. He thus places the end in the beginning in addition to advising knights and Christian wayfarers not to make too much of the first dragon that they slay. Since what we see is not simply the defeat but the eradication of error it is apparent that the end will only be at the end of time. Between the beginning of the author's poem and the end of a poem that cannot be the author's, there lies the maximum space, not only for deferral, but for those purposive movements which infiltrate deferral with the intimations of design and closure. Moreover, the end in the beginning situates in Spenser's poem a segment of that circuitous journey which *Paradise Lost* so influentially invokes and expounds and which in its secular form becomes, for Abrams, an inclusive paradigm of the Romantic consciousness.[5]

[5] The inclusiveness of the paradigm is questioned in this book. It can

Deferral and purposiveness, it has been suggested, are situated within dichotomized arrays on the engagement of which the poem is placed. The common response to such dichotomization is to privilege one family of terms, the second family then being reduced to minor or even to marginal status. It is the "purposive" array that has so far been privileged by Spenser criticism, but the state of that criticism is not necessarily advanced by reversing valuations and privileging the second array. Spenser, in fact, seems concerned to privilege neither array but the balanced attention he gives to both leaves him with the problem of bringing about the sense of an ending within the accumulating likelihood of a stalemate. He achieves this by engineering (with extraordinary skill, which will be studied later) the self-effacement of the poem itself. The vanishing of the poem enables it to remain unfinished without submitting it to arbitration by its purposiveness or by the potentially endless flow of its errancy.

Sin in *Paradise Lost* has a multiple ancestry but Spenser's Error is an important predecessor, identified as such from Newton onwards. Like Error she is to be eradicated at the end of time. Like Error she is encountered at the beginning, not of a quest, but this time of an anti-quest, the aim of which is not to build Cleopolis in the image of Jerusalem, but to re-form the new world in Pandemonium's likeness. These are important lines of connection but they are strengthened because *Paradise Lost*, like *The Faerie Queene*, is a poem of generic contestation. The difference is that the contest is not, as in Spenser, a competition between two ranges of possibility both of which speak for the poem, though in sharply different ways. In Spenser, the poem's dissensions are to be seen in the true poem of finality as manifestations of a single voice. In Milton, the final poem

---

accommodate only a restricted range of the poetry of the unfinished. Keats, Shelley, and Byron, in particular, seem to bring about between them, a significant break-away from the circuitous journey.

will celebrate a world from which the false poem has been ultimately rejected. The dichotomies we attach to Spenser's contest between epic and romance are aesthetic and, as we have seen, *The Faerie Queene* privileges neither array. Those we attach to Milton's contest between tragedy and epic are moral and ontological, and *Paradise Lost* resolutely privileges the epic array. In fact the privileging is entrenched and strengthened by the reduction of the second array to parodic status.[6] This parodic diminution not only shapes the poem's internal dispositions but is strong enough to include one of Milton's principal lines of filiation with Spenser. Sin is Error's true offspring, the fulfillment of all expectations, but she is also the inversion of Spenser's Sapience, "daughter and Darling without end" to Satan as Sapience is the Deity's "sovereign darling."[7] Because of Milton's powerful movement of valorization the structure of understanding he erects is anything but uncertain. The outcome that structure is to judge continues however to be profoundly uncertain, remaining dangerously open to incorporation by the very genre which the valorizing dismisses.

Contestation and deferral are important elements in the constitution of the unfinished, particularly when contestation creates the basis for deferral. Spenser carries this interdependence further by making deferral one of the contesting forces. Deferral in *The Faerie Queene* acknowledges one aspect of createdness, that aspect which can be named and celebrated as plenitude and creativity. Deferral in *Paradise Lost* is more defensively oriented, seeking to maintain a space in which the outcome can remain uncertain and in which human history will not betray itself into incarceration in the tragic form. But Milton is also the exponent of

---

[6] For elaboration of the two arrays see Balachandra Rajan, *The Lofty Rhyme*, London, Routledge and Kegan Paul, 1970, pp. 59-61. For Milton's use of parody see "The Cunning Resemblance," *Milton Studies* VII, Pittsburgh, University of Pittsburgh Press, 1975, pp. 27-48.

[7] *Paradise Lost*, II, 870: "Hymn of Heavenly Beauty," Stanza 27.

another, less troubled paradigm in which the space created by deferral is more confidently occupied by that creative movement which Michael does not fail to chart to Adam, but which, in his sombre exposition of history, seems unendingly undermined by man's destructive propulsions. *Areopagitica*'s master image of the torn body of Osiris puts before us an approximative model of goal-attainment, based on the fragmentation of an original whole and the progressive retrieval through time of those fragments, ending in the reinscription of origin as *telos* at the end of time. The historical basis for this model lay in Puritanism's multiplying dissensions and the desirability of interpreting those dissensions as a creative ferment within which the collective search was to be launched and out of which the redeemed consensus would emerge. The model thus responds to the questions and anxieties of its time, but it does so while maintaining its continuity with a previous form of the unfinished. Like Spenser, Milton makes deferral a space for the achieving of significance and, like Spenser, he occupies that space with the energies of contestation, though the contest is no longer one which offers itself to dexterously ambivalent readings. Truth and Error may be twin sisters but the business of the seeker is to detect the false Florimell in her innumerable masquerades. The privileging of one side enables closure to be prophesied and makes it possible to argue that the search for understanding will progressively manifest the nature of that closure. The model thus promises completion but it also shifts attention from the visionary goal to the endeavour to reach it by insisting that we can know the goal only in so far as it is inscribed in the endeavour.

Truth is self-consolidating in the Areopagitican movement to the whole truth. As the fragments are identified and gathered and the cunning resemblances discarded, we approximate more and more closely to that "homogeneal and proportional" form to be built up from its splintered

components.[8] But the movement forward may be trans-
formational rather than approximative, characterized by
qualitative leaps rather than by incremental adjustments.
Milton's insistence in the *De Doctrina* that the whole Mosaic
Law was abolished by the Gospel[9] may indicate his rec-
ognition of the transformational nature of creative change
in the theatre of history and not merely within the interior
world of the self. The typical view was that the moral part
of the Law was not abolished but that regenerate Christians
were freed from its bondage. This change in the quality of
compliance left relatively undisturbed the continuity be-
tween social structures established by deterrence and struc-
tures maintained by the spontaneous adhesion of a re-
formed community. Milton's point presumably was that
the structures of a transformed society might well be dis-
continuous from those which the fallen mind was capable
of imagining.

The internal correlative of the Areopagitican model is the
reconstitution of the divine image in the self. The impair-
ment, burial, mutilation, and defacement which in sev-
enteenth-century theological literature characterize the state
of the image in fallen consciousness suggest both slow
progress carefully safeguarded and verified and the sudden
illuminations of crucial discoveries. There are transforma-
tional barriers which can be crossed only by the interven-
tion of grace or, as in *The Fall of Hyperion*, by a capacity for
survival that seems both earned and dispensed. In Milton's
understanding, affirmed in *Areopagitica*, the interior recon-
stitution is correlated to creative action in the exterior world.
But the two movements can be uncoupled, as they appar-
ently are in the final books of *Paradise Lost*. When attention
shifts to the interior movement and that movement is de-
prived of its transcendental referent (a dissociation Milton

---

[8] "Areopagitica," *Complete Prose Works of John Milton*, New Haven, Yale
University Press, 1953– , Vol. II, ed. Ernest Sirluck, pp. 549-52.

[9] *The Works of John Milton*, New York, Columbia University Press, 1931-
38, Vol. XVI, p. 125.

did not contemplate), the process of self-formation becomes unstable, increasingly committed to questioning its status within fictions that may well be self-generated, rather than to verifying its status within a fiction that is divinely dispensed.

The Areopagitican model, internalized, is an influential paradigm for the Romantic unfinished. Blake's myth of dismemberment and reconstitution can indeed be read as an immense elaboration of Milton's central image. In Blake the distance between actuality and finality is lengthened since creation is a product of the fallen consciousness, so that even the book of nature must be transformationally rather than metaphorically read. Mental fight, moreover, in so far as it is based on transformational readings of the self, may unfold itself not as a steady progress, but as an endlessly self-revisionary journey. It is no accident that the author of the Areopagitican model himself is required to undertake such a journey if he is to remain a collaborator in the ongoing poem of self-formation. Nevertheless, visionary finality, claimed rather than sought, is a shaping characteristic of Blake's poems and one that powerfully restrains their possibilities of openness.

Wordsworth and Coleridge may also be deemed Areopagiticans in their pursuit of the whole, the whole being given its literary equivalence as the impossibly ambitious œuvre the mind subscribes to but is unable to fulfill. Failure is inevitable, but the fragment is given both its direction and its dignity when it is seen as occupying a place within a structure. The architectural figure Wordsworth uses to describe the structure leaves us in no uncertainty about the place. The fragment is not as yet the aperture through which whatever lies beyond must be discerned nor that ambivalently lit clearing in an area of darkness which it seems to become in *The Triumph of Life*. For Wordsworth and Coleridge the major form of the unfinished is the entire individual literary endeavour, as it is for Shelley when he invites us to think of literary history as a continuing poem

13

of consciousness.[10] The work of a single author presumably finds itself by entering into and responding to that poem. In these participations the individual poem need not announce itself explicitly as a fragment. It is identified as a fragment by announcements made about the whole. The whole can therefore be ennobled by the very magnitude of the poems it establishes as fragments. At the same time the fragment is ennobled and the practicalities of attainment are given status by the impressiveness of the edifice of which they form a part.

Later in this book a distinction is made (arbitrarily because it is needed) between incomplete and unfinished poems. Incomplete poems are poems which ought to be completed. Unfinished poems are poems which ask not to be finished, which carry within themselves the reasons for arresting or effacing themselves as they do. If an unfinished poem were to be finished it would ideally erase its own significance. On this basis *Christabel* can be considered an incomplete poem. At least it can be so classified until it is satisfactorily shown that there are inner tensions in the poem that justify its ceasing when and as it does. On the other hand, *Kubla Khan*, though announcing itself as a fragment, has the ring of closure in its final lines. It may be that, as McFarland suggests, *Kubla Khan* is a collapsed epic, forming with *The Prelude* the base of an isosceles triangle of which *Paradise Lost* is the apex.[11] Granting this, we might ask whether a collapsed epic invites inflation to suitable epic dimensions. If so, *Kubla Khan* is incomplete. On the other hand we might ask if the collapsed state is the true state, a desolate commentary on contemporary epic pos-

---

[10] "A Defence of Poetry," *English Critical Essays. Nineteenth Century*, ed. Edmund D. Jones, London, Oxford University Press, 1940, p. 41.

[11] Thomas McFarland, *Romanticism and the Forms of Ruin*, p. 238. The view of *Kubla Khan* as a collapsed epic was originally offered by E. S. Shaffer. *Kubla Khan and the Fall of Jerusalem: The Mythological School in Biblical Criticism and Secular Literature 1770-1880*, Cambridge, Cambridge University Press, 1975.

sibilities. If so, it could be argued that *Kubla Khan* is unfinished. Further reflection suggests, however, that the poem then falls into the category of the ruin, the expression of a surviving capability that is no more than vestigial in relation to the genre's high achievement. It has yet to be demonstrated (particularly in view of an ending which, in its ominous finality, seems to provide several of the satisfactions of closure)[12] that *Kubla Khan* is a poem truly unfinished, in other words a poem that holds away closure because of undecidable dissensions on which its identity rests.

The major unfinished is justified not by collapse but by incorporation, its participation in a whole that is to be. It is thus with Spenser and in Milton's Areopagitican model. The difference, and it is a crucial difference, is that, with the Romantics, the privileging whole is no longer transcendentally guaranteed but is formulated by the very consciousness that seeks it. A consciousness that both aspires to be privileged and yet finds and names out of itself the source within itself by which it is to be privileged is caught in a self-division from which it may be difficult to escape. In fact, the only logical avenue of escape may be to relinquish the fiction of a privileging source.

In Spenser, Milton, and the early Romantics the movement of procession and return, the reinstatement of origin as *telos*, are inscribed in the unfinished as the sign of its parentage, the credentials of a citizenship that has yet to be decisively claimed. The movement is goal-oriented and the goal stands apart from the movement however much the perception of the goal may be modified by the movement. As the poem of the mind reflects on its own realities, a transformational model of attainment must supersede the approximative model, to record faithfully the crises of growth and the qualitative changes brought about through these

[12] McFarland (p. 225) finds the poem "as fully terminated as any in the language."

crises. Ironically, it is the transformational model which makes possible the decoupling of the movement from the goal. An approximative model is by definition goal-oriented.

The Fall of Hyperion now takes its place in the field as an example of a transformational poem of self-achieving that is no longer goal-oriented. Change is qualitative, registered by the crises of dying into life, but can predicate no more than its own obsolescence. The identity of a new state cannot be projected from the previous state. It is not known but found by enduring the rites of passage into its newness. Such a model does not endow the whole with privileging power, electing instead to treat understanding as emergent and indefinitely self-revisionary rather than as the progressive inscription of *telos*. The balance of power between the fragment and the whole swings towards the fragment in this version of the transformational model. It is a shift of some importance in the history of the unfinished.

The Triumph of Life is a case of a fragment successfully contesting that incorporation which was once seen as the natural destiny of the fragment. It does so by insisting on its givenness, by underlining the resistance of that givenness to decoding and by offering strategies for dealing with its resistance which are then defeated by the poem itself. Like *The Faerie Queene* and *Paradise Lost*, *The Triumph of Life* is a poem of contestation, with the contestation now brought forward as the poem's ambivalence about its own identity, its inability to interpret itself. *The Triumph of Life* therefore takes its place with *The Fall of Hyperion* as part of the later Romantic effort to privilege the fragment against the whole, or at least to disconnect it from the whole as a privileging source.

Somewhere in the field we are surveying there should be a place for a poem based on sheer succession, which is not approximative, transformational, or developmental, which is not propelled by its nature to the magnetic north of a final cause, and which is not driven forward by the prospect of emergent understandings or even the hunger for those understandings. *Don Juan* comes closest to being such a poem. The patterns in *Don Juan* are coalescences brought about by the repetitiousness of events, but the repetitions do not accumulate sufficiently to support a theory of repetitiousness. The whole is not privileged since there is insufficient evidence that any whole is being sought, either by the protagonist or by the increasingly dominant authorial voice. On the other hand the fragment is not privileged, except implicitly. Explicit privileging would arise out of the fragment's successful resistance to incorporation. In *Don Juan* there is no clearly discernible incorporative effort.

In keeping with its comic-satiric decorum *Don Juan* is a poem of mockery. It proclaims epic purposiveness at its outset and then deflates that purposiveness by submitting it to the errancy of events. It mocks errancy in its turn by making it apparent that it can exhibit nothing beyond its own perpetuation. The impossible specification is held up to ridicule. The pretensions of the mixed-genre poem are complicated and confounded amid an assortment of generic claims. The *Bildung* principle is queried by the randomness of events and by a hero whose concern seems to be to accept what is offered by the event rather than to interrogate it so as to disinter its meaning. Digressiveness is twice mocked by being doubly located, both in the wanderings of the narrative and by an authorial voice which compounds the wanderings it might be expected to integrate. Appropriately enough, this satire on the unfinished ends by being itself unfinished, but it also implicitly bestows upon the unfinished the status of a literary tradition.

Against the background of the later Romantic valorizing of the fragment Eliot's work can be seen as deeply conservative, notwithstanding its advanced language tactics. His œuvre is the sustained pursuit of a wholeness which gives meaning to experience, establishing the reality of that wholeness through the ineradicable notations of its absence and defining its claims upon the self by exhausting our habitual evasions of those claims. The closures of Eliot's individual poems can be seen as apertures through which the psychic fable of the œuvre makes its way in propounding and unfolding itself. It is the Areopagitican model that we trace, characterized by passage over a transformational barrier—a true dying into life in *Ash-Wednesday* to be contrasted with the false deaths of Prufrock, Gerontion, and Phlebas.

Like Eliot, Pound returns to the classic unfinished, writing a poem of contestation, not between genres as in *The Faerie Queene* and *Paradise Lost*, nor as in *The Triumph of Life* within the poem's endeavour to comprehend itself, but between the holistic objective and the fragmentary method. The resolute empiricism means that the whole is no longer inscribed by an exterior finality on the movement that seeks it as an authentication and protection of that movement. The rose exists not at the climax of vision, but as the delusive fiction or perhaps the disinterred form yielded enigmatically by the steel dust. That final form may be coincident with the deep form of consciousness is a proprosition related to the presence of the divine image in the self, but the divine image posits a transcendental safeguard which Pound shows no eagerness to accept. By insisting that all understanding must be compounded from fragments, that all connections must arise from the natural cohesions of givenness, Pound sets up a secular incorporative effort against which is pitted the resistance of the fragment, its reluctance to yield the language of wholeness except in jagged and splintered intimations. Moreover, the intimations can only be recognized as intimations by a self which chooses to discern them as such and which has no ground for its discernment other than itself and the hoped-for concurrence of its prospective audience. The whole is still offered as the destiny of the fragment. The just city, Dioce, not Cleopolis, is still to be built, not in the image of Jerusalem, but rather in the image of a fully formed human consciousness. The fragment's resistance to incorporation is a formidable *de facto* questioning of this claim. That the claim continues to be maintained *de jure*, that it is contested rather than defeated are reservations which save the poem from subsiding completely into its stream of fragments and which enable it to remain unfinished, still poised, though precariously, on its basic engagement.

Marvell stands on the margin of the unfinished with poems that are extraordinarily well-finished. Unlike unfinished poems, which resist closure, Marvell's poems are hospitable to closure in their formal balances. But that very hospitality obliges us to ask what settlement has been achieved by closure and to receive uncertain answers to that question. The equities encouraged by Marvell's poetry include that most dangerous of all equities, parity between the proposition and its subversion. The poem is thereby centred on its own destabilization. Closure is merely a means of circumscribing a poem that is inconclusive on the page and unfinished in the mind of the reader, since every reading interrogates previous readings. Unfinished poems hold off closure, thus making it clear that closure is inappropriate to the dissensions on which their identities rest. Marvell's poems, based on similar dissensions, accommodate closure in order to make evident where closure fails to work.

As has been indicated, the unfinished is based on contestation, or upon a movement of deferral, initially arising out of contestation, but capable of being uncoupled from that engagement. Contestation and subversion are sisters but not twin sisters; there is a distinction of some importance to be made between them. Contestation interrogates a proposition by confronting the mind with an alternative. In fundamental contestations (for example Milton's view of how the knowledge of good is attained by a fallen consciousness) the proposition can be only apprehended in relation to the alternative. Subversion undermines a proposition without putting an alternative before us. A con-

19

tested understanding is advanced by its interrogation. A subverted understanding is overthrown or frustrated by being subversively questioned. Marvell's poems may seem to be based on contestation (withdrawal versus involvement being the most pervasive pairing) but since each side in the contest is undermined not simply by the other side but, more significantly, by its own rhetoric of self-affirmation, Marvell's patterns have to be seen as subversive. Though formally closed, they are more radically indeterminate than some of the paradigms of the unfinished we have studied.[13]

The models indicated can be seen as occupying positions in a theoretical field and as related by virtue of their location in that field. But they are historically as well as spatially linked. Poems of generic contestation excite contestations which are other than generic and so open the way to later poems based on more fundamental dissensions. The privileging of the whole leads naturally to the whole's being placed in engagement with the part, initially on the basis that the fragment seeks the whole or can be decoded so as to disclose it (a proposition that is revived as late as Pound),

---

[13] We might ask whether poems as precisely poised in their stand-offs, as Marvell's yield aesthetic satisfaction, or whether they merely resign us to their nullity, to the futile made endurable within the well-wrought urn of form. Sextus Empiricus provides us with a basis on which to discuss this query. In the *Outlines of Pyrrhonism* he describes the sceptical stance as "the ability to place in antithesis, in any manner whatsoever, appearances and judgements and thus—because of the equality of force in the objects opposed—to come first of all to a suspension of judgement and then to mental tranquillity." *Scepticism, Man and God: Selections from the Major Writings of Sextus Empiricus*, ed. Philip P. Hallie, Middletown, Wesleyan University Press, 1964, pp. 32-33. The description goes beyond merely countenancing parity between the proposition and its subversion; it encourages that parity with the reassurance that the result will be calm of mind rather than paralysis. When Sir Thomas Browne tells us that he has "runne through all sorts of philosophies but found no rest in any" he is aware of the "rest" paradoxically offered by scepticism's apparent restlessness: "the wisest heads prove at last almost all scepticks" (*Religio Medici*, II,8).

but later in a manner that raises the question of the fragment's resistance to the very incorporation which it was supposed to seek. Meanwhile, the forces of scientific empiricism and of religious experientialism lead to the Areopagitican model in which a final cause is progressively manifested by the gathering cohesion generated between fragments. Models of progressive movement, approximative or transformational, towards an incorporating whole, then become internalized with the disappearance of a worldview that was once capable of liberally providing metaphors for poetry. Newton may demand the muse as Marjorie Nicolson assures us, but the muse is not that of the Romantic poets. It is not only Blake and Yeats for whom the garden perishes when the mechanical bride is born from the side of Locke.[14] The rehabilitation of the literary in the real must now come from an interior journey and so it is over the abyss of the self (as Wordsworth makes clear in the Prospectus to "The Recluse") that the "omnific word" of literary creation hovers. Both the interiorization, and the disengagement of the movement of self-formation from a privileging whole to which it was once oriented, make the journey radically self-questioning, increasingly destabilized by its unavoidable concern with the status of the fictions it must invoke to sustain or even to discover itself. Yet the trend towards the valorization of the fragment once set in being cannot easily be reversed, since it registers the widely recognized alienation of the self from the increasing dehumanization of social and technological aggregates. There are reasons for the route that has been followed, and literature does not fail to speak for those reasons. The insistence on the fragment's autonomy is by now a part of the psychic politics of the threatened self. There need be no question that the self is threatened, not least by incorporation into its own inventiveness.

[14] W. B. Yeats, "Fragments," *Collected Poems*, London, Macmillan, 1950, pp. 240-41.

In his most recent book,[15] Edward Said distinguishes between filiation, the relationship of a text to its ancestry, and affiliation, the relationship of a text to its environment. The previous paragraph can be read as an outline of how affiliation helps to shape filiation. Contemporary circumstances may not be an ingredient in the literary problem a text inherits; but they affect the direction in which the problem is pushed and the subsequent problems which the direction taken may generate. This interaction is particularly noteworthy with the long poem since one of the long poem's principal commitments is the accommodation of the text to the contemporary world. Affiliation in other words, is part of its filiation. Changes in the character of the long poem or in the relative status of its components are intrinsically more than formal rearrangements and matters such as the cost of change, the reality of progress, the relationship of the individual to the collective, and the betrayal of knowledge by its pursuit are not simply topics on the long poem's agenda. Rather, they are disclosed as embedded in the structures and in the basic interrogations from which the long poem wrests its identity. More amply, the long poem's increasing resistance to its own integrative energies questions not simply the possibility but the desirability of totalization. Such resistance cumulatively comes to constitute a socio-political as well as a literary statement.

The variety of authors studied in this book and the range of literary history covered has made it desirable to situate the poems we are to examine as paradigms in an organizational field. Perhaps this introduction would be more fully fitted to its subject if it were to end by contesting its own endeavour. Our concern, we might say, should be with the poems and not the field. Although the design of relationships between the poems may be enlightening and even aesthetically pleasing in its disengagements and

[15] Edward W. Said, *The World, the Text, and the Critic*, Cambridge, Mass., Harvard University Press, 1983.

22

flement of the actual is once again faced. There is of course a difference between the open form of truth and the uncompletable yet growingly self-evident structure Milton makes real in the shape of his work. But the consolidations which end his poems are not conclusions. They are opportunities to renew the effort of self-making.

In Eliot the endings are disasters subverted into significance as Prufrock drowns, as Gerontion is driven to his sleepy corner, and as the thunder intones its benediction in an alien language over the cultural clutter assembled by the poem's bewildered hero. The œuvre advances through catastrophes that arrange themselves to make new beginnings possible. Failure is the ironic form of enlightenment. All defeats are inconclusive, not only because defeats in the wasteland manifest themselves less as heroic frustrations than as the continuance of aimlessness, but also because of the gathering consolidations found to be taking place under what initially seems the "drifting wreckage." We can see this in Section II of *The Dry Salvages* where the fall of progression into addition, of continuity into stark repetitiveness, is brought out by a rhyme structure totally and destructively open, which seems capable only of being endlessly echoed. Such purified pointlessness might be difficult to bear if it were not in its turn undermined by the movement of significance which it does not wholly succeed in excluding. Meaning does not prevail; but at least it can be said that it survives and by surviving rules out the inverse conclusiveness of a world built around the absence of meaning.

It should be apparent by now that both the confident close and the stuttering irresolution are more than what they seem to be. The œuvre builds itself on the awareness that the stuff of experience is not fully revealed in its texture, that the part is seen differently through its membership in the whole. Vehement finalities can conclude a poem by subjecting it to a boundary; but their very vehemence may summon into existence another poem with a contrary

transferences, the poems are obviously more than the positions they occupy in the design. The individualities of utterance by which they surround and justify their situatedness ought not to be slighted. More fundamentally, we might ask whether a movement characterized first by deferring and then by resisting wholeness is best examined by placing it within an organizational whole. Can we profitably subject to structural integration a variety of detections that are potentially post-structuralist? The importance of such questions should not be minimized, but the counter-affirmation they incite, to wit, that we should be more than fragmentary in our response to fragments, is also a proposition that we need to acknowledge. To place a poem in a design is not necessarily to intrude on its particularity. Indeed our awareness of the richness and specificity of a poem may be impoverished if we ignore its participation in an overall design. The poem's appropriation of that design may be a main voice of its individuality. Thus a study of the unfinished, like the works it examines, must walk a line of engagement between competing claims. It must endeavour to be a book. It must also yield what is appropriate to the errancy of texts and to the discoveries made possible by that errancy.

Andrew Marvell: The Aesthetics of Inconclusiveness

THE DANGER of a chapter on the aesthetics of inconclusiveness is that it may end in an inconclusiveness that is anything but aesthetic. I had thought of safeguarding myself against this danger by subtitling this chapter "Some Preliminary Evasions." This kind of anticipatory deflation, it will be remembered, was regarded by the new critics as a sign of maturity. However recklessness is more in vogue today than ironic self-insurance, so like Marvell, though without Marvell's agile elegance, I must proceed to definitions that are "begotten by despair/Upon Impossibility." Indeed in the interests of controlled over-statement, I shall proceed to talk of forms of inconclusiveness, disdaining the more prudent word, "types."[1]

Let us begin unexpectedly with Dante. The *Divine Comedy* will seem unpromising terrain for a searcher after inconclusiveness, but reflection will show that the very structure of the *terza rima* encloses a continuing lack of completion. The rhyme sandwich, if we may use so disrespectful a description, contains or, better still, prophesies the next rhyme and the infinite linkages which are thereby solicited make the pattern a pioneering model of open form. The verse calls for continuation out of its nature. Continuation

Quotations from Marvell's poetry follow the text of *The Poems and Letters of Andrew Marvell*, ed. H. M. Margoliouth, Oxford, The Clarendon Press, 1952.

[1] The pages which follow profit from Barbara Herrnstein Smith's *Poetic Closure*, Chicago, University of Chicago Press, 1968, and from Frank Kermode's *The Sense of an Ending*, New York, Oxford University Press, 1968.

24

is not necessarily inconclusive, though it is insistently so in the second section of Eliot's *The Dry Salvages*. In Dante we have not yet reached the point where there is no end but addition. But continuation posits a local inconclusiveness from which one can advance into finality, or towards a receding horizon, or into a world which is all before one where to choose but where no choice can be trusted to lead anywhere. The journey can be differently perceived; but something has been said once and for all by a rhyme structure whose very nature predicates the journey.

Milton elaborates the poetry of continuation with firm closures that point beyond themselves, providing a model for Eliot's final finding that "to make an end is to make a beginning." The endings undermine their own conclusiveness with the "bright-harness'd" angels of the Nativity Ode "in order serviceable" for the greater work ahead, the "uncouth swain" of *Lycidas* facing the future with "eager thought," Adam and Eve wandering hand in hand into an open world of peril and opportunity, and Christ returning to his mother's house on earth, having stood on the pinnacle of the father's house of heaven. The "private" return, the scaling down to the world of the ordinary, advises of what lies beyond the poem for its hero and of what may also lie beyond it for ourselves. The open endings of poetry help to remind us that the remaking of the self is a continuing enterprise which the acts of the imagination both mirror and help to advance. Milton tells us in *Areopagitica*, through the Osiris image, that history moves to a conclusion but that the conclusion will be outside history. The poem as an act of mimesis fully responsive to understanding is both an affirmation and an incomplete statement of the pattern so far as it is known and a moment of finding by which the pattern is both verified and advanced towards completion. "Calm of mind, all passion spent" is by no means an attainment of autumnal tranquility. It suggests rather gathering into a much needed clarity, a necessary reassurance of design before

25

field of force. A characterization of Yeats will be detected by many in this preamble, and it must be acknowledged that Yeats is indeed the master of a poetry of stances on a wheel of possibilities. A poetry of stances is basically inconclusive since every stance is formed by acts of exclusion which become in their turn the origin of other stances. Poems in patterns of continuity open into other poems by taking into themselves elements which they do not fully organize, or by reaching into a centre which other forms of insight are used to penetrate. In an œuvre of stances on the other hand, a poem summons other poems into being by virtue of what it omits. Poems respond to and complete themselves by the creative enmities they seek and by the alliances of undermining into which they enter. If man can embody truth but cannot know it, then one man in his time must play many parts.

Hitherto we have looked at poems or structural units which are inconclusive because they promise or threaten something beyond themselves. The movement towards understanding, the approach to the meaning by different routes which reshape the approach, the interlocking of stances vigorously limited, the partly open rhyme schemes of consummation, and the totally open rhyme schemes of numbing additiveness, the baffled self-consciousness seeking to decode itself by dint of its own bewilderments all present us with local events within structures of continuity. They are inconclusive because they require relationship with the overall embodiment they help to bring into being. We could oppose to a poetry of continuity a poetry of arrest of which the *Ode on a Grecian Urn* might be a crucial example. Frozen potentiality is the form of this "cold pastoral." The other side of fulfillment can be extinction. Yeats recognizes this relationship in declaring that "The herald's cry, the soldier's tread/Exhausts his glory and his might" but for him there is tragic joy in the exhaustion, as well as the knowledge that any new movement of creativeness must find its birth amid the ruins of an old one

Whatever flames upon the night
Man's own resinous heart has fed.[2]

Yeats, to use Marvell's phrase, makes the sun run, exulting in what he elsewhere calls the thundering away of time. Keats's urn attempts to make the sun stand still. Its unravished achievement touches rather than enters becoming, teasing us out of thought by teasing us into shapes of possibility. The town it portrays can be by a river, by the sea-shore, or amid the mountains. It does not divulge the reason for its emptiness. The poem poses questions which are aesthetically pleasing because they admit of more than one answer. It would seem that the urn is not segregated from history in thus refraining from its narrative force. It remains a sylvan historian, capable of intimating wild ecstacy through the withdrawals of its quietness. Keats is too considerable a poet not to be aware of the losses that are necessary as the urn maintains its distance against what Yeats was later to call the "pushing world." If the lover is spared the ravages of time, he is also denied the fulfillment of the moment. More significantly, the town, emptied of its populace on a happy morning, is bleakly described as "desolate." Indeed the very nature of the urn invites us to contemplate the spectacle of the permanence of art perpetually confronting the permanence of mortality. The "foster child of silence and slow time," adopted rather than generated in that hushed tenuousness with which being approaches becoming, bears witness continually to the triumph of time and of the uncreating silence. Art is constituted around its own undoing. We can thus read sadness as well as felicity into the urn's abstentions from history. The point is that we can revise our reading even as we make it. The poem is like the object it contemplates, interpreting it, but arresting its interpretation, poised between detachment and entry with a precariousness that seems the condition of its cogency.

[2] W. B. Yeats, *Collected Poems*, p. 240.

The reader's response can be an important element in a work of calculated inconclusiveness. Herbert writes "Prayer" as a catalogue, carefully omitting those verbs which are in language the main instruments of narration and causality. It is a poem purified by being without an argument. The final "something understood" calls on the reader to discover within himself the implied cohesion between the prayer's components. Thus the phrase covers not only the structure of relationship but the act of making by which that structure is reached. We are brought to the eventual and essential understanding that prayer must be an act and not a recital. Herbert's lyric is a striking early example of a genre which might be called the "do-it-yourself" poem and Eliot, who quotes it for a different purpose,[3] may not have forgotten it in minimising his own use of connectives in *The Waste Land*. The "do-it-yourself" poem is inconclusive because it solicits completion by the reader. When more than one way of completion is made available the possibilities of inconclusiveness can be particularly interesting.

In outlining various forms of inconclusiveness, the accommodations of the word may seem to have been stretched. Some stretching is perhaps desirable if we are to free ourselves from the containment of the Aristotelian postulate that a whole must have a beginning, a middle, and an end. Much of poetry can be read as a quiet questioning of this postulate, a resistance against it as much as a contribution to it. Actuality, even when freed from what are classically called "accidents," does not always exhibit that plot structure which the work of art is supposed to discover in it. An aesthetic of inconclusiveness serves a corrective purpose because it can be more receptive to the obstinancies of the actual, to the ongoing nature of the poem of process,

[3] T. S. Eliot, "George Herbert," *British Writers and Their Work No. 4*, ed. Bonamy Dobree and J. W. Robinson, Lincoln, University of Nebraska Press, 1964, p. 65.

to the ironic response, the response that is "vacillating" in Yeats's sense, or the response seeking to formulate itself.

We now come to the curious case of Marvell. Perhaps it should be made clear at the outset that the statements which follow apply not to all Marvell's work but only to certain poems, frequently anthologized, which are widely regarded as distinctively Marvellian. There can be little doubt that these poems are inconclusive. "Coolly elusive," the phrase so often used to evoke the quality of Marvell's accomplishment, testifies to the difficulties of adequate characterization. Joseph Summers, in introducing a selection from Marvell's work, offers three readings of each of the better-known Marvell poems, making clear by his language which reading he prefers, but indicating that the other readings are possible and even plausible.[4] Even the titles of two fairly recent books on Marvell—*The Resolved Soul* and *Marvell's Ironic Vision*—suggest radically different assessments, both sustained by attentive scholarship, of the kind of poet with whom we are dealing.[5] These wide variations in reading have a point to make. It can be argued in response to them that Marvell's poems are inconclusive not because they take place within larger patterns of settlement to be negotiated by the poet, or negotiated between the poet and the reader. They are inconclusive because a controlled uncertainty is the objective of the poem rather than its enmeshment, because the play of forces within it is so arranged that the poem can settle down in more than one way.[6]

"Ironic" is another term frequently applied to Marvell's

[4] Joseph H. Summers, ed., *Marvell*, New York, Dell Publishing Co., pp. 14-15.

[5] Harold E. Toliver, *Marvell's Ironic Vision*, New Haven, Yale University Press, 1965; Ann E. Berthoff, *The Resolved Soul*, Princeton, Princeton University Press, 1970.

[6] It is, of course, now argued by several critics that all poems settle down in more than one way. Such critics would have to distinguish a Marvellian poem from others by the range of permissible settlements it demarcates and by the strategies of demarcation.

poetry, but irony in poems often implies its own weight, or exists in order to be overcome by affirmative forces which the irony serves to validate. The alliance of levity and seriousness is supposed to intensify and not overturn the seriousness. With Donne and Yeats the deflationary risk-taking can be read as endeavouring to dramatize the range of facts with which the overall understanding is able to co-exist. The poem as a performance is made convincing by the degree to which it undertakes to threaten itself. The revisionary energies of *Lycidas*, the poem's anguished dismantling of its assumptions, raise the stakes for which the game is being played.[7] Eager thought becomes not only possible but significant when we have confronted and civilized the power of the meaningless. With Marvell it is not easy to agree upon the nature of the understanding that has emerged, prevailed, or survived. In fact it is not clear whether the purpose of his poems is to arrive at a finding or to display a pattern of forces.

Marvell's most celebrated poem provides a spacious arena for compliment. From the Humber to the Ganges and from the deluge to the last judgement gives room enough for the expertise of praise. It is in fact the very size of the exaggeration which undermines the enterprise, putting before us with amused civility the disproportion between means and ends. "Vegetable love" grows with the slow pace of empires, though not through conquest as an empire does and as a lover hopes to do. There is a touch of monstrosity here to contend with the surface elegance.[8] Yet the hyperboles of praise are esteemed as well as dismissed.

[7] This sentence refers to a view of *Lycidas* further developed by the present author in *The Lofty Rhyme*, London, Routledge and Kegan Paul, 1970, pp. 45-55.

[8] Notwithstanding Legouis as quoted by Margoliouth (p. 253), "vegetable love" does seem to refer to the Aristotelian division of the soul into vegetative, animal, and rational. In terms of this division, a vegetable love is an impropriety. Since growth is the property of the vegetable soul, Marvell's use of the impropriety to suggest the corpus of praise expanding inertly like some enormous cabbage, seems expertly comic.

31

"Lady you deserve this State;/Nor would I love at lower rate" is at once an urbane concession to the postponements of the love game, a reminder that the suitor is fully adept at playing it, an appreciation of the lady's reticence, a mockery of that reticence, a recommendation to inhabit a world of reality rather than one of convention and an acknowledgement that reality might be barbarous were it not for the civilizing force of convention. This is the characteristic Marvell tone, complex and even treacherous, subverting what it alleges and, at the same time, questioning its own subversion.

Carpe diem exercises do not begin with the *blason*. Marvell starts with a convention and then proceeds to dismantle it (in the carefully qualified way which has been outlined) before making his approach to another convention. The tactics put us on notice that "realism" is not necessarily to triumph. The *carpe diem* injunction is in any event unusual because of its incorporation of the metaphysical shudder in a manner generally and justly admired. In thus turning from urbanity to grimness the poem confronts us with the destructive forces that loom behind all ceremonies, whether of sophistication or, as Yeats would have it, innocence. Space is a desert now, instead of a fertile land of compliments. The epochs of praise now stretch into a sterile eternity.[9] Time's winged chariot hurries threateningly closer in an image that seems mockingly ornate as if conventions of embellishment previously played with were offering the poem their deadly consequences. Spaciousness shrivels into the narrow grave. The "none I think, do there embrace," savagely conjectural, metamorphoses polished bantering into macabre taunting. Yet we have to ask what is implied by a situation in which honour and lust are alike exposed to mortality and in which lust is declared as the probable driving force behind an earlier zeal for compliment. The

[9] "Vast Eternity" picks up and grimly consummates the "Vaster than Empires" of line 12.

Biblical echoes of dust and ashes provide no sanction for the satisfying of desire. It is the triumph of time that lives at the heart of the poem. That triumph cannot be thwarted. All that can be done is to retrieve the moment from it and intensify the meaning of the moment. The *carpe diem* exercise always had desperation as a suitably muted context but Marvell endows that context with predatory urgency while proceeding again, in typically Marvellian fashion, to undermine the retrieval that he offers.

As Eliot and others point out,[10] the poem might have ended there. In other writers the exhortation to seize the day has not called for an anatomy of seizure. But a previous convention has been set up to be dismantled and the one that has replaced it is not any more sacrosanct. It is deconstructive energy that characterizes the poem rather than the choice of one possibility or another. To devour time may be to turn on one's tormentor. But it is also to become the enemy. At point after point the imagery suggests that liberation can be the subtlest of victimizations, that we are born again as that which we repudiate. The winged chariot is responded to by "am'rous birds of prey" who "sport" presumably in those very deserts from which the courage to act had purported to deliver us. Actively to "devour" rather than passively to "languish" is not to escape the end but to accelerate its arrival. If we console ourselves by declaring that we have at least taken charge of our destiny, the destructive comment is that our destiny may have altered because of the manner in which we were permitted to take charge of it. We may concentrate all our strength and sweetness (the ingredients of Samson's riddle) into the "ball" which is the substitute sphere of perfection,[11] but

---

[10] T. S. Eliot, "Andrew Marvell," *Selected Essays*, London, Faber and Faber, 1934, p. 296.

[11] In the introduction to his selection of Marvell criticism, John Carey lists eight differing explanations of the "one ball." The possibility offered here is not among them. John Carey, ed., *Andrew Marvell*, Harmondsworth, Penguin Books, 1969, p. 63.

there is little sweetness in the "rough strife" and the tearing, the forcing of those "iron gates" which as "iron wedges" in *The Definition of Love* contributed so elegantly to love's geometry. "Tear," "devour," "strife," and "prey" provide a telling reiterative context for "am'rous." The savagery of engagement and the frivolity of abstention from engagement dispose themselves around that mocking grave which is now seen as common to both courses. The poem ends with what it is able to salvage. We can make the sun run, even if we are not able to make it stand still. To abstain from action is to surrender one's destiny to time. To act is to discover that self-realization cannot be wrested from the space of seizure, the intense moment when the flame should burn at its brightest. If the sun runs, then time reasserts itself even in our command of it. We declare ourselves only in what we accomplish; but the accomplishment is always a betrayal of the intention.[12]

To his Coy Mistress is probably Marvell's most destructive poem. Its strength is that having turned against itself in

[12] Christopher Hill quotes Bishop Joseph Hall: "A good man must not be like Ezechia's sun that went backward, nor like Joshua's sun, that stood still, but David's sun, that (like a bridegroom) comes out of his chamber, and as a champion rejoiceth to run his race." *Puritanism and Revolution*, London, 1958, p. 347; quoted Carey, ed., *Andrew Marvell*, p. 82. Legouis (Margoliouth, p. 255) comments that "the difference between David's sun, which runs of its own accord, and Marvell's, which will be compelled to run, strikes me more than the resemblance." It is not clear that an allusion to Psalm 19, 4-5 is intended; if it is, we would have to recognize the contrast between a situation in which the sun runs so that the firmament can display the glory of its maker and one in which it runs to signify the limited (and perhaps self-destructive) control over events that is possible in the desert of reality. We therefore cannot take it that the conclusion of the poem endorses Bishop Hall's advice, or for that matter that it rejects Milton's consistent curbing of the temptation to seize the day, evident not only in "Comus" and in *Paradise Regained* but also in Sonnet VII ("How Soon Hath Time . . .") and Sonnet XIX ("When I consider"). Marvell's poem is designed to resist simplification and like other poems which are fundamentally self-critical, it is also a critique of its own allusiveness.

the expected manner of ironic poems, it then turns against its own internal objections, leaving us with the desert that is the poem's centre both actually and numerically. *To his Coy Mistress* is inconclusive because of its consistent, subversive energy. Marvell's other poems do not demolish themselves as thoroughly as this one and one might even say that the typical objective is the stalemate or stand-off as much as the demolition. But even in poems that press less closely than this one to the desolation of reality Marvell remains the most accomplished of English subversives.

The Definition of Love is an exercise in geometry, countering Donne's "Valediction," where separation argues for relationship. Here Fate and Love, opposition and conjunction, the outreaching soul and the separating wedges, cooperate to design a pattern of forces in which neither alliance can be perceived as dominant. Hemispheres mirror each other in Donne and join together in the perfection of the sphere. In Marvell, parallel lines mirror each other and remain endlessly separated by the perfection of their mirroring. The definition might seem a salvaging from defeat (or a witty refusal to agree to a lover's demands) until we allow ourselves the possibility that the poem because of its basic inconclusiveness can find its locus of satisfaction only in its geometry. Fulfillment would collapse that very geometry in which inconclusiveness is stylized and celebrated.[13] So too would the directing of the design by hope, and that is why the poem spurning reliance on hope's "Tinsel Wing," chooses instead to generate its diagram from despair. We make these statements on the basis that the poem is not simply about star-crossed lovers[14] but to some degree about a world the nature of which is that the ideal cannot be completed in the actual. On this basis we can see how the presence of absence and the creative po-

[13] Stanza VI envisages in suitably catastrophic terms, the possible collapse of this sustaining geometry.

[14] J. B. Leishman, *The Art of Marvell's Poetry*, London, Hutchinson, 1966, p. 65.

tential of impossibility are put before us in the modern manner as forces on which definitions may reliably depend. We may prefer a solution or a failure that is more heroic but the poem presses the advantage of a fictive world that is not corrupted by success or failure, where the diagram of forces can be studied without the distraction of the triumph of either force.

In the *Horatian Ode* the force of change embodied in Cromwell is presented in images of catastrophe the effect of which is

> To ruine the great Work of Time
> And cast the Kingdome old
> Into another Mold

The pleading of "antient Rights" in this context is a complaint by "Justice against Fate." Change may be desirable but the cost of change is not to be minimized. And if progress (or that creative change which the poem officially celebrates) is put forward in images of disaster, resistance to progress is presented in images of decorum and self-control. This double undermining haunts the remainder of the poem notwithstanding its celebration of Cromwell's victory over the Irish, his coming victory over the Scots, and his Adamic union of "contemplation and valour."[15] There are ironic reversals as one might expect with Marvell. He who stood for Fate against Justice is now both good and just. He who relinquished the "inglorious Arts of Peace" must now maintain his power by the same "Arts" by which he gained it.[16] Milton's sonnet to Cromwell should echo in

---

[15] *Paradise Lost* IV, 297.

[16] Occurrences of the thought, which is a commonplace, are noted by Margoliouth and Duncan Jones, pp. 302-03. But here as in *To his Coy Mistress*, a critique of the thought is called for by the questioning and supporting dispositions of the poem. Kermode notes that Lucan and Horace "also celebrated, at a crucial moment of history, the destruction of ancient rights and the casting of the State into another mould . . . certain ancient rights have been repressed, the king has died well but his

the reader's mind, but Marvell's version is befittingly am-
biguous. Perhaps the poem invites us to admire a final
figure who has recovered some of what he gave up in
himself and who has assimilated some of what is praise-
worthy in his opponents. But the poem's underminings
are extensive enough to leave uncertain how much weight
is to be given to the poem's official statement and how
much to the subversion of that statement.

This discussion can be further complicated, and a com-
plication is duly suggested. Cromwell is, as is often ob-
served, presented as a force of nature. Charles is a "Royal
Actor" on a "Tragick Scaffold."[17] Marvell's underlining ought
to advise us that the king is a participant in a work of art.
The nature-art relationship cross-biases (to use Herbert's
helpful word)[18] the poem's other relationships, making a
statement of its "findings" even more difficult. Art, we
may say, must answer to nature; but nature particularly
when it is that "rude heap together hurl'd" that lies outside

---

manners were those of an *ancien régime*, now superseded." *The Classic*,
London, Faber and Faber, 1975, p. 65. What must be must be; the problem
is to determine the weight Marvell gives to the costs and risks of its being.
The reference to "Justice" and "Fate" makes the invited response more
complex. We are kept aware, by the classical connection, that Olympian
justice was subject to fate. A Christian god, on the other hand, can declare
that "What I will is Fate" (*Paradise Lost* VII, 173). It is tempting to argue,
as Wallace does, that justice must yield to providential will. John M.
Wallace, *Destiny His Choice: The Loyalism of Andrew Marvell*, Cambridge,
1968, pp. 69-84. See also Frank Kermode, ed., *The Selected Poetry of Marvell*,
New York, New American Library, 1967, Intro. The main difficulty facing
this reading is that (apart from the exemptions of mercy) the divine will
stands above fate to implement Justice rather than overrule it. We can
circumvent this difficulty by "demoting" justice to the civic and social
level, while raising fate to the status of divine providence. Unfortunately
Marvell's capitalization of both terms, for what it is worth, resists our
placing them on separate planes.

[17] Margoliouth (p. 299) observes that "Scaffold" was "in use to denote
'stage.'" It was in fact so used in Foxe's *Book of Martyrs*, making all the
more noteworthy its application to Charles in a poem praising Cromwell.

[18] Herbert, *Affliction*, 1, line 53.

the boundaries of *Appleton House* must also answer to the civilizings of art. Perhaps we cannot creatively ruin the great work of time without having planted bergamots in gardens. If tradition is linked to art, then the nature-art relationship comments upon the relationship between tradition and the new in ways that further modify the main ways of the poem.

Gardens trouble Marvell as well as soothe him and it is not just to his troubles to say that he is a poet of pastoral sensibilities or even a poet putting the pastoral mode to ironic use. The relationship between the garden and the world outside echoes the relationship between reality and a fictive world and invites us to ask what fictionalizing accomplishes. We can say, probably rather emptily, that gardens are organically related to nature. We might add, slightly more specifically, that gardens represent a cooperation of the natural and the human. Marvell, as a subversive, is not reluctant to suggest that man, the ordering force in the garden, is also the principal force of disorder in it, whether as "Luxurious Man" contriving unnatural relationships, or as the mower doing to the grass and eventually to himself what Juliana does to him. Art too has its displacements and misplacements in addition to its purer renderings. But it is the protective garden, the enclosed and therefore manageable space, with which Marvell is concerned as a counterpart to the protective fiction. The organic relationship sustains us here in insisting that art cannot escape from life. The space of enclosure reconstitutes what it nominally excludes. Thus in *Appleton House*, the formal gardens ironically re-enact the Civil War and the wilder, less explored areas beyond provide a background of history—the deluge, the passage through the Red Sea, and the Crucifixion. The vantage point in the journey through history is, in the modern manner, that of the experiencing self, so that the meaning of the landscape is not described but discovered—through Alice-in-Wonderland alterations of scale that become convincing as part of the fictive experience.

At this point we ought to be able to tell ourselves consolingly that the worlds of withdrawal and involvement, or in aesthetic terms of the fictive and the actual, are different in degree rather than in kind. But the simulation of the Crucifixion makes us wonder not just whether the distance of withdrawal is too great, but whether the impulse to withdraw does not always create too great a distance of withdrawal. This likelihood becomes manifest in the garden of Marvell's poem of that title where the "enormous bliss" of Milton's Paradise is reduced to the comic prodigality of "What wond'rous Life is this I lead." All things served man in the original garden but they did not do so by crushing themselves against his open mouth. If it is objected that the fish in "Penshurst" exhibit similar behavioural characteristics and that this is a respectable classical trope, we can only reply that it needed a Marvell to expose its latent outrageousness.

The mind is its own place and can only be lessened by responses limited to external stimulations.[19] The next stage of withdrawal is to the Paradise within, the ocean of imagination, the interior garden of Adonis, the repository of the forms of all created things. The mind is now not tied to that exterior reality which it has succeeded in originating fully within itself. It can in Bacon's reproving phrase, "join that which Nature has severed and sever that which Nature

---

[19] Margoliouth (p. 268) reads these lines as describing a withdrawal from the lesser (physical) to the greater (intellectual) pleasure. Leishman (*The Art of Marvell's Poetry*, p. 312) agrees and adds that the language reflects the Aristotelian division between pleasure and happiness. He nevertheless concludes that "Marvell's clumsy inversion, here as often elsewhere, has produced an unintended ambiguity." Rosalie Colie agrees that the primary meaning is "from lesser pleasure" but also argues for Empson's "diminished by pleasure." *My Ecchoing Song*, Princeton, Princeton University Press, 1970, p. 149. The Empsonian view and its subversive consequences are part of the effect here; the ambiguity is anything but clumsy.

has joined"[20] much in the manner of "Luxurious Man." It can also create its own "seas" which are other than the ocean of the forms of the actual and its own worlds which are other than golden counterparts to bronze ones. The capabilities of the imagination here verge on the irresponsible and we are made aware of the hubris latent in the creative enterprise. The world of art is a mimesis of the real world but through its inherent auto-intoxication it is also a continuing subversion of that mimesis. "Annihilating all that's made/To a green Thought in a green Shade" puts before us the achieved harmony of the work of art through its counterpart, the creative tranquility of the garden, but we are not expected to forget the still-persistent force of "annihilating." Nevertheless and despite its comic undertones, the world of withdrawal can remain a place where the soul, like a bird about to take flight, can wave the "various Light" in its plumes, preparing to blend the colours into the white light of eternity. Thus the poem negotiates its subtly shifting balances between the affirmation and the undermining. It undermines itself again in the mildly preposterous suggestion that to live alone in Paradise is to possess two Paradises in one. There is a text in Genesis to challenge this proposition of which *Paradise Lost* has made even the modern reader aware. Adam's eloquent plea for companionship in Eden which is Milton's elaboration of the Genesis text makes evident the demand of the human identity for enrichment and completion in acts of social relationship. That society is "all but rude" to the "delicious Solitude" of the garden is not exactly a statement that the fictive world is anti-social. Nevertheless the word "delicious" does comment on the latent self-indulgence of the artistic impulse, just as "annihilating" comments on the latent destructiveness of what begins as a withdrawal from destructiveness. On the other hand we

[20] "The Advancement of Learning," *The Works of Francis Bacon*, ed. Spedding Ellis and Heath, Vol. III, London, Longman and Co. etc., 1859, p. 343.

have to remember that poetry can have its beginning in disengagement and even in the refinement of disengagement into solitude. The inconclusive conclusion is that the energies which constitute the fictive world are also instrumental in undermining what they create. The fictive and the actual stand in what is potentially a reinforcing rather than a contending relationship; but the nature of mind may be such that it contributes to the contention in seeking the reinforcement, brings about the mimesis in constructing the protection, and subverts the validities of withdrawal through the very manner in which withdrawal is made.

It is apparent that *The Garden* is another one of those poems which must be resignedly described as "elusive." That word, in Marvell criticism, has come to connote exasperation as well as admiration. Marvell might not have been displeased with this mixed response, which is not irrelevant to the piece of work that is man. The fact is that poems which seek to display a field of force rather than to pass judgement on its dispositions must resist conversion into that poetic argument which the reader, seeking conclusiveness, attempts to win from the work. Marvell achieves this resistance through extensive underminings which themselves contribute to the depiction of the field. However, when poems are as fully subverted as Marvell's, it becomes difficult to ascertain whether the centre of gravity lies in the surface understanding or the overturning effort; and one's sense of the centre of gravity may reasonably shift from reading to reading. An inconclusive poem of this kind, moreover, permits the reader to cast himself in more than one role and to enter the poem as the potential ally of either the proposition or the subversion. The resultant elasticity of interpretation will not console the seeker after tidiness, though Marvell is anything but an untidy poet. Yet there is a justice in a strategy which presents the fictive world as subverted by the very impulse of withdrawal which forms it and as calling for a correction by the actual which is in turn self-subverting, necessitating a retaliatory correction by the fictive. Since Marvell's tone is ironic rather

41

than absurdist the indecisiveness of this disposition of forces is not driven to its conclusion of futility. Indeed the containing form of the poem, its elegance of enclosure, leads to a degree of aesthetic and actual acceptance which is far other than the diagram might cause one to expect.

Art begins in a counter-thrust against the "pushing world,"[21] a withdrawal into an enclosure of order where the force of the actual can be reflected but diminished in intensity to what the form can tolerate. Marvell can put before us the comedy and even the irrelevance of withdrawal, but it is a fictive world which he both seeks and mocks. It requires a more powerful poet to tell us that the betraying fictions may be those not of art but of existence, the banalities of a life measured with coffee spoons, and to find the poetic commitment demanding an advance from a time "reckon'd with herbs and flow'rs" to one threateningly measured "under the oppression of the silent fog." These statements point to Eliot but it is Yeats who has given us the most uncompromising account of the deconstructive onslaught of the mind against those fictions which are its assurance of safety. Civilization, Yeats tells us is "hooped together" in the fragile artifice of fashion, brought under the "rule" of a passing social order and given a "semblance of peace" by the "manifold illusion" which protects that order. Nevertheless "man's life is thought" and thought despite its terror of itself, is inexorably driven to tear apart its own safeguards. Man cannot cease

> Ravening through century after century
> Ravening, raging, and uprooting that he may come
> Into the desolation of reality.

The "desolation of reality" stands in a line of descent from Keats's core of "eternal fierce destruction"[22] and Marvell's

---

[21] W. B. Yeats, "Certain Noble Plays of Japan," *Essays and Introductions*, London, Macmillan, 1961, p. 224.

[22] "Dear Reynolds, as last night I lay in bed." *The Poems of John Keats*, ed. Jack Stillinger, Cambridge, Mass., Belknap Press of Harvard Univer-

deserts of eternity. Keats wished not to look too far into that core. Yeats is telling us that the tragic nature of man leaves us with no choice but to look. "We have put a golden stopper into the neck of the bottle. Pull it Lord! Let out reality."[23] No text expounds more eloquently than "Meru" the compulsive terror of the passion to demystify and no poet shows more convincingly than Yeats how the imagination seeks the dream and the dream's destruction. "Desecration and the lover's night," the repeated line that ends *A Full Moon in March*, confesses much through its violent juxtaposition.

Marvell does not move forward like Eliot, into the meaning that can lie only beyond the perilous flood. He does not like Yeats advance to "an act of faith and reason" that enables one to "rejoice in the midst of tragedy."[24] His is the cautious tenancy of an uncertain middle ground, between the betrayals of withdrawal and the treacheries of involvement. The desolation of reality is a presence and sometimes a threatening presence in this middle ground; but it is kept within limits by the propitiations of irony. An area of inconclusiveness is thus occupied and made into a proper space for poetry. If Marvell is conscious of the fictive comedy, he is conscious also of how it can protect us.

> Stumbling on Melons, as I pass,
> Insnared with Flow'rs, I fall on Grass.

---

sity Press, 1978, p. 244. The poem is better known by the title of "To T. H. Reynolds Esq." which Stillinger (p. 601) describes as "surely Woodhouse's own addition."

[23] *The Ten Principal Upanishads* put into English by Shree Purohit Swami and W. B. Yeats, London, Faber and Faber, 1937, pp. 16-17.

[24] *Letters on Poetry from W. B. Yeats to Dorothy Wellesley*, New York, Oxford University Press, 1940, p. 13.

❧

The Faerie Queene:
How the Poem Vanishes

THIS CHAPTER BEGINS with a necessary distinction. It proposes to use the word "incomplete" to describe works of literature which it is possible and proper to complete and the word "unfinished" to describe works of literature which have evolved in such a way as to make it improper to finish them. The impropriety is relative. An unfinished work might be a work which it would be possible to finish and which might be satisfactory in its finished state. But that state should be less satisfactory than the state in which the author chose to leave it.

There is no ground for this distinction in the dictionary. This may not be the only occasion on which the English language enables us to reverse Thomas Sprat's complaint that the number of words is in excess of the number of things. But arbitrary though the distinction may be, it is needed to keep in order what follows. Briefly, it is proposed that *The Faerie Queene* began as a poem that was incomplete and ended as a poem that was unfinished.

Spenser's poem stood in print before its public for nineteen years before attaining its final inconclusiveness. During this period it passed through three stages of evolution. Each of these stages enables the poem to offer the reader a different view of its status, actual or prospective. These differences are not necessarily, or even characteristically, changes of intention. They play with as well as against each other. The poem accepts what it has made of itself but on the basis of that acceptance it also proceeds to occupy a future which cannot be simply an extension of what has been made.

The initial 1590 edition of *The Faerie Queene* consisted of the first three books of the poem accompanied by dedicatory matter, commendatory verses, and the letter to Raleigh. How much and in what ways the letter matters have been, as might be expected, the subjects of wide dispute. The letter is our only advice on the possible final shape of a poem of which half remains permanently unsung. It is therefore natural to regard it as the poem's fore-conceit or, less ambitiously, as its blueprint.[1] The extent of detail in the letter and the fact that it is by the author of the poem rather than by another party encourage us to treat it as a firm commitment. On the other hand, the poem deviates from the letter to an extent which can be regarded as either inconsequential or of considerable significance. If we take the latter view it can be argued that the letter should be treated not as a blueprint but as a tactful warning against the betrayals likely to be found in any blueprint. The suggestion made here is that the letter is to be read in both ways, i.e., as contesting the claim it puts forward. We are invited to read it in both ways by the editorial staging, in other words, by the nature and placing of the document.

The letter, we must remind ourselves, is a letter. It is moreover not an epistle dedicatory, but a communication from the author to a friend. The reader is admitted to the content of the communication but the content is overheard and not announced. The pattern proposed is therefore tacitly provisional. It can be seen as a way and perhaps as *the* way of looking at the poem, but it is also measured by the poem it looks at. Since it is itself subject to a critique it is not an unambiguous vantage point. These observations may seem to lay undue weight upon the form of Spenser's disclosure but he is by no means inexperienced in the di-

[1] A. C. Hamilton, *The Structure of Allegory in "The Faerie Queene,"* Oxford, The Clarendon Press, 1961, pp. 50-52.

plomacies of placing the reader in relation to the poem. *The Fowre Hymnes* also makes use of a letter (this time an epistle dedicatory) to suggest a way of reading the poems which the poems themselves seem designed to question as much as to confirm. The subtleties of that particular placing of the reader deserve detailed consideration that is not possible here. The case is cited only to suggest that Spenser was both interested and expert in manoeuvres of the kind that are being described.

As has been already suggested, the positioning of the letter is important in controlling its impact. We might expect an overall statement of pattern to precede the poem of which it is the basis, particularly when only a quarter of the poem has been completed. The letter to Raleigh follows the first three books of *The Faerie Queene*, thus requesting the reader to pass through the poem in order to attain the schematic. By then he is in need of some guidance because of the poem's extraordinary givenness, its reticence in expounding itself, and the persistent intimations of structure (notably in the symmetries between Books I and II)[2] which suggest how fully it might reward decoding. "Dark conceit" is a phrase which accurately encapsulates the experience of passing through the poem. The letter reassures the reader that there is more to be said and that all will come together in the saying. It offers the poem's principles of cohesiveness for someone "pricking on the plaine" in pursuit of these principles. Yet the reader is also entitled to wonder whether some of the principles have been rendered obsolescent in the process of attaining them. Having read three legends "exercising" the virtues of holiness, temperance, and chastity through the trials to which these virtues are subjected he may be surprised to learn that these attributes are intended to come together in "the

[2] Woodhouse, "Nature and Grace in *The Faerie Queene*," *ELH* XVI (1949). Reprinted in *Elizabethan Poetry*, ed. Paul J. Alpers, New York, Oxford University Press, 1967, pp. 345-79 and esp. pp. 353-54. A. C. Hamilton " 'Like Race to Runne'; The Parallel Structure of *The Faerie Queene* Books I and II," *PMLA* 73 (1958), pp. 327-34.

image of a brave knight, perfected in the twelve private moral vertues, as Aristotle hath devised." Only one virtue is Aristotelian. Another is Christian and the third Christian-Platonic.[3] Again the reader who comes to the letter from the third book might well feel that "the loue of Britomart, the overthrow of Marinell, the misery of Florimell, the vertuousness of Belphoebe," and "the lasciuiousness of Hellenore" form the main part of the book. The letter informs him that these are "accidents" rather than "intendments." Britomart's rescue mission, which is presumably the book's "intendment," is not given to her until the penultimate canto. We are entitled to wonder whether the poem, as it proceeds, will not be taken over by its accidents. These divergences seem at least as important as the one usually quoted, namely the introduction of the babe with blood-stained hands who in the letter is brought by the Palmer to the court of Faery and in the poem is entrusted by Guyon to Medina after the suicide of his mother. Taken in themselves these disagreements may be of no great consequence. A writer should be allowed this much elasticity of intention. But the disagreements are magnified by the juxtaposition of poem and letter, by the author's unwillingness to devise a means of elucidation other than the letter, and by the placing of the letter at a point where the authorial claim must be subjected to the literary experience. These tactics suggest not that the letter must be accommodated to the poem but rather that the poem must stand in an unstable connection to any potential specification of it. A degree of inconclusiveness has been introduced into the relationship between the poem's flow and its pattern.[4]

[3] Quotations from the Letter and from FQ follow the J. C. Smith/A. C. Hamilton text as printed in The Faerie Queene, ed. A. C. Hamilton, London and New York, Longman, 1977.

On the matter of the Aristotelian virtues, various ways have been offered for reconciling the letter with the poem. A critique of these ways is not called for in this chapter since its hypothesis is that the letter is purposefully at odds with the poem.

[4] Isabel MacCaffrey at one point recognizes the poem's natural incon-

This inconclusiveness, as much as the letter itself, is part of the advice being offered to the reader.

Six years pass and three more books are published. A poem in instalment form (and this may be the first one in the language) holds intriguing possibilities but the instal-

---

clusiveness "For the imagination every end is necessarily a new beginning, and the open-endedness of Spenser's poem is expressed in a pattern of reiterated inconclusiveness. . . . A poetic structure is a procrustean bed on which life lies uneasily; the abrupt conclusion to Book IV is, among other things, a sign that the poet has allowed Proteus to triumph over Procrustes." *Spenser's Allegory, The Anatomy of Imagination*, Princeton, Princeton University Press, 1976, pp. 330-31. Though the recognition is important, I would prefer a more neutral vocabulary. My chapter, moreover, is concerned with the engagement of two forces rather than with the triumph of one over the other.

Although Angus Fletcher's later view (*The Prophetic Moment*, Chicago, Chicago University Press, 1971, esp. pp. 51-58) is that *The Faerie Queene* is satisfactorily closed he does draw attention in *Allegory. The Theory of a Symbolic Mode* (Ithaca, Cornell University Press, 1970, pp. 174-78) to the tendency of allegory "toward infinite extension." "Arbitrary closure," a device he finds conspicuous in *The Faerie Queene*, is characteristically used to overcome this tendency. This chapter treats the poem's closures not as arbitrary, but as expressing the natural purposiveness of inherited epic. Equally, the poem's extension of itself is bound up with the natural errancy of romance. By declining to privilege one or the other tendency, the poem posits a dialectic of difference rather than the dialectic of negation posited by *Paradise Lost*.

Judith Dundas approaches recognition of this dialectic when she observes that an "either/or choice of artistic means was historically difficult for Spenser and . . . temperamentally impossible, simply because the only finality he knew was beyond his work and beyond the here and now." "*The Faerie Queene*: The Incomplete Poem and the whole Meaning," *MP*, 1974, p. 264. However Dundas treats "fluidity, or expressive form" as complementing, rather than contesting "restrictive, containing form" (p. 265). The latter is distinctly privileged. For Renaissance artists, purpose is the clue to meaning (p. 258). Spenser's poem is the "embodiment," even if incomplete, of the intention stated in the letter to Raleigh (p. 259). "Creation itself proceeded by the imposition of restrictive form" which is thus given a cosmic as well as a literary sanction (p. 260).

Also to be read are Susanne Woods, "Closure in *The Faerie Queene*," *JEGP* 76 (1977), pp. 195-216, and Stanley Stewart, "Sir Calidore and 'Closure,' " *SEL* 24 (1984), pp. 69-86.

ments are too substantial and the interval between them too great to permit suspense of the Perils of Pauline variety. There is time for thought, and easy arithmetic makes it evident that twelve more years will be needed to complete a twelve-book poem and thirty-six more for that twenty-four book version the letter holds out as a distant promise or threat. The logistics of continuation have to be seen as onerous. A reiterated narrative form of the kind which carries forward the first two books could become crushingly monotonous if it is indefinitely multiplied. On the other hand, substantial deviations from that form would place the accidents in competition with the intendments. The poem is not sustained as *Paradise Lost* is by the momentum of a great argument. It is a pattern of virtues, and problems will arise in the sequential disclosure of a pattern. A work of literature must maintain unpredictability. In this case it is obliged to do so within a pattern that is naturally repetitive. Increasingly it will find its nature contested by different and diverging claims upon that nature.

We can argue that Spenser invites us to take cognisance of these difficulties by deleting the letter from the 1596 edition. This is not to say that the letter had become an embarrassment. We are invited, rather, to reflect on the relationship between pattern and flow (and in the end between mutability and constancy) in a manner not possible within the constraints of the letter. It was the letter which had introduced us to this relationship and which must now stand aside while the implications of the relationship are more searchingly explored.

The decision, it is being argued, was deliberate and results in the text's renegotiating its relationship with the reader, not by denouncing its past but rather by working towards a fulfillment of its history which is not quite that promised in the letter's methodical closures. As an aesthetic conjecture this may be preferable to the view that Spenser discarded the letter because it had become superfluous and because its implementation could be entrusted to the poem. We can argue that the author had become tired of the letter as a directing device and felt that it interposed a needless complication in the relationship between the reader and the literary work. If we say this we have to remember that in the year in which Spenser made the withdrawal, he also published the *Fowre Hymnes* with a dedicatory epistle at least as sophisticated in its interpositions as the letter to Raleigh.[5] The moral seems to be that the letter was withdrawn not to simplify matters but to allow the poem the proper complexities of the debate within itself.

Aesthetic conjecture is always more plausible when it rests on more than one support. There is another major deletion in the 1596 edition which sustains the same purpose as the deletion of the letter to Raleigh. Five stanzas ending the third book and described by J. C. Smith as "glorious," including one which is "the most rapturous" that Spenser "ever wrote" were replaced by the three final stanzas of Book III in the text now before us.[6] The original five stanzas brought not just the third book but the whole

---

[5] In his dedicatory epistle to the *Fowre Hymnes* Spenser observes that the first two hymns, circulating in manuscript, had inflamed the passions of those too young to know better. No reference to these ill effects has survived. He had thought of calling in the hymns but apparently the manuscripts were too numerous and too widely dispersed. Despite this alleged profusion no manuscript has come down to us. He now offers "instead of those two Hymns of earthly or natural love and beauty two others of heavenly and celestial" though that does not prevent him from conveying the two harmful hymns he was seeking to replace into the prominence of print from the obscurity of manuscripts. Having attracted to the two poems a degree of attention that might otherwise have been avoided he now proposes "at least to amend and, by way of retraction, to reform them." A variety of reading strategies is thus suggested in the epistle dedicatory but since the epistle itself may be offered as a fiction subject to an uncertain degree of discounting, the status of these strategies is in doubt and their relationship to the four poems provisional and unstable.

[6] Hamilton, p. 401. J. C. Smith, ed. *The Poetical Works of Edmund Spenser*, Oxford, The Clarendon Press, 1909, Intro. p. xvi.

first edition to a joyous conclusion in the reunion of Scu-
damour and Amoret. It is a decisive, happy ending and
the only one in *The Faerie Queene* to be attained by human
effort. The hermaphroditic figure it cites not only embraces
the lovers but can be invoked by the poem itself as the sign
of its destination. The authorial voice responds to this hap-
piness in the final stanza by abandoning its previous image
of a storm-beaten ship making harbour and using instead
the image of a team of oxen ploughing a furrow and at-
taining the rest a good week's work has earned:

> Now cease your worke, and at your pleasure play;
> Now cease your worke; tomorrow is an holy day.

The "holy day" promises a time for reflection and for un-
derstanding, followed by the confident renewal of pro-
ductive labour, and holds up the union of Scudamour and
Amoret as an earnest of what the untilled ground will yield.

In the 1596 edition the happy ending is relinquished.
After Britomart has spent a night and two days in the house
of Busyrane, Scudamour's "expectation to despaire did
turne" (XII, 45). He believes that Britomart has been con-
sumed by the wall of fire which prevented his own entry
even though at an earlier point he saw her "past the fire/
safe and untouched" (XI, 26). Lovers are capable of show-
ing more patience, but patience was never Scudamour's
strong suit. He departs with Britomart's squire to search
for "further aide." There is no evidence of his having re-
turned with the aid. "Where let them wend at will, whilest
here I doe respire" is the author's casual closure of the
episode and the "respiring" as a substitute for the previous
edition's "holy-day" is a diminution from which it is hard
to escape.

It would be a simplification to say that Spenser abandons
the constituents of his earlier happy ending. The lesson
really lies in the manner in which he retrieves them. The
hermaphroditic icon finds its home in the temple of Venus.
Scudamour may not find Amoret but Florimell is married

to Marinell and the Thames is joined to the Medway, with
the rivers of the world and their attendant fertilities offering
their collective tribute to that marriage. The "holy day"
becomes the "Sabaoth Sight" in the last line of the unfin-
ished poem's exit. But the temple of Venus lies in the mythic
distance and the poem's having promised us, now with-
holds from us, the replication of that mythic iconography
in a human event. Amoret and Scudamour were reunited
by human effort. The union of the Thames and the Medway
is an event in symbolic geography, and Marinell and Flor-
imell are brought together only by intercession with the
gods. Were it not for that intercession, Florimell's fate as
well as her incarnate vulnerability might still remain summed
in a single line from *The Waste Land*: "And still she cried
and still the world pursues." The "Sabaoth Sight" invokes
a closure beyond time and may even be suggesting that
no closure within time is possible in any fictive world that
tries to remain responsive to the actual. The retrievals do
not simply tell us that the poem is changing its direction.
They advise us that it may be reconsidering its nature.

As we look back from a revisionary watershed the con-
tours of the land behind seem to alter. The departure of
the Redcrosse knight from Una for his pledged six years
of service with the Faerie Queene had looked forward to
a destiny beyond time, the Sabbath of the true church,
and, in an interim of productive labour, the sustaining of
Cleopolis in the image of Jerusalem. The pursuit of fame
and the performing of illustrious deeds are legitimate and
even commendable if they are apprenticed to a higher real-
ity which it is their purpose to translate into human en-
deavour. As we look back on the episode from a vantage
point further on in the poem's self-formation, we wonder
whether what is taking place is a translation or an exile.
The Redcrosse knight's interview with the hermit had sus-
pended itself carefully between these alternatives and we
can now see the suspension asserting itself as part of the
life of the poem. Sidney's proposition that the end of all

learning is virtuous action and the Augustinian proposition that existence is a pilgrimage or trial through which we assert our claim to a higher citizenship, both bear upon the exercise of virtue but bear upon them in ways that are deeply different. A poem such as *The Faerie Queene* must submit to the difficult task of maintaining a tenancy between these two propositions. It must discover itself in the actual. Yet as part of that discovery it may be driven to repudiate the very actuality in which it discovers itself. That the Redcrosse knight does not return to Una while the poem lasts may be a loose end which a twelfth or a twenty-fourth book would have tied up. It may also be a fundamental statement.

Looking further back from the Redcrosse knight's departure to the very first of *The Faerie Queene*'s countless battles we find again that the shape of events has altered. In 1590 one could read the destruction of Error as a pre-figuration of triumphant closure—a prefiguration cumulatively endorsed by the Redcrosse knight's slaying of the dragon, the destruction of the Bower of Bliss, and the union of Scudamour and Amoret. In 1596 one could be struck by the over-conclusiveness of that first brief battle in which not only Error but the entire brood of Error are destroyed. If the claims of the event are accepted the poem that follows becomes unnecessary; if they are not accepted there is no reason why any subsequent promise of finality should not prove to be equally delusive. The poem's inconclusiveness and its resistance to closure can be just as much in keeping with the first episode as the structural and narrative energies which move the poem towards closure. How exactly the overall reading will run will depend upon a play of forces that is now carefully indeterminate. The end may be in the beginning, but that is no great assurance of security when the beginning is exposed as fundamentally ambivalent.

The three books of the first edition are built upon a fairly straightforward narrative movement. A mission is assigned, there are initial victories, a delay resulting from a fall into adversity, and a rescue followed by the completion of the mission.[7] Some of these components are discarded in the third book. The mission is assigned rather late and the delay and rescue are omitted. But the swift and decisive completion of the mission makes it possible to argue that the characteristic rhythm is being preserved and that the compressed version we see is merely a variation designed to avoid monotony. A standard rhythm in the exercise of virtue contributes to symmetry in the pattern, and the rhythm itself as it is repeated and varied, will acquire additional weight as symbolic action. In addition its maintenance, notwithstanding surprises, contributes to cumulative closure.

As we proceed into Book IV it becomes evident that the modified structure of Book III is not an exception but a precedent and that the poem is beginning to build up resistance to closure. Book IV even begins by announcing that it is about a character who is not to be found in the book.[8] It is true that the character can be arrived at by combining some of the other characters but we have to ask what is implied by this ingenuity beyond sheer boredom on the part of the author.[9] We take it that the autonomy of the poem is being underlined by a negligence too striking to be credible as negligence.

There is certainly no lack of autonomy in Book IV. The narrative line is virtually submerged or, to put it more tactfully, richly embroidered by the episodic overlay, and

[7] The special status given to Book I by Woodhouse ("Nature and Grace in *The Faerie Queene*") and others means that its action is primary, not that it is unique. It can therefore be mirrored or distorted in other actions which must then be read in relation to the action of holiness.

[8] Thomas P. Roche, Jr., *The Kindly Flame*, Princeton, Princeton University Press, 1964, pp. 16-17.

[9] Spenser may be putting it to us that the centre of attention in Book IV is to be found in the sum of its inter-personal relationships rather than in any single person. Such a view would also amount to a departure (however felicitous) from previous promises of design.

the accidents compete with the intendments to a degree which makes discrimination more than difficult. Epic, some will say, is yielding to romance and friendship is a collective not an individual virtue, best defined by exhibiting the varieties of friendship. There are always reasons for Spenser's doing as he does. My point is simply that what he does moves the poem in the direction of intractability. If the intractability comes about in the natural course of events it is all the more difficult to argue that the gathering inconclusiveness ought to have been otherwise.[10]

As if conscious of his responsibility to keep autonomy within manageable limits, Spenser returns to the standard rhythm in the fifth book. Indeed, he enables us to argue that the central two books of the 1596 edition yield in varying degrees to the episodic in contrast to the flanking four which preserve the standard movement. The mirror pattern, it could be said, deftly joins the individual virtues of the first three books, with the social and civic virtues of the last three.[11]

The symmetry is probably intentional. If it were not, we could make less of the way in which it is undermined. The forces of undermining are present from the beginning in the poem's natural copiousness. It is both nourished and threatened by its plenitude. The felicities of that plenitude, its sustaining of poetry's creative celebration, are strikingly expressed at the outset of the final canto of Book IV as the poet comes to the end of his recital of rivers:

> O what an endlesse worke haue I in hand
> > To count the seas abundant progeny,
> > Whose fruitful seede farre passeth those in land,

---

[10] For a post-structuralist view of inconclusiveness in Book IV see Jonathan Goldberg, *Endlesse Worke. Spenser and the Structures of Discourse*, Baltimore, The Johns Hopkins University Press, 1981. More persuasive is Patricia Parker's consideration of errancy, deferral, and dilation as pervasive elements of romance in Spenser's poem. *Inescapable Romance*, Princeton, Princeton University Press, 1979.

[11] The mirror pattern is noted by Roche, *The Kindly Flame*, pp. 200-01.

> And also those which wonne in th'azure sky?
> For much more eath to tell the starres on hy,
> Albe they endlesse seeme in estimation,
> Then to recount the Seas posterity:
> So fertile be the flouds in generation,
> So huge their numbers, and so numberlesse their
>   nation.

There is happiness in being defeated by abundance, in apologizing as the poet does in the next stanza, to any river which may have passed unnamed in the multitude of rivers. Generation in the third book was mythically located in the garden of Adonis, and Spenser can now rejoice in *Venus genetrix* in her display of creative exuberance, as Milton rejoices in the "enormous bliss" of Paradise. But Paradise was destroyed and in Spenser's poem also we have to ask how long the fictive enclosure can be relied on to safeguard its contents. In celebrating plenitude we may be agreeing to accommodate the plenitude of destructiveness as Spenser in fact seems obliged to do in proceeding to the legend of Justice. At an intermediate point, we can note that in celebrating the naming power of poetry the poet is also raising the question of how much profusion his structures can accommodate. The nation of the poem cannot be "numberlesse." Nature has time and space for closures beyond what is given to the poet. His patterns and the limitations he accepts are the signature of his ordering power. Yet their presence and their shaping capability involve safeguards whose lifting may be difficult. More particularly, the poet in exercising social and civic virtues is undertaking to reduce the distance between the fictive and the actual. So far the enclosure of the poem has been both constituted and protected by that distance. When the virtue exercised is individual, the enclosure of the poem can be matched to the enclosure of the self. External engagements can be mirrored in timeless relationships such as the struggle of the church with the world or the pursuit of right action in the field of moral choice. The poem can speak as commentary and yet maintain its integrity, the purified play of forces within its containment. When the virtues exercised are civic, it is not simply that the distance between the fictive and actual is diminished. The engagement across that distance is also particularized. The poem moves closer to the contemporary, and that is its gain. But it also faces the difficulty of translating the contemporary into the poetic in a way other than that of repudiation.

That these difficulties harass Spenser in the fifth book is evident. His previous proems looked back to the antique age, but did so to celebrate its latent presence rather than to lament its absence. Indeed the proem to Book II had suggested that faeryland might remain to be discovered as Peru, the Amazon, and "Fruitfullest Virginia" had been discovered. In the proem to Book V the world has declined into an age of stone, a fourth stage of degeneration beyond the three mentioned by Ovid.[12] The irregular motions of planets, much cited by Elizabethans as evidence of decay, are according to Spenser most marked in the case of Saturn, since Saturn reigned over a world of natural goodness and universal peace in which "No warre was known, no dreadful trompets sound." The language is echoed in the fourth stanza of Milton's Nativity poem, but Spenser is not using the familiar phrases to define the restorative power of a great event. Rather, he is indicating the distance that separates the contemporary from an ideal both fictive and antique and thus doubly removed from the present it seeks to reconstitute. Yet though Astraea has long departed from us, as poets never tire of pointing out, she has left us Artegall, trained to administer justice among beasts before

---

[12] The stones cast by Deucalion and Pyrrha, after the deluge (*Metamorphoses*, Book I) make the restoration of the human race possible. But they also testify to that part of our nature which is to triumph in an age of stone. Milton's use of the story (*P.L.* XI, 1-14) points to a situation where stoniness in the heart has been removed by prevenient grace. Spenser's use points in a quite different direction.

graduating to the more difficult human problem. Less fortunately, she has also left us Talus. Artegall's endeavours are a sign that the actual, for all its plenitude of destructiveness, is not to be repudiated by the fictive. But it also cannot be transformed into the image of the fictive. It can be flailed into acceptable shapes but the violence bespeaks the poem's difficulty in engaging itself creatively with what it cannot disregard.

Artegall's sword (V, 1, 9) was used by Jove against the Titans. Given Spenser's earlier setting up of the age of Saturn as a model of justice the weapon must be found not altogether immaculate. In fact Chrysoar is used no more than twice—at the outset of Artegall's mission when he slays Pollente (II, 18) and at its conclusion when he kills Grantorto (XII, 23). In between, Britomart kills Radigund and Arthur kills Gerioneo as well as the monster, with its family resemblance to Error, under the church altar. The rest belongs to Talus and Talus is a troubling force within the poem, not sufficiently dealt with by those who argue that justice needs power, that an age of stone demands a man of iron, and that power attending on justice in a degenerate time must sometimes be brutally applied. The rationale the reader seeks is poetic rather than political. If the world of the actual is perceived as yielding nothing to the fictive, the poem must retreat into its enclosure, denying itself the sustenance of engagement, or surrender to the actual, or await the divine deliverance, or claim its fulfillment at the end of time. Between protective isolation and dissolution in the destructive element, the only alternatives are those of indeterminacy. A concord fiction (to use Frank Kermode's invaluable term) may be implied but the time and the manner of closure into concord remain matters on which the poem can make little comment.

Engagement with the actual proceeds on the hope that it is possible to reclaim the actual in the poetic image. In Book V the mythographic locus of that hope is Britomart's vision in the Temple of Isis. Like any dense mythic-iconic complex the Isis-Osiris relationship will not yield easily to methods of exposition which are necessarily sequential and analytical. However the authorial voice offers a reading of the complex, and a helpful priest a reading of Britomart's vision which are presumably designed to be reliable.

Isis, representing that lunar principle Yeats associated with self-realization, has a crown of gold signifying "powre in things divine" (6, 7). Britomart in her vision later wears a similar crown (13, 6). One of Isis' feet is set upon a crocodile whose "wreathed taile" enfolds the goddess. The other is set on the ground. The posture symbolizes suppression of "both forged guile,/And open force." In Britomart's vision a tempest rises through the temple, fans the holy fire at the altar, strews the embers on the ground, and starts a conflagration which threatens the temple. The sleeping crocodile awakes and "gaping greedy wide" (15, 5) devours the flames and the tempest. Then "swolne with pride" (7), like the clergy in Milton's *Lycidas*, he attempts to devour Isis. She beats him back. Pride turns to "humblesse" and lust to suing for "grace and love." Isis accepts the crocodile's overtures and "enwombed" of him brings forth a "Lion of great might" (16). The priests explain that the crocodile is Osiris and also represents Britomart's "righteous knight" and "faithful lover" (22.3). Isis' clemency restrains the "stern behest" and "cruell doomes" of Osiris. The knight will subdue the "troublous stormes" and "raging flames" that threaten Britomart's succession of her "sires Crowne." She will share the kingdom with him and beare him a son "That lion-like shall show his power extreme."

The priest tactfully says nothing about the assault of Osiris upon Isis, about the ambivalences of the relationship, or about the consequences of translating the engagement between clemency and justice into erotic analogues.[13]

---

[13] See Jane Aptekar, *Icons of Justice. Iconography and Thematic Imagery in Book V of "The Faerie Queene,"* New York, Columbia University Press,

Spenser is presumably reminding us that the interplay between justice and its containment is not merely civic but cosmic, as it is indeed in the third book of *Paradise Lost*.[14] More so than Milton, Spenser sees cosmic forces in erotic terms. In particular the resemblance between Isis wreathed by the tail of the crocodile and Venus in her temple with her "feete and legs together twyned/ . . . with a snake whose head & tail were fast combyned" (IV, X, 40) suggests that we are looking at related myths. One has social and political consequences which are not present (or not drawn out) in the other but the pattern of forces is not fundamentally different.

It is not easy to read the fifth book as an implementation of its central myth. Talus is significantly not admitted to the temple of Isis (VII, 3, 8-9) but it seems clear that the relationship between Isis and Osiris ought to be reflected in the relationship between Artegall and Talus. In fact it is Talus rather than Artegall who dominates the first part of the book. In the second canto, for example, Artegall kills Pollente but is unable to enter the castle. Talus has to devise an entry (11, 20). Munera cannot be found until Talus finds her (25). Talus then carries out on her a judgement from

---

1969. "The temple of Isis is the temple of justice. And justice is as ambivalent as is sexual energy. . . . The crocodile represents the energy (which resembles and derives from and in part *is* sexuality) which justice uses and abuses; without this . . . energy there would be no justice" (p. 107). This may well be Spenser's view or rather his mythic assimilation of the savagery of justice in the actual world. Nevertheless, the principles of justice can be thought of more temperately, as for example in *Lycidas*, 78-84. See also Elizabeth Bieman "Britomart in *The Faerie Queene*," *UTQ*, XXXVII (1968), pp. 156-74. According to Kathleen Williams "The fierce and at first inimicall beast Osiris/Artegall, now tyranically wrathful, now fawning, is to become, with Britomart, complete justice, the union of opposed principles, operating as the instrument of destiny." "Venus and Diana. Some Uses of Myth in *The Faerie Queene*," *ELH*, XXVIII (1961), p. 108.

[14] An exploration of the cosmic-erotic in *Paradise Lost* is offered by Michael Lieb in *The Dialectics of Creation*, Amherst, University of Massachusetts Press, 1970.

which Artegall does not dissent but which it is not clear
that he made (26, 27). In the next episode Artegall exposes
the fallacious arguments of a leveller giant who seems to
be anticipating Burnet's history of the earth.[15] Talus de-
stroys the giant, apparently on his own initiative (49-50).
The "lawlesse multitude" rises in anger. Artegall is reluc-
tant to soil his hands "In the base blood of such a rascall
crew." On the other hand, he can hardly retreat before
them. He asks Talus to ascertain their grievances and sug-
gest a truce (52). Talus disposes of the problem in his by
now customary fashion. In Canto IV Artegall reacts in much
the same way to an Amazonian mob bent upon hanging
Terpine:

> Yet though him selfe did Shame on womankinde
> His mighty hand to shend, he *Talus* sent
> To wrecke on them their follyes hardyment:
>
> (IV,24, 3-5)

Artegall does not profit from Terpine's tale of woe. Like
Milton's Adam he is weak/Against the charm of beauty's
powerful glance (*P.L.* VIII,532-33) and falls precipitately
into that very "shame" which he undertakes to avenge
(54). Britomart's behaviour in requiring Talus to desist from
the slaughter of the followers of Radigund (VII,36) is more
in accord with the lessons learned in the temple of Isis.
This said, it should be added that Artegall's attitude to
Talus changes markedly after his release from capitivity.
He commands him to "recoyle" from the slaughter of a
mob of refractory peasants (XI,65) and wills him to restrain
his "rage" against the forces of Grantorto (XII,8). His finest
hour comes when after killing Grantorto, he dissuades Talus
from administering a lesson to Envy, Detraction, and the
Blatant Beast who have gathered upon the "strand" to

---

[15] Don Cameron Allen, *The Legend of Noah*, Urbana, University of Illinois
Press, 1963, pp. 95-96; Marjorie Nicolson, *Mountain Gloom and Mountain
Glory*, New York, W. W. Norton, 1963, pp. 153-54, 184-270.

upbraid him (XII, 38-43). The Beast is needed for another book but Artegall is doing more than merely cooperating with the author. Some degree of change in his character must be conceded though the change requires care in reading to detect.[16] On the whole Book V remains dominated by the flail and the mob. They answer each other but not as Isis' rod beats back the aroused Osiris. Indiscriminate repression responds to faceless rebelliousness. It is a world in which chivalry seems on the verge of irrelevance.

The world of *The Faerie Queene* is a fallen world but till now not fallen to a point where it cannot be reformed. Because it is fallen it can be engaged with actuality. Because it is not too far fallen it can be engaged with the forms of the imagination and its managing myths. Essentially Book V seems to recognize a distance between the ideal and the actual which may make impossible this intermediate tenancy, thus placing the fictive centre at a point where it is divested of its negotiating force. Withdrawal from an environment such as that of Book V is necessary if the fiction is to be reinstated and its ordering capability reaffirmed. Yet the withdrawal may have to be of such an extent as to preclude or limit involvement seriously.

Justice might be unnecessary if courtesy were to prevail. Nominally, courtesy is a civic quality, but its cosmic sanction is decorum, the exemplary manners of the perfect poem.[17] Mutability will later exhibit some lack of courtesy

---

[16] T. K. Dunseath (Spenser's Allegory of Justice in Book Five of *"The Faerie Queene,"* Princeton, Princeton University Press, 1968) emphasizes Artegall's development. Aptekar (*Icons of Justice*) argues otherwise. The distinction between Briton knights and knights of Faerie, made influential by Harry Berger (*The Allegorical Temper: Vision and Reality in Book II of Spenser's "Faerie Queene,"* New Haven, Yale University Press, 1957), can lead to the conclusion that Briton knights "grow" but Faerie knights do not.

[17] ". . . by the end of the [sixth] book, poetry will turn out to be something remarkably like courtesy, the practice of courtesy itself becoming a form of artistic creation . . . criticism of the court is also in this context criticism of the state of Elizabethan letters." Humphrey Tonkin, *Spenser's Courteous Pastoral*, Oxford, The Clarendon Press, 1972, p. 17, p. 25.

in her claim to justice and will be told that there is an order in change which change must learn to respect. Courtesy is basically a fictive virtue, to be located in an antique age or a pastoral remoteness. Justice can accommodate itself, though uncomfortably, to the brute facts of distance from the desirable. Courtesy cannot do so without extinguishing itself as courtesy.

It is instructive to begin a consideration of Book VI with two views of its nature. Kathleen Williams, who apart from A. C. Hamilton is the most persuasive advocate of the structural cohesiveness of *The Faerie Queene*, has the following remarks on the legend of courtesy.

> It has an absoluteness, a finality of self-existence, which separates it from the other books although it develops their themes so naturally. . . . For four books (if one omits the orderly first where the One Truth is guide) the knights have been struggling from one crisis to the next, seeing only from tree to tree of the wood of the world. Suddenly we are out, and we can see what the forest is, perhaps even what is there for and why we should ever have been in it.[18]

Harry Berger's view is to put it mildly, not the same:

> The contrivance of the narrative, the inconclusiveness of the adventures, the gradual flawing of the romance world, the failure of chivalric action—these dramatize the claims imposed by actuality on the life of the imagination. They also reveal the poet's awareness that the problems of life cannot be solved by poetry, cannot even be adequately represented in the simplified forms of Faerie.[19]

[18] *Spenser's World of Glass*, Berkeley, University of California Press, 1966, pp. 189-90.

[19] Harry Berger, "A Secret Discipline: *The Faerie Queene*, Book VI" as reprinted in *Edmund Spenser. A Critical Anthology*, ed. Paul J. Alpers, Harmondsworth, Penguin Books, 1969, pp. 266-67.

The temperate critic might begin by maintaining, however tritely, that the truth must be between these extremes but, schooled by the history of the poem, he must then ask if the vision on Mount Acidale is the poem's bower of bliss or its temple of Venus. He may reasonably adopt the second answer but he should not be able to free it of the first one. Calidore's world is certainly one in which an effort is made to keep destructiveness within manageable limits. Artegall, we are told, perhaps ironically, needed only the assistance of Talus, the two being enough "t'encounter an whole Regiment" (V,i,28; V,XI,36). Other knights have their squires and palmers. Calidore alone is bound by a vow to accept no assistance in the fulfillment of his mission (II,37). His confident handling of a hostile crowd (I,24) and of a band of brigands (XI,46-49) contrasts with Artegall's irresolution before mobs. Arthur (VI,23-24) disposes of Turpine's followers with equal ease, and Calepine (VIII,49) deals similarly with a gathering of cannibals. The Salvage man, righteously aroused to punish injustice, is, unlike the early Talus, restrained by Arthur (VI,39-40; VIII,28-29). He responds to the restraint not out of hierarchical deference, but as natural nobility responds to courteous guidance. Even the Blatant Beast is unable to cause concern to either Calidore or Timias (III,26; VI,16) though he does succeed in temporarily carrying off the mischievously named Serena as she wails her way from disaster to catastrophe. This is a world in which the "sib to great *Orgolio*" (VII,41) is diminished to a quasi-giant, Disdain, whose main function is to execute Cupid's judgement on a hard-hearted lady. It is a world in which "chances oft exceed all humaine thought" (III,51), in which Pastorella is a cousin to Shakespeare's Perdita and in which Calepine pursues and kills a bear (IV,18), reversing Shakespeare's most famous stage direction.

The poem subscribes to this world but we have to ask how far it is committed to that subscription. Is it involved in a truancy similar to Calidore's? If so, we have to recognize that Calidore's diversion is singular. Other knights fall into adversity and are rescued. Only Britomart proceeds upon her mission undistracted. The delay is presented un-ambiguously and not as competitive with the mission itself (X,2). Calidore is divided between the delay and the mis-sion, persuaded to one yet unable to disavow the other, not simply because of the pastoral beguilements, but be-cause the vision seen upon Mount Acidale is precisely that which will be attained by destroying the Blatant Beast. The poem is similarly ambivalent, with the authorial voice be-moaning Calidore's truancy—and then pointing out that he cannot really be blamed for it (X,1-4)—and the author as Colin Clout, participating in the very spectacle that Cal-idore is exhorted to pass by. There is charm in a situation in which the poet follows one course while reproaching the hero for not following another, sympathizing mean-while with the hero's dilemma. But the consequence, de-liberately invoked, is that the poem is committed to two courses, each of which it both retreats from and accepts. In its vacillation between withdrawal and involvement, the balance Spenser contrives is strikingly Marvellian.

Marvellian insinuations are strengthened by the "one sight" viewed by Calidore on Mount Acidale, a sight by which the "goodly, glorious gaze" of the world's blan-dishments is dimmed (X,4). Much commentary has been bestowed upon this "sight," with special attention given to the choreographing of the graces and the identity of the fourth grace.[20] The varieties of erudition displayed scarcely bear out Kathleen Williams' statement that "there is noth-

---

[20] Thomas Roche's notes in his edition of *The Faerie Queene* (Harmonds-worth, Penguin Books, 1978, pp. 1126-28) are particularly helpful here. See also Tonkin, *Spenser's Courteous Pastoral*, pp. 136-42, 230-64, and Ber-ger, "A Secret Discipline," pp. 273-76. If Tonkin's view (pp. 140-41) that the fourth grace is effectively the fore-conceit of the poem is accepted, the relationship between the fore-conceit, the author as Colin Clout, and Calidore as the representative of the poem, becomes particularly inter-esting.

ing to explicate in the legend of courtesy, little to interpret, no need to demonstrate the fineness of its quality."[21] Given the scope of this chapter attention will be restricted to one matter, the disappearance of the four graces and the hundred dancing maidens.

They disappear when Calidore rises out of the wood and approaches them (17,18). Their vanishing into thin air may reproach Calidore's lack of courtesy, a courtesy better displayed in III,20 when he comes unwittingly upon a jolly knight who is seeking "To solace with his lady in delight." In the earlier episode Calidore had craved pardon for his offence against the virtue he was supposed to exemplify. In the present one he merely says he is "Right sory," puts the event behind him, and seeks enlightenment on the meaning of the spectacle.[22] We might conclude that he is being let off lightly. More summary treatment is given to a later voyeur, this time upon Mount Arlo, which is dedicated to Diana as Mount Acidale is dedicated to Venus (*Mutabilitie* VI, 46-55; *FQ* VI,X, 9).

Spenser may be saying something more substantial than this. To identify what he is saying it may be helpful to turn to a poet much closer to our time, T. S. Eliot. In *East Coker* a dance takes place to the accompaniment of a "weak pipe" which may be Colin Clout's pipe grown feebler. The dance, signifying matrimony and betokening concord, is described in archaic language which holds it away from the reader. The words are presented as quoted rather than real (they are in fact quoted from Thomas Elyot) and the world they invoke is therefore placed before us as fictive and "antique." It is consequently vulnerable to scrutiny and can be viewed only if unlike Calidore, "you do not come too

---

[21] *Spenser's World of Glass*, p. 191.

[22] Tonkin notes that Calidore's recognition that he "rashly sought that, which I mote not see" is an "admission for the first time, not of luck-lessness but of imperfection." The acceptance of responsibility is slow in coming. Eight stanzas of elucidation by Colin Clout are needed to make Calidore understand the extent of his transgression.

close." Eliot repeats the caution in order to underline it. Moreover, even when the "sight" is preserved by maintaining an appropriate distance from it the natural evolution of the dance translates its courtly grace, first into movements that are heavily bucolic and then into a grimmer dance of dung and death.[23]

The poet in *East Coker* seeks to abandon the poetic enclosure, the artificial world of protective language stereotypes, and to move forward into the painful renegotiation of the covenant of language with reality. "The poetry does not matter," he tells us. The dancers have disappeared like the graces and maidens. They are all gone under a hill which may or may not be Mount Acidale.[24] More resolutely than Spenser and perhaps because a world of war leaves him with no alternative, Eliot is committed to the search for the design of the real in the injustice of the actual, a search which for the poet, is unavoidably a language-quest, "the intolerable wrestle/With words and meanings."[25] The Blatant Beast is of a different complexion here, wounding us not with invective but with platitudes. Spenser, less determined to "fare forward" than Eliot, keeps his poem deftly divided between the heroic enterprise and that world of fictive purity which is, complicatingly, both the alternative to and the possible eventual objective of that enterprise. The relationship between the creative deed and the contemplative attainment, discussed between the Redcrosse knight and the Hermit in Book I (X, 46-48) is renegotiated here with imaginative understanding substituted for religious insight. As might be expected, the pattern of relationships is complex, quite other than the "transparency" Kathleen Williams sees and not quite the straightforward flawing of the romance world Harry Berger discerns. That world is indeed vulnerable. Its profusion of

[23] *East Coker*, I.
[24] *East Coker*, II.
[25] *Ibid*.

contrivances will not bear serious scrutiny. The whole of it and not merely its centre of insight can maintain itself only "if you do not come too close." Yet it is to be desired as well as disassembled. The poem seeks both responses, merging them in its central episode and refusing to supersede its ambivalences by a heroic undertaking subversively depicted as intermittent, distracted by recurrent abductions and rescues, and in the end, inconclusive. It cannot even be said that the quest, however erratic, results in acts of self-formation similar to those which the Redcrosse knight and Guyon undergo. Yet the poem does not solicit the abandonment of the endeavour it discounts any more than it seeks the relinquishment of that pastoral centre which vanishes as one approaches it. Between the fragility of the desirable that is by now unavoidably fictive and the uncreative obduracy of the actual, it maintains that continued and precarious truce which it seeks to put forward as the consolation of honesty.

The last twenty stanzas of the 1596 edition deal with the defeat of the Blatant Beast. It is a brief end to a pursuit that has been overlaid with distractions. Calidore has actually been absent for five of twelve books and the poet has found it necessary to point out how insistently the knight has been hunting the Blatant Beast while the reader and the poet were engrossed in other matters (IX, 2-6). The beast is now run to earth in a monastery, suggesting that there is no protection even in seclusion.[26] He is subdued without undue difficulty. Since his weapons are largely verbal, he offers little trouble to the knight of courtesy. Symbolically, the beast does not wound Calidore and Calidore strikes no actual blow at him but pins him down with his shield until his virulence is exhausted. It is fitting that Spenser's most intriguing monster should embody the extraordinary de-

---

[26] Tonkin (p. 152) comments that "the unprotected monastic life, cut off from the normal protection afforded by a properly functioning social system, is a natural prey for a force which thrives on isolation."

structive force of language misused. Courtesy is possible without language as the Salvage Man shows us, but language is the cementing force in civilized relationships and so is the central objective in any attack on the standards of civilization.

The beast has been compared to the beast in Revelation. It bears some resemblance to that animal. Indeed there are few literary beasts in the Renaissance that do not, just as there are few literary harlots who do not remind us of the great whore of Babylon. The real link with Revelation is in what happens to the beast rather than in how the beast looks. The beast is bound and it breaks loose. In Revelation commentary the breaking loose initiates a period of religious turbulence which will intensify until the beast is destroyed. Things must get worse before they can get better and they may not get better until the end of time. By making the earlier binding relatively easy and indicating how the subsequent efforts of Pelleas and Lamorache were useless (39), Spenser is able to suggest the extent to which the power of the beast was waxing even in Arthur's time. In the thousand years that have passed between the courts of Arthur and Elizabeth the capabilities of the beast have presumably grown in proportion. It should be noted that a thousand years was the conventional period of "binding."[27] Spenser makes it the period for which the beast has been loose. In so doing he is able to comment on the state of his own times with a deadliness all the more effective because it is only implied. The final attack is on poetry, the citadel of courtesy. The question is whether poetry can survive except by an act of segregation from the contem-

---

[27] See Naseeb Shaheen, *Biblical References in "The Faerie Queene,"* Memphis, Memphis State University Press, 1967, for resemblances between the Blatant Beast and the Beast in revelation. The binding and the breaking loose (Rev. XX,2; XX,7), have been indefatigably elaborated and expounded. Ernest Lee Tuveson in *Millennium and Utopia* (Evanston and London, Harper Torchbooks, 1964, pp. 1-70) provides an initiation into this bottomless subject.

porary so far-reaching that it can only be self-destructive. Can it on the other hand, maintain itself in a world in which the Blatant Beast has flourished for ten centuries? The poem ends poised between two possibilities both of which are potentially hostile to its survival.

The final battle in *The Faerie Queene*'s last complete book can be profitably related to the poem's opening encounter. The Blatant Beast is spawned by Typhon and Echidna (VI,vi, 9-13), and Echidna's resemblance to Error has been noted in Spenser commentary. Error's vomit of "bookes and papers" (I,20) and the "black as inke" complexion of her progeny (I,22) make it apparent that the Blatant Beast is indeed one of her most talented children. The contrast between the total destruction of Error and its brood and the Blatant Beast roaming at large for ten centuries after its nominal defeat is therefore particularly effective. If the mirror relationship suggested by Roche between the first and second three books is admitted, it is hard to avoid the implication that the last battle is the undoing of the first.

The inconclusive subduing of the beast invokes and strengthens other inconclusivenesses. Amoret has yet to find Scudamour, Britomart must be united to Artegall, and the Redcrosse knight must return to Una. The reader must await these developments in a time which he now knows will not be that of the poem. He had to wait six years for Guyon to recover his horse. Meanwhile the unfinished stories should not be taken as the narrative sign that the poem has defeated itself by its helpless hospitality, by accepting more than it is able to unify. A tighter containment might be possible but the exclusion of everything outside that containment would weaken the poem while facilitating its closure. The natural plenitude of the poem has been allowed its consequences and while the poem has not mastered those consequences it also has not succumbed to them. In fact its own self transcendences—the garden of Adonis, the temple of Venus, the temple of Isis, the sight upon Mount Acidale—have drawn a line at a mythic elevation that can be seen as running in an ongoing though not necessarily parallel relationship to the fictive flow over which it stands in appraisal.[28] Though the pattern cannot be closed—at any rate not in this poem—it is intimated too often and too firmly to be thought of as abandoned by events. The form of the unfinished as the poem progressively comes to it is to admit the forces of redemptive change and fictive idealization as they declare themselves within and against the actual, to characterize the pattern of their interplay with events, to make gestures towards a prospective settlement but also to persuade us that the scope of acceptance is such that the actual settlement must lie outside the time of the poem. If the scope were more restricted, the poem should strike us as being false to itself, as having settled its conflicts by contrivance. If the shaping energy were less sustained, the continuing movement of the poem would signal not its formation but its collapse. The poem must be shaped sufficiently and the contest within it must be contained sufficiently for it to remain a work of art. But the nature of what it includes must also be such that it is not a work of art allowing of closure.

So far it has been argued that the first edition of *The Faerie Queene* was a poem announcing itself as incomplete. Its decisive and indeed ardent happy ending was an earnest of a more comprehensive closure to come. The outlines of that closure were indicated in the letter to Raleigh that followed the happy ending. Though the poem deviated from the letter it did so to the extent of contesting rather

---

[28] Alastair Fowler observes that "it could be shown that all the generative couples of Books III-IV—Venus and Adonis, Florimell and Marinell, Amphitrite and Neptune, Tethys and Oceanus, Thames and Isis, and the rest—find a common relation in the primary conjugates Isis and Osiris." *Spenser and the Numbers of Time*, London, Routledge and Kegan Paul, 1964, pp. 213-14. See also A. Kent Hieatt, "A Spenser to Structure our Myths," *Contemporary Thought on Edmund Spenser*, ed. Richard C. Frushell and Bernard T. Vandersmith, Carbondale, Southern Illinois University Press, 1975, pp. 99-120.

than overthrowing the letter's status as a projection of the poem's possible future. In the second edition the poem defined itself as unfinished rather than incomplete. It did so in several ways. The letter was discarded and the happy ending was replaced by an inconclusive climax that looked forward to the inconclusive climax of the sixth book. The scope of acceptance was widened. In particular the brute world of the book of justice was juxtaposed with the contrived world of courtesy creating a distance across which engagement was difficult and establishing alternatives neither of which could be indefinitely sustained. Unfinished narratives were allowed to accumulate, lending weight to the gathering inconclusiveness. Shifts, indeed breathless shifts, from one suspended narrative to another were multiplied so as to retard and distract the forward movement.[29] Thus the available signals were used steadily to indicate that the poem might no longer be one which it was fitting to complete.

The general disposition of Spenser scholars is to treat *The Faerie Queene* as incomplete. Two statements, contrasted in a way that is frequent in Spenser criticism, will serve to illustrate the common assumption. According to C. S. Lewis,

—the poet broke off with many of his greatest triumphs still ahead. Our loss is incalculable; at least as great as that we sustained by the early death of Keats.[30]

On the other hand, according to Northrop Frye, the six books of *The Faerie Queene*

---

[29] See Berger, "A Secret Discipline," p. 265, for what he terms the "deliberate casualness" of Book VI.

[30] *The Allegory of Love. A Study in Mediaeval Tradition*, Oxford, The Clarendon Press, 1936, pp. 336-37. Elsewhere Lewis observes that *The Faerie Queene* "is a poem of a kind that loses more than most by being unfinished. Its centre, the seat of its highest life, is missing." *English Literature in the Sixteenth Century*, Oxford, The Clarendon Press, 1954, p. 380.

form a unified epic structure regardless of how much might have been added that wasn't.[31]

Lewis and Frye differ considerably on the cost of incompleteness but both agree that the poem is incomplete. The view offered here is that the poem is by now nearly as complete as it ought to be, but that in achieving that near-completeness, it has announced itself as a poem not to be finished. One more strategic desirability remains. If the poem is not to attain its closure it should ideally effect its disappearance. The disappearance, if properly brought about, would provide us with a highly finished form of the unfinished, on which it would not be easy to improve.

The poem's disappearance now becomes the last act in the drama of the relationship between the poem and its audience. When the 1609 version appeared with the appended cantos, the poem had stood before the public for nineteen years. Its author had been dead for ten years. The posthumous circumstances strengthen the propriety of those fragments to which the vanishing poem is now being reduced. They also make the disposition of what remains an editorial rather than an authorial act so that the poem, even as it vanishes, is also being taken over. The poem's demand for autonomy, its dissociation from the author's proclaimed intention, which began with the deletion of the letter to Raleigh, now seems to be proceeding to its limits. In the end the poem and the author stand in debate, with the author's words appended as a postscript to a postscript, distanced even further from the poem by the withdrawal from poetry which it advocates.

In the edition of 1590 a canto on generation had stood at the centre of a final book on chastity. The 1609 fragment offers us "Two Cantos of Mutabilitie: which both for forme and matter, appeare to be parcell of some following book of *The Faerie Queene* under the legend of Constancie." The

[31] *Fables of Identity. Studies in Poetic Mythology*, New York, Harcourt Brace and World Inc., 1963, p. 70.

editorializing is suitably guarded. It refrains from suggesting that the book to which the mutability cantos could belong might be the seventh book and it presents as conjectural even the possibility that the two cantos might be part of a book. Given this reticence, the grounds on which the conjecture is offered is significant. It is because of their "forme and matter" that the mutability cantos appears to be part of a book on constancy. "Forme" one might reasonably argue, applies not simply to the stanza but to the elevation, to the manners of the poem as distinct from its substance. The mutability episode can be seen as part of the poem because it is at the same mythic level that the Garden of Adonis, the temples of Venus and Isis, and the "sight" upon Mount Acidale occupy. The proposition as to "matter" is more provocative. It recognizes an ontological paradox far deeper than the paradox of Book III. In doing so it suggests that the nature of the legend within which the mutability cantos are located ought to be such as to invoke this paradox. Then in an act of numbering which is offered rather than justified and which may be either the author's or the editor's, it locates the cantos at the subversive centre of a book on constancy that must somehow contain their explosive force. Thus the poem has been opened out to a maximum range of acceptance and the editorializing has distinctly suggested that this opening out is part of the poem's nature.

The suggestion is not unjust. The poem's widening of previous acceptances, its importation of its own past into its subversive present, are evident when we recall the relationship between change and the quasi-eternal once typified in the figure of Adonis.

> All be he subject to mortalite,
> Yet is eterne in mutabilitie,
> And by succession made perpetuall.
> (III,VI, 47)

In the garden, mutability had made no claim against this structure of relationships. In the final cantos, it challenges the structure to the extent of claiming sovereignty over it, thereby arguing in effect that structures are either not attainable at all or open to replacement as soon as they are attained. Since the revolutionary demand is not made *in vacuo* but within the unfolding of a poem, it is really being implied that the balance of forces within the poem itself has changed to an extent calling for radical reassessment. In other words, the poem's forms of quasi-permanence—specifically the mythic and the fictive—have not succeeded in assimilating the poem's occurrences. Its "intendments" are unable to cope with its "accidents."

Raised to the status of an Olympian debate, the poem's interrogation of itself has been daringly extended. Indeed, it has been advanced to a point where it almost seems to presage challenges to come in literary history of the Apollonian principle by the Dionysiac. The issues raised, of course, are cosmic rather than literary but in a literary work they must be framed to question the nature of poetry as part of the nature of order.

Nature's judgement of Mutability's claim is a restatement of the relationships prevailing in the garden. The emphasis there had fallen on the plenitude of generation, on the diversity propagated by the "Father of all formes" (VI,47). It falls now on the purposiveness of change and on the manner in which all things "worke their own perfection" through the mutations they undergo (VII,58). The dilation of being and the "turning to themselves" which Nature sees as the principle of change evidently invoke the neo-Platonic procession and return. Raphael in expounding the scale of nature to Adam (*P.L.* V, 469-70) has the same thought in mind.

To argue that there are principles of change is to disallow Mutability's claim, which is that change itself is the only principle. It is the proper answer but the circumstances in which it is rendered undermine the authority of the findings. Nature's judgement takes less than two stanzas (58-59) to articulate. Jove's statement of his case is restricted to one stanza (48). Mutability's claim proceeds for fourteen stanzas (14-27), is documented by witnesses for nineteen stanzas (28-46), and then continues for a further nine stanzas (47, 49-56). The weight of evidence and the failure of both the judge and the contestant to deal with the evidence specifically, entitle us to wonder whether nature's verdict is to be regarded as a finding or a fiat. On the other hand Mutability's argument is undermined by her highly structured advocacy of her own case and by her presentation of a pageant of witnesses when a rout or a rabble might have been more appropriate. The poet has in fact achieved a Marvellian stand-off with one side subverted by its peremptoriness and the other by its inability to practise what it preaches. The reader has no real conclusion in his hands. All he has is the disappearing poem.

Under the complexities of debate, the means for disappearance are being carefully prepared. Six books have been succeeded by a fragment and the fragment is now to be succeeded by a sub-fragment. Two cantos have diminished to two stanzas. The disappearance of the graces from Mount Acidale has been followed by the disappearance of Nature from Mount Arlo. All that is needed for the poem's disappearance is a *raison d'être* for its exit. That basis is provided by Nature's argument for dilation and return. If we translate that summing-up into its literary equivalent, we can say that the poem issued from a meta-text into which it must now withdraw. The complete cycle of dilation and return is achievable only by the meta-text. The poem can provide us with intermittent reflections of that cycle, with intimations of how the meta-text might proceed. But since its capacities for dilation are limited, it cannot bring what it reflects to a close. It lives in a world of significant mutability. Full closure is the privilege of the meta-text. A poem is properly unfinished when it has brought itself to a point where its completion necessitates a duration longer than the poem can command and when the text from which it issued can be fittingly invoked for the conclusion not attainable within the world of the poem. This is the point which *The Faerie Queene* has reached. In particular, by implicitly raising the literary question within the cosmic question of how a poem can be "eterne" in its own mutability, it has prepared the way for its absorption into a poem larger than itself.[32]

The authorial voice speaks in the penultimate stanza in conventional accents of world-weariness.[33] Mutability "beares the greatest sway" in all things other than the rule of heaven itself. Nature's statement of purposive change is not so much dissented from as bypassed. In fact, Nature at this point is not even mentioned. It is mutability to whom the author responds and whose supremacy he seems eager to admit. Time's "consuming sickle" dominates a flowering which is no more than the luxuriance of pride. The image reaches back to the garden of Adonis where time was a destructive force in the procession of things (III,VI, 39-41). The force was controllable then. It is overpowering now, and its destructive supremacy seems to argue clearly that the moment has come to say farewell to the world's vanities, including the vanity of poetry.

The poet does remember Nature's verdict in the final stanza but his recollection is distinctly partial. Nature had said that the last change would be into the changeless and the poet looks forward into a realm "when no more *Change*

---

[32] See *Eterne in Mutability: The Unity of the Faerie Queene. Essays published in Memory of Davis Philoon Harding*, ed. Kenneth John Atchity, Archon, Conn., Hamden Books, 1972. While recognizing Spenser's inconclusiveness, the contributors treat that inconclusiveness as calling for a reversal of traditional views of the poem. Thus Jean McMohan Humez suggests that "to 'complete' anything so long and so comprehensive in its progress [as *The Faerie Queene*] may be simply to stop at a good moment." Susan Fox observes (pp. 28-29) that the "dangling states" of the love affairs in the poem are "allegorical disasters as the poem now stands. . . . Since allegory dictates the structure of *The Faerie Queene* in the first place, allegorical disaster is also structural disaster. . . . It is probably in its very incompleteness that the over-riding plan of the poem is most evident."

[33] The stanzas have all the characteristics of allusive closure as defined by Barbara Herrnstein Smith. *Poetic Closure*, pp. 172-82.

shall be." Nature had said that all things "stedfastnes doe hate" and the poet seeks a world of "stedfast rest." His aspiration is for a state not "eterne in" but "contrayr to Mutabilitie." In dismissing the temporal in favour of the eternal and literature in favour of an understanding beyond literature, it is perhaps an ingenious extra touch that the poet should quarrel with his own poem. It seems even more apt that he should decline to subscribe to a philosophy of purposive change that appears, among other things, to justify the sequential nature of language, its bringing about of permanence through "succession." The tactic, we might say, adds zest to an otherwise routine dismissal. Wit is being shown even in cosmic farewells. The flourish and its propriety should be admitted but we should also note that the crucial part of nature's judgement is being ignored rather than contested. The juxtaposition of two verdicts is pluralistic; but it stops short of becoming self-contradictory.[34]

Indeed, the two statements approach each other under their interlocked differences. Nature's judgement and Mutability's case have already been shown to be undermined. The author's underlining of the vanity and transience of things is similarly not quite as resolute as it seems to be. The counter-movement may at first strike us as fragile but since we are dealing with only eighteen lines, one line can be significant in its revisionary force. Nature had said that "all things stedfastnes doe hate." The poet alters this to "all that moveth, doth in *Change* delight." The word "delight" recalls the joyous plenitude of the Garden of Adonis and since the poet has already made full use of the de-

---

[34] Spenser's pluralism is examined by Carol V. Kaske in "Spenser's Pluralistic Universe: The View from the Mount of Contemplation," *Contemporary Thought on Edmund Spenser*, pp. 121-49. The case for pluralism, as Kaske recognizes, amounts to more than compiling a catalogue of "discrepancies." There must be a pattern in the discrepancies, mobilized around alternative formulations in the poem's view of itself. The poem should be unable to commit itself entirely to either formulation.

structive presence of time in that garden, his response to the garden's main aspect is fitting, though ambivalent. Delight in change may be the imagination's last infirmity, the final vanity of *homo ludens*. But given the force of attachment exercised by "delight" and the substitution of delight for hatred, it seems reasonable to conjecture that the poet is justifying as well as dismissing himself. Moreover deeper reading suggests that "moueth" has more than one meaning. A poem moves us by delighting us through its changes, and when it ceases to delight it ceases to move. The poet's playing with a familiar critical tag (and one which aptly suggests the achievement of his own poem) invites us to look warily at his dismissive gestures.[35]

It is important to establish these ambivalences since they have a bearing on the final two lines of the poem. The tapering down of the poem to its vanishing point is carried out with a persistence that ought to delight as well as move the reader. Two cantos, as we have already pointed out, diminish into two stanzas. Two stanzas reduce themselves to two lines linked by a repetition that detaches them slightly from the rest of the stanza. The two lines call our attention to two letters within a repeated word. In the third and last

---

[35] Donald Cheney comments that the reader is at no point "permitted to forget the mixture of opposing attitudes with which Mutabilitie is being viewed. One pole of this opposition is the Christian *contemptus mundi*, the feeling of exhaustion and disdain for this world and intense longing for the combination of absolute delight and absolute rest to be found through death in the 'Sabaoths Sight' hinted by Nature. At the other pole is the artist's delight in the inexhaustible variety and movement of his creation; a delight which is apparent from the moment he begins to unfold his legend, in the effortless tracery of the stanzas as in the *copia* with which character, incident and theme are anatomized." *Spenser's Image of Nature: Wild Man and Shepherd in "The Faerie Queene,"* New Haven, Yale University Press, 1966, pp. 246-47.

Judith Anderson (*The Growth of a Personal Voice: "Piers Plowman" and the "Faerie Queene,"* New Haven, Yale University Press, 1976, pp. 198-203) draws attention to syntactical ambiguities in the poet's final words in the last two stanzas. This, as well as the opposing attitudes with which Mutability is viewed, should cause us to look warily at the poet's dismissals.

repetition of the word the two letters become a single one. The spelling differences and their implications have been much discussed in Spenser commentary and we must not forget that the 1611 editors preferred to make the spelling uniform. Nevertheless if the 1609 spelling is admitted, the last two lines become a climactic subtlety in the poem's disappearance.

We are, however, dealing with something more than an exit gesture of extreme dexterity. The question to be asked is about the nature of the "Sabaoth Sight." Is it the sight *of* or the sight *from* the still point? The sustained, dismissive rhetoric of the final two stanzas seems to suggest the former. Yet as we have already indicated, that rhetoric may be undercut by its recognition of how life delights in change. Moreover, spelling in Spenser's time, in so far as it can be standardized, uses "Sabbaoth" to refer to the day of rest and "Sabaoth" to refer to the Lord of Hosts. The "Sabaoth sight" therefore could be the sight *from* the still point. It might be one more turn in Spenser's ambivalences if, in seeking stillness, we were to return to motion.[36]

Of course the sight *of* and the sight *from* the still point need not be separated and the spelling may finally be advising us of that through the discriminations it entices us into making. Spenser can be illuminated by authors of our own century. We have already quoted *East Coker* in connection with the Sight on Mount Acidale. The words which clarify Spenser's final words are to be found in the second section of *Burnt Norton*. "At the still point, there the dance is" is Eliot's strenuous finding and even more emphatically

[36] This crux has been extensively discussed. No decisive resolution is proposed here. Any such resolution would be out of place in a chapter concerned throughout with the engagement of alternatives. The view that the Sabaoth Sight is the sight from the still point, advanced in the eighteenth century by Upton, has been revived more recently by Don Cameron Allen ("On the closing lines of the *Faerie Queene*," *MLN*, LXIV, 1949, pp. 93-94).

he tells us that except for the still point "There would be no dance, and there is only the dance." Yeats' *Byzantium* is also a poem that can be profitably pondered. Its tactics follow those of Spenser's final stanzas in their commitment to a dismissive rhetoric vehement in its repudiation of the "fury and the mire of human veins." The golden bird of Byzantium is "More miracle than bird or handiwork." It is cast in "glory of changeless metal" and scorns aloud "common bird or petal." The language here and throughout the poem proclaims the otherness of being from becoming and yet, through the very force of its segregating strenuousness, testifies to the impossibility of total disengagement. In repudiating the world of generation, poetry unavoidably recreates what it scorns. On the other hand, the dance on the emperor's pavement in Byzantium though ultimately real is incapable of being actualized. It is "An agony of flame that cannot singe a sleeve." The poem siting itself upon that pavement, looks out with fascination on "That dolphin-torn, that gong-tormented sea" where images beget fresh images. It is the sight *from* the still point, of the teeming world of generation, of time and language begetting the unceasing flood of images of the eternal, that dominates the poem at its close.[37] Spenser may not proceed as far as this but his poem too, in its intricate course, has made its commitments to the world of generation from which it cannot seek final disengagement. The sight from the still point is the sight of that completed poem of divine creativeness into which the author's unfinished poem has been absorbed. The last dismissal may be that of language but in the course of that dismissal language ironically reasserts its claim.

The mechanics of presentation of *The Faerie Queene* make the reading of it an exercise rich in opportunities. We might almost say that the poem's ideal reader should be divided

---

[37] Yeats, *Collected Poems*, pp. 280-81.

in himself or should teach himself to vacillate between different ways of taking hold of the poem. He must refrain from withdrawing the poem into its schematization. Equally he must refrain from letting the schematization dissolve in the fictive flow. Like Frye, Hamilton, and Williams he must accept the poem's invitation to spatialize it, to stand away from its immediacy in its pattern-constituting hinterland. It is an invitation strengthened by the letter to Raleigh which helpfully seems to offer us the poem's principles of spatialization. On the other hand the reader must also be conscious of the manner in which the poem resists the letter it seeks to implement. Like Alpers and Hough he must respond to *The Faerie Queene*'s other invitation—to move with its immediacy and to recognize how it discourages pattern-making by its proliferating encounters, its involvement in its own plenitude, and its deflection of the abstract by the actual. The two main ways of reading *The Faerie Queene* can be thought of as complementary but are perhaps better thought of as necessary defences against each other. The compleat reader must seek not the sum but the engagement of both ways of passing through the poem.[38]

[38] Hamilton, *The Structure of Allegory in "The Faerie Queene"*; Williams, *Spenser's World of Glass*; Frye, *Fables of Identity*, pp. 69-87. Hough's view (*A Preface to the "Faerie Queene,"* London, Duckworth, 1962) is mixed. He considers (p. 93) the letter to Raleigh to be relevant "formally and externally" but not "to the real nature" of Spenser's work. The essence of *The Faerie Queene* is "immanent" in its "multitudinous local effects, not in an over-riding plan which could be abstracted and schematically displayed" (p. 94). The suggestion seems to be that the true pattern of the poem emerges from its flow. The claimed pattern is one the flow is free to modify. Alpers (*The Poetry of "The Faerie Queene,"* Princeton, Princeton University Press, 1967) is more decisive. According to him, the search for structure in *FQ* has "faced us in the wrong direction" and "made us regard our own theories and interpretations rather than the poem" (p. 107). We must talk of organization rather than structure. The unity of *FQ* is to be described "in terms of habits of mind, both the poet's and the reader's" rather than "in terms of a fixed structure" (p. 119).

Neither of the main groupings indicated succeeds in responding fully to the poem. Hamilton's present view is that "no genuine response to

There are other ways of thinking about the engagement upon which the poem situates itself. It can be regarded as poised between the purposiveness of Virgilian epic and the errancy of Ariostan romance with each inheritance coming increasingly to represent an essential component of the poem's self-declaration, its mediation between pattern and flow, between the movement to closure and the resistance to closure. Since the poem has to work through an engagement which is too much part of it for the engagement to be arbitrated, it can ask with propriety to remain unfinished.

In short, if the reader is asked to be pluralistic it is because the poem is pluralistic. It is divided between intention and autonomy, with autonomy claiming, as it must, the right to revise and yet to retrieve intention. The text's evolving versions of its status take it in a direction which it has not ruled out but which is not in the main line of its hopes for itself. Yet as we ponder the direction, we cannot but appreciate its propriety to the poem's natural forces, to the privileges sought out by its own momentum. The foremost of these privileges is to remain unfinished. The evolving engagement between pattern and procession traced by *The Faerie Queene* both in its own dispositions and in the invitations it issues to the reader situates the poem around an internal dialogue about its nature which it can initiate and explore but not conclude. The end is therefore properly posthumous with the author speaking from another dimension, addressing the poem as another self, and dismissing a life-work in the name of that "rest" which the dismissal promises, only so that, in the last evaporation of word-play, he can retrieve the disowned self in its perfecting. As a model of the unfinished, *The Faerie Queene* is manifestly rich in implications. It might be excessive to say

the poem is ever wrong, only incomplete" (*The Faerie Queene*, General Introduction, p. 8). It follows that any way of reading *FQ* that is advanced will be productive only to the extent that it engages itself with other ways of reading it.

that these implications directly affected the future course of the unfinished since a more recent vocabulary of criticism has had to be called on to identify the play of crucial forces in the poem. Yet the very manner in which the poem opens itself to that vocabulary says something and probably something important about the nature of the imagination's continuity.

Areopagitica and the
Images of Truth

IN THE EPILOGUE to *Comus* the Attendant Spirit leads us
through an ascending series of marriages, the highest of
which is the union of the soul with virtue. Preparatory to
that final relationship, in which the mind finds its destiny
in the good, is the marriage of Cupid and Psyche. Youth
and joy are the outcome of that marriage, an outcome un-
derwritten by a heavenly commitment. Both the local real-
ities of the language and the previous dispositions of the
masque put it to us that youth and joy find their identities
as the children of that discipline represented by the Lady
rather than as the brood of that indulgence which Comus
represents. A fulfilling relationship with the world beyond
the "starry chime" is the condition, not the countermand-
ing, of a creative relationship with the world of events.

In *Areopagitica* we pass to a different understanding and
to a different aspect of the legend of Cupid and Psyche.

Good and evil we know in the field of this World grow
up together almost inseparably; and the knowledge of
good is so involv'd and interwoven with the knowl-
edge of evill, and in so many cunning resemblances
hardly to be discern'd, that those confused seeds which
were impos'd on *Psyche* as an incessant labour to cull
out, and sort asunder, were not more intermixt. It was
from out the rinde of one apple tasted, that the knowl-
edge of good and evill as two twins cleaving together
leapt forth into the World. And perhaps this is that
doom which *Adam* fell into of knowing good and evill,

85

that is to say knowing good by evill. (*Complete Prose* II, 514)[1]

There are twins here, but they are not youth and joy, or even knowledge and virtue, those twins of "divine generation" born of that love whose "first and chiefest office begins and ends in the soule" (*Complete Prose* I, 892).[2] What we see instead are the offspring of human fallibility, knowledge joined indivisibly to the betrayal of knowledge, symbolizing not the fulfillment beyond the dark wood, but the ever-present confusion within the wood itself. The emphasis now falls on the "incessant labour" and the interwoven entanglements, the unrelaxing vigilance that is needed to cull out the seeds of our true flowering. Yet it would not be just to say that a previous response has been rendered obsolete in this sombre yet onward-urging reminder that the legend of Cupid and Psyche has more than one face. Root images haunt the literary imagination be-

---

[1] References to Milton are to the *Complete Prose Works of John Milton* (New Haven, Yale University Press, 1953–), cited as *Complete Prose* and to the Columbia University Press edition of Milton's works (New York, 1931-40), cited as *Works*.

[2] Milton's preoccupation with twins and sisters deserves to be noted. We begin at the level of fallen awareness with the knowledge of good and evil cleaving together. We rise to Youth and Joy at the level of natural plenitude, creatively apprehended. At a higher level, we come to Knowledge and Virtue, the twins of divine generation and at the apex, beyond and before generation as we know it, are Wisdom and Urania.

The eighth chapter of *Proverbs* provides the basis for Milton's Wisdom and we can also remember that in Spenser's *Hymn of Heavenly Beauty*, Sapience is "The sovereign darling of the Deity." However neither the Bible nor Spenser provides Wisdom with a sister and it is the sister who is Milton's muse. Wisdom moreover is "Eternal Wisdom." Augustine's distinction between eternal and created wisdom (*Confessions*, XII, 15) is probably at the back of Milton's mind. Since Urania both converses and plays with Wisdom, two functions of poetry, knowledge (attained in conversation) and utterance (liberated in play), are being pushed back to the borders of the ultimate. The association between utterance and knowledge implicit here, is explicit in "The Reason of Church Government" (*Complete Prose* I, 820-21).

cause of what they comprehend, because disparate recognitions are brought together in a cohesion both baffling
and authentic, which the writer finds himself called upon
to expound and explore. The mind learns by submitting to
the interrogation of these images, by responding to the
different aspects of their nature as they confront the mind
at each stage of its growth.

Milton sees truth through the lenses of more than one
image, but some early statements of its self-vindicating
quality will serve as the first part of an instructive contrast.

> The very essence of Truth is plainnesse and brightnes;
> the darknes and crookednesse is our own. *The Wisdome*
> of *God* created *understanding*, fit and proportionable to
> Truth, the object, and end of it, as the eye to the thing
> visible. If our *understanding* have a film of *ignorance*
> over it, or be blear with gazing on other false glister
> ings, what is that to Truth? If we will but purge with
> sovrain eyesalve that intellectual ray which *God* hath
> planted in us, then we would beleeve the Scriptures
> protesting their own plainnes and perspicuity. . . . ("Of
> Reformation," *Complete Prose* I, 566)

In avoiding what he derisively calls a "paroxysm of citations" Milton quotes only Athanasius in support of his
conviction.

> The knowledge of Truth, wants no humane lore, as
> being evident in it selfe, and by the preaching of Christ
> now opens brighter than the sun. (*Ibid.*)

If the structure of truth is not naturally discerned it is
only because its radiance is avoided.

> . . . they feare the plain field of the Scriptures, the
> chase is too hot; they seek the dark, the bushie, the
> tangled Forrest, they would imbosk: they feel them
> selvs strook in the transparent streams of divine Truth,
> they would plunge, and tumble, and thinke to ly hid

in the foul weeds, and muddy waters, where no plum-
met can reach the bottome. . . . Wherfore should they
not urge only the Gospel, and hold it ever in their
faces like a mirror of Diamond, till it dazle, and pierce
their misty ey balls? (*Complete Prose* I, 569-70)

If the light is all that is needed for the dismissal of dark-
ness, the Word is all that is needed for the dismissal of
Babel.

But let them chaunt while they will of prerogatives,
we shall tell them of Scripture; of custom, we of Scrip-
ture; of Acts and Statutes, still of Scripture, til the quick
and pearcing word enter to the dividing of their soules,
& the mighty weaknes of the Gospel throw down the
weak mightines of mans reasoning. ("The Reason of
Church Government," *Complete Prose* I, 827)[3]

Affiliations with the Ludlow masque offer themselves
invitingly in these statements. The dark and tangled forest
recalls Comus' habitat. The "false glisterings" on which
the understanding can gaze recall the "orient liquor" in
Comus' glass that "flames and dances in his crystal bounds."
The "transparent streams of divine truth" are reminiscent
of Sabrina's lodging "Under the glassy, cool, translucent
wave." Elsewhere in "Of Reformation" (*Complete Prose* I,
535) Milton refers traditionally to "spotlesse *Truth*." It is a
phrase which in this context cannot but recall the unblem-
ished form of chastity and the birth of Youth and Joy from
the unspotted side of Psyche. Milton's early understand-
ings of the nature of error and truth thus connect them-
selves to the images of error in "Comus" but not in such

---

[3] This passage is among those discussed by Stanley Fish in *Self-Con-
suming Artifacts* (Berkeley, University of California Press, 1972), p. 274.
Fish's overall view is that the rhetorical strategies of "The Reason of
Church Government" decisively undermine that very reason which the
title and the pseudo-structure allege. For purposes of this chapter it can
be said that the merely ratiocinative is dismissed to establish a higher
coherence to which reason must be answerable.

a manner as to revise those understandings. It is to *Paradise Lost* and to the final phase of Adam's education that we must turn for a more radical rereading of these images.

> . . . to nobler sights
> Michael from Adam's eyes the film removed
> Which that false fruit that promised clearer Sight
> Had bred; then purged with euphrasy and rue
> The visual nerve, for he had much to see;
> And from the well of life three drops instilled.
> So deep the power of these ingredients pierced,
> Even to the inmost seat of mental Sight,
> That Adam now enforced to close his eyes,
> Sunk down and all his Spirits became entranced.
> (*Paradise Lost* XI, 411-20)

In the eighth book of *Paradise Lost* Adam also sinks down "Abstract as in a trance" but his "internal sight," uncorrupted and therefore in no need of renewal is able to see Eve born as Youth and Joy were born to Cupid and Psyche. The rationally desirable becomes the actual in the prelapsarian universe. "Whatever is, is right" but whatever is right also is.[4] Adam, whose "Colloquy Sublime" with God had established the rightness of Eve's creation, is witness to the implementing of this principle. Imagination leads us to the nature of reality even if a short period of deprivation (significantly placed within the dream itself) intervenes between the dream and its fulfillment. For fallen Adam, remedial measures need to be instituted before mental sight can function even partly. "If we will but purge with sovrain eyesalve that intellectual ray which *God* hath planted in us" is Milton's hopeful cry in *Of Reformation*. The understanding has been created fit and proportionable to truth the object and end of it, in a nice blend of the theory of ac-

---

[4] This is to restate the principle of plenitude as elaborated by A. O. Lovejoy in *The Great Chain of Being* (Cambridge, Mass., Harvard University Press, 1936). The phrasing intentionally echoes Pope's *Essay on Man* II, 294.

commodation with the Greek view of the sufficiency of reason. The knower is matched to the knowable and all that is necessary is to remove by our own, not very onerous efforts the film of ignorance over the eye of the mind. In *Paradise Lost* that film is removed not by any effort of man, but through the ministrations of an angel. When that is done, the visual nerve must be purged with euphrasy and rue and only then can three drops from the well of life be instilled. These carefully planned measures are needed to pierce to "the inmost seat of mental sight" suggesting that truth is no longer seen as a "mirror of Diamond" dazzling and piercing the misty eyeball. Even then, the "intellectual ray which *God* hath planted in us" needs much guidance from Michael before it can adequately interpret what it is assisted to see. The light is discerned not as itself, but in the course of its contention with darkness. Good and evil grow up together indivisibly in the field of this world.

A further example can be offered of a root image which the later Milton sees in a different light. "It is my habit day and night," he wrote to Diodati, "to seek for this idea of the beautiful, as for a certain image of supreme beauty, through all the forms and faces of things . . . and to follow as it leads me on by some sure traces which I seem to recognize" (*Works* XII, 27). He compared the search into which he was drawn by his "vehement love of the beautiful" to the "labour" with which "as the fables have it" Ceres was said "to have sought Proserpine." It is ardour rather than labour which dominates this pursuit, but when Milton returns to the image in *Paradise Lost*, the sense of how it addresses us has changed.

> Not that faire field
> Of *Enna*, where *Proserpin* gathering flours
> Her self a fairer Floure by gloomie *Dis*
> Was gatherd, which cost *Ceres* all that pain
> To seek her through the world.
>
> (*P.L.* IV, 268-72)

Milton's multiple similes are carefully thought out in their implications. The sequence of which these lines are a part tells us that Paradise is a place of metamorphosis, that it is a place of protection that does not fully protect, and before all that it is a place of loss. As we look narratively forward yet backward in our own psychic biographies to Eve, the fairest flower and her gathering by Satan, the world becomes the theatre of history and the searching Ceres the energy of the desolation within us. We are not led on by "sure traces," by the presence of a supreme idea "through all the forms and faces of things." Rather we are haunted by the absence of a creative principle which, because it is lost, can be only dimly discerned. "All that pain" is authentic because of what it unchallengeably takes for granted. The finger points and we cannot avoid acknowledgement.

As Milton proceeds from the diagram to the experience, from the golden world of design to the bronze world of actuality, he is enacting a progress that is not unfamiliar. Yet it is not sufficient to say that politics helped Milton as it has assisted others, in the discovery of original sin. To seek beauty and to proclaim it as truth is a natural trend in the poetic imagination but one which the imagination must come to question in the very course of its pursuit. In finding access to the structures it sees as authentic, the fictive capability also finds itself obliged to bring those structures into engagement with the world. The actual may then be perceived not simply as repudiating the real but as placing in doubt even its claim to reality. The problem the imagination then faces is to outlive its own subversion without collapsing into an irresponsibility which would achieve survival only at the cost of protective incarceration in the fictive. The responsible imagination (and the imagination *is* constituted between answerability and self-delight, between radical innocence and subversive experience) must succeed in finding and inhabiting a ground for mediation between the actual and the authentic.

The movement from the beauty of truth to the pain of seeking truth makes the inclusive and intricate structures of order which Milton builds subject to threatening erosions. Yet we never lose the sense of a shaping purpose, the conviction through all these disturbances, that "It shall be still in strictest measure eev'n." (Sonnet VII). "Light after light well us'd they shall attain/And to the end persisting, safe arrive" (*P.L.* III, 196-97) is a later version of this measured progress. The syntax does what it ought to do in postponing safe arrival to the end of the assurance and the emphasis falls properly on the persisting effort as it did earlier on the strict rhythm of things. The dance is now the struggle but the struggle is not without its consolations, its controlled movement to an objective that is more and more clearly discerned. An intermediate statement nicely balances the effort and the serenity.

> Lady that in the prime of earliest youth,
> Wisely hast shun'd the broad way and the green,
> And with those few art eminently seen,
> That labour up the Hill of heav'nly Truth.
>
> (Sonnet IX)

The smooth-flowing movement of the passage, its lack of what is admiringly called muscularity, can make us insufficiently aware of its not inconsiderable verbal energies. "Prime of earliest youth" with its intensification of apparent opposites, is effective in suggesting that wisdom is not necessarily the product of experience. It is the product of the right commitment, resolutely made. "The broad way and the green" probably remembers Virgil as well as Matthew: VII, 13-14, and also looks forward to the causeway built by Sin and Death, "broad/Smooth, easy, inoffensive down to hell" (*P.L.* X, 304-05).[5] "Green" has other possi-

---

[5] The ease of the descent into Hell is touched on in the two passages cited. The difficulty of the ascent is touched on in *P.L.* II, 432-33 and III, 20-21. *Aen.* VI, 126-29 seems to stand equally behind all four passages though it is cited only in connection with II, 432-33 (from Newton onwards).

bilities called out by the context. It is the colour of youth, of growth, and of the promise that is expected to flower. But it is also the colour of fallibility and is therefore wisely shunned in the prime of youth. Appearance is not reality and the pacing of the passage puts before us the steady, undistracted rhythm of the mind committed to reality. There is labour in the ascending of the hill, as the language clearly tells us, but the labour is subdued to be no more than the converse of the gentle, yet dominant, urging forward.

There are many ways up the hill and Donne's way must be quoted, though there can be few readers to whom it is unfamiliar.

> On a huge hill,
> Cragged and steep, Truth stands, and hee that will
> Reach her, about must, and about must goe;
> And what th'hills suddennes resists, winne so;[6]
>
> (Satire III)

Donne's hill is a challenge rather than a destiny, an incitement to conquest, warily approached in the searching and circling movements of a mind estimating its adversary and attempting to form a feasible plan of assault. The repeated "about must" exactly conveys the vigilant reconnaissance, going over and solidifying its first findings. But all stratagems are subject to the experience of the encounter, the "suddenness" inherent in the outline of the actual, however carefully that outline may be charted. The nature of the hill becomes known through its resistance and in the storming effort by which that resistance must be overcome. This is not the self-evident truth, or the truth processionally attained, as in Milton's sonnet, by the committed mind advancing upon its destiny. It is a view in which the basic dispositions of the structure of truth are made real through the intensities of crisis.

Guiding generalizations should seem necessary by now

---

[6] The text used is from *The Satires, Epigrams and Verse Letters of John Donne*, ed. W. Milgate (Oxford, Clarendon Press, 1967).

to the readers of this chapter who have watched its explorations proceed about and about a certain hill. It would be comforting to say that Donne is the poet of process, of structures found and disengaged from experience, and that Milton is the poet of justification, of structures made answerable to experience. The distinction is valid enough to be discussable and Milton's synchronic view of truth in his earliest pamphlets, a view to which the Puritan mind was powerfully attracted,[7] does seem to argue for unchanging structures of understanding, which the divine has purposefully accommodated to the human and within which experience can be obliged to fall. Unfortunately for those comforted by clear-cut discriminations, Milton's most memorable and complex image of truth will not fit easily into the mould.

> Truth indeed came once into the world with her divine Master, and was a perfect shape most glorious to look on: but when he ascended and his Apostles after him were laid asleep, then strait arose a wicked race of deceivers, who as that story goes of the *Egyptian Typhon* with his conspirators, how they dealt with the good *Osiris*, took the virgin Truth, hewd her lovely form into a thousand peeces, and scatter'd them to the four winds. From that time ever since, the sad friends of Truth, such as durst appear, imitating the careful search that *Isis* made for the mangl'd body of *Osiris*, went up and down gathering up limb by limb still as they could find them. We have not yet found them all, Lords and Commons, nor ever shall doe, till her Masters second comming; he shall bring together every joynt and member, and shall mould them into an immortall feature of lovelines and perfection. . . . They are the troublers, they are the dividers of unity, who

---

[7] Boyd Berry draws attention to the "compulsive rage" of the Puritans for "order, system, and orthodoxy." *Process of Speech*, Baltimore, The Johns Hopkins University Press, 1976, p. 87.

neglect and permit not others to unite those dissever'd peeces which are yet wanting to the body of Truth. To be still searching what we know not, by what we know, still closing up truth to truth as we find it (for all her body is *homogeneal*, and proportionall) this is the golden rule in *Theology* as well as in Arithmetick and makes up the best harmony in a Church; not the forc't and outward union of cold and neutrall and inwardly divided minds. (*Areopagitica, Complete Prose* II, 549-52)

Several lesser images are gathered and reviewed in this controlling statement. The truth is self-evident, but self-evident only as a living whole which was catastrophically lost and must be laboriously recovered. The truth is progressively regained in a cohesive forward movement, with each discovery making the next discovery possible. Nevertheless human effort can only approximate, not constitute, the truth, and a final act of integration remains reserved for a force of coherence beyond time. The torn body is sought in the field of the world as Ceres sought Proserpina; the church of the imagination is linked with the true church and the pursuit of beauty with the building of truth in the deep affinities between Osiris and Orpheus. The light shines not to dazzle the beholder nor to dismiss the darkness but to make possible that collective effort by which the darkness is to be subdued: "The light which we have gained, was given us, not to be ever staring on, but by it to discover onward things more remote from our knowledge" (*Complete Prose* I, 550). In the balances and proportionings of the image, the revealed and the achieved, the structures deciphered by human effort and the structures set forth in eternal dispensations are placed in relationships which give each other meaning and which are in that deep sense, homogeneal.

In contemplating this central image, we relate it first to other images used by Milton which are less inclusive or which differ in their emphases. The unspotted truth, the clear waters of truth, the hill of truth and the dazzling light of truth have their sanctions in both convention and the Bible. The torn body of truth is less frequently encountered, though Milton is doing no more than following and developing the interpretation offered by Plutarch (*Complete Prose* II, 549, n. 222).[8] One result of the introduction of a relatively new style of seeing is that our sense of the more traditional images is altered. We are persuaded to think of the stream as flowing, of the light as guiding, of the hill as continually being ascended, of the unspotted form as cleansed rather than virginal. The principle of an evolving consciousness, arising from the consolidations of its own past and putting into a progressively built relationship the eternally present and the historically attained, is brought dramatically into the field of inquiry. The resultant revaluations encourage us to attempt the further exercise of moving forward from the image so that we can respond to it not merely as an advancement of seventeenth-century attitudes but also as a foreword to the modern awareness. If the waters of truth flow "in a perpetual progression," so too does the stream of literature. When Yeats repeatedly compares to a "perfectly proportioned human body" that Unity of Being which literature and culture strive to attain, he is remembering a tradition in which Milton's image is a crucial element.[9] When T. S. Eliot unexpectedly tells us

[8] A. Bartlett Giammati has brought out the extent to which images of fragmentation and reconstitution occupy the Renaissance humanist view of its relationship to the classical past. "Hippolytus among the Exiles: The Romance of Early Humanism," *Poetic Traditions of the English Renaissance*, ed. Maynard Mack and George de Forest Lord, New Haven, Yale University Press, 1982, pp. 1-23. The transference of these images from the secular to the sacred and from humanism to the Puritan "dissidence of dissent" is noteworthy.

[9] For some of Yeats's many references to Unity of Being see Balachandra Rajan "W. B. Yeats and the Unity of Being," *The Nineteenth Century*, CXLVI (1949), pp. 150-61. See also "Yeats and the Renaissance," in *Chaos and Form*, ed. Kenneth McRobbie (Winnipeg, University of Manitoba Press, 1972), pp. 159-70.

that there is in Donne's poetry hardly any attempt at or-
ganization but only a "puzzled and humorous shuffling of
the pieces," he may be really characterizing not the Dean
of St. Paul's, but the author of *The Waste Land*.[10] Never-
theless in reading the present into the past, Eliot invites
us to connect the past to the present and to estimate the
distance travelled on the road away from the source. Those
who gathered the pieces of the body of Osiris had some
sense of what they were seeking. Today's puzzled and
humorous shuffler is too deep in exile to retain any memory
of the lost design. Indeed, the first task in the rehabilitation
of his consciousness may be to achieve the recognition that
a design was lost. Milton's image should evidently be seen
as an early statement of the dismemberment myth, a myth
of which Blake's poetry is the most organized and elaborate
literary declaration. It might be added that the doctrine of
the dissociation of sensibility which has been so influential
in our time is fundamentally an application of the dismem-
berment myth to cultural history.[11]

At this stage it may be desirable to ask ourselves how
these discriminations and linkages bear upon the concerns
of Christian humanism and the ways of access to the truth
which that humanism registers. To observe in response
that a Christian humanist is a Christian who is also a hu-
manist may well be taken as a sign of exhaustion. Never-
theless there is a tension implicit in the phrase, and *Paradise
Regained* with its crucial scrutiny of the limits of learning
can be read as one of the works designed to keep us prop-
erly aware of that tension. It is a tension increased by the
Reformation insistence on the inward and overwhelming
nature of the experience of relationship to the divine. Such
an experience requires no frame of reference. It may enter
history but it is a disclosure outside history. It is self-in-

---

[10] "Donne in Our Time," *A Garland for John Donne*, ed., Theodore Spen-
cer (Cambridge, Mass., Harvard University Press, 1931), p. 8.

[11] This particular doctrine has to be read as a cultural version of the
loss of Eden as well as a cultural version of the dismemberment myth.

terpreting and self-authenticating. The angel speaks to the naked, thinking heart, and we can even argue that it speaks more clearly to a mind devoid of cultural distractions.

A position as extreme as this does not need to be consistently held for us to recognize its attractions and even respond to its pull. The flight from the alone to the alone—to use the phrase Plotinus made immortal (*Enneads* VI, IX, XI)—is part of a longing built into the nature of man, though there is a further part of that nature which calls on him not to reject but rather to temper that longing, making it responsive to that stubborn historical effort which is a condition of our creative fulfillment. Truth can be the dazzling diamond, the indisputable structure unchallengeably revealed, but it is also the torn body, sought fragment by fragment in the field of the world. To the Christian visionary Athens can seem the enemy simply because it is the noblest of all distractions. Nature, as Geoffrey Hartman has shown us, can seem to stand in a similar relationship to the Romantic search for reality. Nevertheless we should seek not the rejection of Athens, but its rebirth in the marriage of Jerusalem and Albion; and we must similarly come to terms with an ultimacy that both dismisses nature and is disclosed in nature.[12] Milton's mind directs itself to this

---

[12] Geoffrey Hartman, *Wordsworth's Poetry, 1787-1816*, New Haven, Yale University Press, 1964. In later editions of his book Hartman has rightly discouraged misreadings of it which take him to be saying that Wordsworth regards nature as an enemy. Such an awareness has to be regarded as one among other *loci* of consciousness rather than as an exclusive destination of consciousness. The mind, to know itself fully, "must pass through a stage where it experiences Imagination as a power separate from Nature" (p. 44). The Simplon experience and the Snowdon experience are to be placed in relationship as "two rival highpoints of *The Prelude*. In one, imagination breaks through to obscure the light of nature; in the other the poet seeks imagination directly via the light of nature" (p. 63). The result is "a twofold revelation that could have been sevenfold as in John the Divine" (p. 67).

Dismissal of nature and disclosure in nature are propositions jointly maintained, in their bearing upon language, in Raphael's preamble to his account of the war in heaven (*P.L.* V, 563-76). The simultaneous presence

overall awareness, and now that laments about his aban-
donment of history are becoming less frequent, it may be
opportune to suggest that the earlier work, with its view
of the truth as self-evident, final, and synchronically re-
vealed, is less committed to the flow of time than the later
work with its essentially evolutionary view of understand-
ing, of truth diligently gathered in the movement of his-
tory.[13]

Models of truth may seem to have only a distant rela-
tionship to a poetics of indeterminacy but reflection indi-
cates that the model in *Areopagitica* is fraught with conse-
quences for such a poetics. The insistence on a lost whole
progressively reconstituted means that the synchronic view
is not abandoned but is announced instead as a point of
origin. A familiar strategy of the imagination is to histori-
cize the fictive, thus generating a poetry of retrieval, the
end of which is the reinstatement of origin. Progress to-
wards such an end is, according to Milton, cumulative, the
closing up of truth to truth and the advancing to what we
know not by virtue of what we know. But it requires only
an adjustment and one which the later Milton might have
been prepared to make, to regard such progress as inher-
ently self-revising. We move forward, in other words, not
through successive approximations but rather through suc-
cessive transformations.

---

of both possibilities is explored in "Osiris and Urania," *Milton Studies XIII*,
Pittsburgh, University of Pittsburgh Press, 1979, pp. 221-35.

[13] In *The Christian Revolutionary: John Milton* (Berkeley, University of
California Press, 1974), Hugh Richmond puts forward what seems a sim-
ilar view of the later poems. However the distinction in Professor Rich-
mond's book is between an arrogant and allegedly platonic commitment
to reason which characterizes the earlier poems and the acceptance of
education through experience which characterizes the later ones. The
distinction offered here between historical and visionary modes of un-
derstanding seems more adaptable to the evidence. Moreover, the point
I would like to make is that Milton's work is distinguished not by its
adhesion to either mode, but by its attempt to maintain a tenancy between
them. In defining the nature of this tenancy *Areopagitica* is a crucial doc-
ument.

The search for truth in *Areopagitica* is a collective endeavour, a common undertaking of the elect community. It posits a text decoded by a privileged group of readers in the manner persuasively secularized by Stanley Fish. Indeterminacy is unavoidable because the decoding can only be ratified by debate among the privileged and because the debate remains continuously subject to the admission of new evidence and to changes in the decoding capability brought about by assimilation of the evidence.

The original Puritan claim was to a systematic, self-authenticating truth, a text which might even be over-determined not only to the extent of offering its own reading but of ruling out alternatives to that reading. The one right reading prescribed by the chosen language is of course, a familiar shaping principle in a world whose passing today's criticism either mourns or celebrates. Under the pressure of the "dissidence of dissent" the Puritan claim likewise could be sustained no longer. An Eden happily free of ambiguity became fraught with pluralistic possibilities. The multiplicity of sects which Edwards and Pagitt resonantly deplored[14] then had to be legitimized as a creative ferment out of which was to emerge that reading consensus which is once again held before us as a horizon. The Puritan problem was to construct an intermediate model of the attainment of truth which retreated from absolutism without altogether renouncing it and without capitulating to the relativities of history. Between the proposition that Jerusalem is the same at all times and all places[15] and the proposition that Jerusalem can be perceived (and unavoidably, partly perceived) only through the means of access offered by time and place, some mediating tenancy had to

[14] Thomas Edwards, *Gangraena*, London, 1646; Ephraim Pagitt, *Heresiography*, London, 1654.

[15] See Berry, *Process of Speech*, p. 142. "When the Puritans removed the process of history and the matrix of chronology from life on earth, they in effect implied that everything is always the same; Israel of the past equals Israel of the present equals Israel of the future."

be found. *Areopagitica* responds to this dilemma, preserving the fragile liaison between the simultaneous truth and the language of temporality.

> Immediate are the acts of God, more swift
> Than time or motion, but to human ears,
> Cannot without process of speech be told,
> So told as earthly notion can receive.
>   (*Paradise Lost* VII, 176-79)

Raphael is here facing the problem of how the creation, that perfect poem, the coherence of which lies beyond sequential statement, is nevertheless to be "told" within the restrictions of narrative. The "homogeneal" truth is a similar poem with history as the potential narrative of its disclosure. The lost wholeness, the fragment-by-fragment recovery, the figures of postponement such as the culling of the confused seeds by Psyche, the separation of the wheat from the tares and the building of the house of God from many timbers and diverse quarries constitute the narrative as a fiction of concord in which progress is reassuringly continuous, but completion indefinitely deferred. When we internalize this collective search, we have the basis for a poetry of self-formation in which the lost whole is the divine image and the movement of self-formation is measured by the progressive recognition and restoration of that image. As we proceed further, secularizing what we have internalized, we find ourselves obliged to relinquish certain crucial reassurances. The divine image and its presence and perfecting within us can no longer form the basis of correlation between outer reality and inner self-making. Divested of this safeguard, the poetry of self-formation will be driven to interrogate the status of its fictions, recognizing them as possibly no more than fictions. Demystification in other words, is the natural consequence of secularizing the Areopagitican model. It is therefore apparent that the model has not only a place but an important place in the evolution of a poetics of indeterminacy.

101

Nevertheless the Areopagitican model is distinctly transitional. It attempts to mediate between history and the eternally present that is taken to be affirmed in history, between the Osiris principle of the search and the Urania principle of vision. The point is that the text authenticated by the search is a continuous text and not a series of random disclosures; its widening interrelationships are in fact the evidence that a totally inclusive text exists. Such an understanding gives status to the fragment, making it incomplete not because of its nature, its innate resistance to unification, but because of its limits, the boundaries which constrain it and which can be broken open only by its participation in a larger totality.

The distinction which has just been suggested between a fragment defined as less than complete and a fragment defined as other than complete is anticipated by the consequences of Derrida's proposition that "To write is to have the passion of the origin."[16] One consequence is that "Totalization can be judged impossible in the classical style; one then refers to the empirical endeavour of either a subject or a finite richness which it can never master. There is too much, more than one can say."[17] The strategies of deferral which maintain totalization in the classical manner not *on* but *as* the horizon of possibility and which depict non-closure as approximating rather than avoiding a final inclusiveness are examined at length in this book as part of the tradition of the unfinished and as the raison d'être of the Areopagitican model. Literary history places before us both the subversion of this model by the later Romantics and the efforts of high modernism to restore it. In this context the romantic subversion can be seen as proceeding to Derrida's other possibility in which non-closure is brought about not by the magnitude of the literary field, but rather

[16] Jacques Derrida, *Writing and Difference*, trans. Allan Bass, Chicago, University of Chicago Press, 1978, p. 295.
[17] *Writing and Difference*, p. 289.

by its character.[18] The loss of an authenticating centre leads to a succession of substituted centres, each relinquishing the wholeness which it claims or seeks since its own self-examination can only reveal the irreducible absence at its heart. The play between substitutions not only inhibits totalization but must eventually take the place of that totalization which it cumulatively excludes rather than defers. It must survive as the animating energy in the very field which it evacuates by the mutations of absence. Literary history bears witness to these possibilities but the manner in which it bears witness can remain a matter for debate. Is the movement shaped by historical and eventually non-literary transformations which deprive us of an authenticating centre, or is it implicit in that self-scrutiny which the act of writing must bring to bear on itself? Is classical non-closure a testimony, no longer sustainable, to the magnitude of a design which the human imagination can gesture towards but cannot hope to encompass, or is it a mystification to be stripped away, a fiction of the authentic which literature must disregard in the compulsive search for its own authenticity? Are the subversive potentialities of the fragment restricted to questioning that passion for origin in which literary history once cast it as a participant, or can the fragment withdraw further, asserting its own givenness and refusing even to engage itself with that passion? As these questions are raised, the Miltonic moment seems to present itself sub-textually as a deferral of their threats even while it valorizes by its own explicit deferrals the whole to which it is dedicated, the promised consummation to which understanding moves. The compositions and decompositions of Keats's two Hyperions, the question mark of Shelley's poem of consciousness are troubling possibilities, but on a still-distant horizon.

[18] *Ibid*.

꩜

Paradise Lost:
The Uncertain Epic

THE PROBLEM of the genre of *Paradise Lost* seems to have been a problem from the day the poem was published. Dryden may have said that "this man . . . cuts us all out and the ancients too"[1] but it did not take long for the caution of the critic to make its inroads on the generosity of the poet. In the *Preface to Sylvae* (1685) the objections are stylistic—to the "flats" among Milton's elevations, to his "antiquated words" and to the "perpetual harshness" of their sound. But eight years later in the *Discourse concerning the Original and Progress of Satire* the qualifications become more substantial. The earlier objections are repeated and Milton's lack of talent in rhyming is added to them. But we are also told that Milton's subject

> is not that of an heroic poem properly so called. His design is the losing of our happiness: his event is not prosperous like that of all other epic works; his heavenly machines are many and his human persons are but two.[2]

In the Dedication to his translations of the *Aeneid* (1697) Dryden begins by saying that "a heroic poem, truly such, is undoubtedly the greatest work which the soul of man is capable to perform."[3] Homer and Virgil are sovereign in

[1] *Early Lives of Milton*, ed. H. Darbishire, London, Constable, 1932, p. 296.

[2] *Of Dramatic Poetry and other Critical Essays*, ed. George Watson, London, J. M. Dent, 1962, Vol. II, pp. 32, 84-85.

[3] *Ibid.*, II, p. 223.

the genre. "The next, but the next with a long interval between was the *Jerusalem*."[4] Spenser would have had a better case than some continental claimants to the succession "had his action been finished, or had been one." Milton's title would have been less suspect

> if the devil had not been his hero, instead of Adam; if the giant had not failed the knight, and driven him out of his stronghold, to wander through the world with his lady errant; and if there had not been more machining persons than human in his poem.[5]

Dryden, it will be observed, gives his objections force by both repeating and extending them. To earlier statements about the unfortunate outcome and the excess of heavenly machinery in *Paradise Lost* he now adds the suggestion that an action dubious in its epic propriety may also be constructed round the wrong hero. The persistence of crucial objections and the adding of related ones thus come to constitute a platform from which the genre of the poem can be interrogated.

Much can be discerned from Dryden's platform. The unfortunate outcome exposes Milton's poem to consideration as tragic rather than epic. If Satan is the hero, he is the hero within an anti-quest that invites us to view *Paradise Lost* as anti-epic or parodic epic. Addison's response to Dryden argues that no hero was intended but suggests Christ, if need be, as the hero. This defence of the poem converts it into a providential epic but one which engages the human only at its periphery.[6] It thus undermines one of Dryden's objections but only at the cost of underlining

---

[4] *Ibid.* For further statements on the sovereignty of Virgil and Homer in the genre see II, p. 167; II, p. 195. Spenser (II, p. 150; II, pp. 83-84) is Virgilian. But Milton, though Spenser's "poetical son" (II, p. 270), is Homeric rather than Virgilian (II, p. 150).

[5] *Ibid.*, II, p. 233.

[6] *Milton, The Critical Heritage*, ed. John T. Shawcross, London, Routledge and Kegan Paul, 1970, p. 166.

another. The Romantic reinstatement of Satan as the hero is of course, not an endorsement of Dryden. It attacks the question of what the poem is by suggesting that there is a poem other than the official one in which the real nature of Milton's accomplishment is to be found. Generic uncertainty is compounded by viewing *Paradise Lost* as an act of creative subversion in which the true poem overthrows the establishment exercise.

The two-poem theory in turn has ramifications which continue into the present. We can simply reverse the romantic valuation and regard the true poem as the official one. The true poem can then stand in relation to the false, as icon does to idol, or as reality to parody within an antithetical universe.[7] We can regard the two poems as confronting each other creatively or, as Waldock would have it, locked in destructive conflict.[8] It can be argued that the two poems only appear as two and that it is the purpose of reader education to bring them into concurrence.[9] Finally, like Woodhouse, we can think of the two poems as engaged with each other through a double protagonist, each functioning within a different genre.[10]

It may be that the course of criticism after Dryden is misguided and that, as John Steadman proposes, Milton is writing an "illustrious" epic fully compatible with Italian neo-Aristotelianism whereas Dryden's criticisms are made from the vantage point of a neo-Aristotelianism that is distinctly French.[11] Certainly neither Aristotle nor the Italians

---

[7] John M. Steadman, *Milton and the Renaissance Hero*, Oxford, The Clarendon Press, 1967. Balachandra Rajan, "The Cunning Resemblance," *Milton Studies VII*, pp. 29-48.

[8] A.J.A. Waldock, *"Paradise Lost" and its Critics*, Cambridge, Cambridge University Press, 1947.

[9] Stanley Fish, *Surprised by Sin*, Berkeley, University of California Press, 1971.

[10] A.S.P. Woodhouse, *The Heavenly Muse*, ed. Hugh MacCallum, Toronto, University of Toronto Press, 1972, pp. 176-94.

[11] John M. Steadman, *Epic and Tragic Structure in "Paradise Lost,"* Chicago, The University of Chicago Press, 1976.

prescribe a fortunate outcome for the epic. But Milton published *Paradise Lost* in 1667 when Italian neo-Aristotelianism was hardly representative of current critical trends. We are accustomed to these gestures of obsolescence in Milton which include the imaginative adoption of a slightly antiquated model of the universe. The voice of the outsider is also a voice from the past, a voice disowning if not excoriating the triviality of the present. Nevertheless the history of reading *Paradise Lost* points to real difficulties which are not disposed of by a more accurate generic assignation. A poem which may be two poems initially or finally, in which there are three possible heroes and even the possibility of two heroes rather than one, is not a poem about which one can be certain.

Some of the problems of placing *Paradise Lost* are interestingly suggested by William Willkie in a preface (1757) to a heroic poem of his own. Willkie is writing about the difficulties of reconciling the untrue with the true, or historical, in an epic poem. Spenser accomplishes this reconciliation through the evasions of allegory. Willkie then notes (remembering Dryden) that in *Paradise Lost* "persons in machinery overshadow the human characters" and adds (remembering Addison) that "the heroes of the poem are all of them immortal." *Paradise Lost* escapes a requirement that looms over epic poetry by being "a work altogether irregular . . . the subject of it is not epic, but tragic . . . Adam and Eve are not designed to be objects of admiration, but of pity . . . it is tragic in its plot but epic in its dress and machinery."[12]

Willkie may be the first critic to recognize that *Paradise Lost* is not only a mixed-genre poem, but a mixed-genre poem with a different protagonist for each of its primary genres. It is true that given Aristotle's views of the importance of plot, the identification of the epic with "dress and

---

[12] *Milton 1732-1801. The Critical Heritage*, ed. John T. Shawcross, London, Routledge and Kegan Paul, 1972, p. 240.

machinery" relegates it to a status which is peripheral rather than central. It is also true that Willkie describes *Paradise Lost* as "altogether irregular," though in an age which was beginning to admire irregularity the observation does not mean that the poem is to be reproached for its generic lawlessness. Nevertheless Willkie's remarks do broach the question of whether it is necessary or even desirable to locate *Paradise Lost* unambiguously within any single genre.

It may be argued that the difficulties surrounding the generic assignation of *Paradise Lost* are difficulties encountered by the reader rather than difficulties to which the author admits. That does not make them any less real, but it may be instructive to look at some of the ways in which the poem announces itself and at the related proposition that the poem always knows what kind of a poem it is. *Paradise Lost* treats itself as "adventurous song" in the first book (13), as "sacred song" in the third book (28) as "song" of which the "copious matter" is the Son's name and arts (III, 412-13) as "Song" related to "celestial song" in the seventh book (12, 30) and as "heroic song" in the ninth book, but only after the audience has been advised that the forthcoming notes of the song will be "tragic" (6, 25). These descriptions are not so divergent as to render reconciliation difficult but they certainly do not suggest resolute consistency in the poem's classification of itself. They suggest rather the desire to have the best of several worlds which is characteristic of a mixed-genre poet.

In the poems that precede *Paradise Lost* Milton's attitude to the inherited genre is powerfully revisionary. We console ourselves by describing it as a strong case of tradition and the individual talent, or by saying, as Reesing does, that Milton strains the mould but does not break it.[13] *On the Morning of Christ's Nativity*, in describing itself as both a Hymn and an Ode, may be initiating Milton's career with

[13] John Reesing, *Milton's Poetic Art*, Cambridge, Mass., Harvard University Press, p. 49. See also p. 135.

a mixed-genre announcement.[14] *Comus* makes use of the antithetical dispositions of a genre new enough to be open to experiment by constructing a staging ground for issues and confrontations we have come to call Miltonic. *Lycidas* directs the capacity of the pastoral for protest into a protest against the pastoral genre itself. Though not exactly a mixed-genre poem it is a poem obliged to accommodate itself to the eruptive presence of an alien genre of which the higher mood is the questioning voice. In each case Milton identifies certain propensities of the genre as giving the genre its style of understanding and then renegotiates the form around those propensities. In each case the ordering power of the genre is made to compass a higher degree of inclusiveness than it has hitherto accommodated. We can expect these creative habits to continue as Milton comes to his most inclusive undertaking.

A primary characteristic of the epic is inclusiveness. When Aristotle differentiates tragedy from epic he does not do so on the basis of the outcome, the agent, or the emotion excited by the literary work. His concern is with the manner

[14] For the poem as a hymn see Philip Rollinson, "Milton's Nativity Poem and the Decorum of Genre," *Milton Studies VII*, Pittsburgh, Pittsburgh University Press, 1975, pp. 165-88. For the poem as an ode see David B. Morris, "Drama and Stasis in Milton's Ode on the Morning of Christ's Nativity," *SP*, 58 (1971), pp. 207-22. For the poem as both see Hugh MacCallum "The Narrator of Milton's 'On the Morning of Christ's Nativity,' " in *Familiar Colloquy, Essays Presented to Arthur Edward Barker*, ed. Patricia Bruckmann, Oberon Press, Canada, pp. 179-95. Milton's reference in "The Reason of Church Government" to "magnifick Odes and Hymns" (*Complete Prose Works*, New Haven, Yale University Press, 1953, Vol. 1, p. 815) suggests that he may have thought of the two genres as strongly related to each other. The relationship may well be in the manner envisaged by Nehemiah Rogers. Rogers writes of hymns as "special songs of praise and thanksgiving." He writes of odes as containing "doctrine of the chiefe good, or mans eternall felicitie" and as being made "after a more majesticall forme, than ordinary." *A Strange Vineyard in Palaestina: in an Exposition of Isaiahs Parabolical Song of the Beloved* (London, 1623), pp. 8-9.

of presentation and the magnitude of the action.[15] The tragic action should confine itself as far as possible to a single circuit of the sun. The epic action can be longer and a month is extended to a year by Italian critics. Although the longer action can support itself by an adequate proliferation of incident, the epic as it graduates from the tale of a tribe to the statement of a civilization, tends increasingly to sustain itself by cultural omnivorousness as much as by narrative complication. The epic and the encyclopedic are thus brought into convergence. In a late epic the encyclopedic interest will involve consideration of the uses of the past, including the past of the epic genre itself. When the generic inheritance is codified to the extent of seeming petrified, the consideration can be revisionary and can extend, as is arguable in Milton's case, into a revisionary treatment of the whole past. A genre can also be enlarged and thus freed from the impending exhaustion of possibilities by incorporating into it the possibilities of another genre not hitherto digested. Mixed genres are thus a natural deliverance from the constraints of a genre which it is necessary to use and which has already been used too heavily. In an epic such absorptiveness can be particularly felicitous since it is clearly the literary application of that principle of comprehensiveness on which the epic has increasingly been based. An encyclopedic epic should include a generic compendium.

Studies by Rosalie Colie and more recently by Barbara Lewalski have drawn attention tellingly to the generic inclusiveness of *Paradise Lost*.[16] Lewalski's suggestion that the various genres in the epic are means of accommodation to

---

[15] Aristotle, *Poetics*, 1449b, 1459b.

[16] Rosalie Colie, *The Resources of Kind: Genre Theory in the Renaissance*, Berkeley, University of California Press, 1973; Barbara Lewalski, "The Genres of *Paradise Lost*: Literary Genre as a Means of Accommodation," *Composite Orders: The Genres of Milton's Last Poems*, ed. Richard S. Ide and Joseph Wittreich, Pittsburgh, University of Pittsburgh Press (*Milton Studies XVIII*), pp. 75-103.

the reader, or of the narrator within the poem to the auditor, also responds to a problem that arises when we think of the epic as a generic compendium. The encyclopedic substance of an epic is a matter of what it contains; the generic variety is a matter of how what is contained is conveyed. Multeity of genres is most convincingly called for when the area of exploration is sufficiently inclusive to require more than one style of mediation or access. The creation, as a fully comprehensive poem, is also a poem that engages us in an adequate variety of relationships. Any mimesis of the perfect original should be similarly rich in means of accommodation or opportunities for engagement.[17]

Nevertheless, it should not be assumed that the purpose, or even the designed purpose, of generic multeity is always to contribute to the overall harmony, to show how many styles of discourse lead us to the one word, or to the unifying capability that is the "one word" of the poem. Multiple genres can provide the ingredients for subversion as well as for synthesis. Their purpose may be to show not the overall concord, but the fragmentation of any single style of understanding that unavoidably comes about when the fictive is brought into engagement with the actual. I am

[17] Tasso describes the writing of a poem as "a work almost godlike that seems to imitate the First Maker." *Discourses on the Heroic Poem,* tr. Mariella Cavalchini and Irene Samuel, Oxford, The Clarendon Press, 1971, p. 97.

For the creation as the perfect poem see also S. K. Heninger, *Touches of Sweet Harmony,* San Marino, Huntington Library Press, 1976, pp. 290-94. Number, weight, and measure are among the characteristics of this poem. Reynolds, for example, describes the church as God's temple and the world as his palace in which he is "a God of Order, disposing everything in Number, Weight, and Measure, so sweetly as that all is harmonious, (from which harmonie, the philosophers have concluded a Divine Providence)." Edward Reynolds, *A Treatise of the Passions,* London, 1640, p. 75. When Marvell says that Milton's verse "created like thy *Theme* sublime/In Number, Weight, and Measure, needs not *Rhime*" (*Poems and Letters,* ed. Margoliouth, p. 132), he is thinking of the creation as a perfect poem. It could be argued, however, that the creation does rhyme in its "correspondences."

not suggesting that Milton's use of mixed genres was governed by this principle or that it proceeded to this point irrespective of the original principle by which it was governed. On the other hand it is not easy to argue that his poem is the unperturbed implementation of a "great idea" or fore-conceit, as the creation is in the seventh book of *Paradise Lost*. A blueprint for the epic must have existed in the author's mind particularly if, as Gilbert long ago argued,[18] the poem was not written in the order in which it unfolds. But the blueprint cannot have been unaffected by the stresses and strains within the poem and by the poem's reconsideration of itself during the deeply frustrating decade of its formation.

If many genres are to be fitted together harmoniously in a poem they must be subject to a primary genre which is unambiguously proclaimed and clearly dominant. When a primary genre is subject to revisionary treatment and when its status is further undermined by another genre asserting a claim to primacy, the subordinate genres are as likely to reflect this central confrontation as to soothe it.

In 1642 Milton was asking himself "whether those dramatic constitutions wherein Sophocles and Euripides raigne" were not "more doctrinal and exemplary to a nation" than the epic undertaking by which he was fascinated.[19] We know from Phillips that *Paradise Lost* began as a tragedy and that Milton showed Phillips the first ten lines of Satan's address to the sun as the planned beginning of the drama he intended to write.[20] The draft of "Adam Unparadiz'd" in the Trinity manuscript shows us the dramatic nucleus

---

[18] Allan H. Gilbert, *On the Composition of* "Paradise Lost," Chapel Hill, University of North Carolina Press, 1947.

[19] "The Reason of Church Government," *Complete Prose*, Vol. 1, pp. 812-15. Milton's "whether" reflects the continuing controversy about the status of epic and tragedy relative to each other. The Renaissance and more emphatically, Dryden (see n. 3, above) found epic the higher of the two genres. But Aristotle (*Poetics*, 1462a) had declared in favour of tragedy.

[20] *Early Lives of Milton*, pp. 72-73.

in which *Paradise Lost* began. Even though the poem moved away from the nucleus it continued to remain engaged to its origins.

The ten books of the first edition of *Paradise Lost*, read as five acts of two books, are tragic in several of their dispositions. In the fourth act the creation is undone by the fall. The fifth act gives us the tragic aftermath of the fourth, the expansion of evil into space and its extension into history. The repentance of Adam and Eve, sandwiched between two huge movements of destructiveness, simply does not have the importance which the twelve-book version succeeds in winning from it. It is true that Christ's victory is the climax of the third act but this matters less when Satan's victory is so effectively dominant in the fifth.

If this reading of the tragic weight of the ten-book structure is not erroneous we can regard the twelve-book version as designed, among other things, to take corrective action. The creative forces are underlined slightly in the poem's contest of energies. Christ's presence in the poem is strengthened by a three-part structure of four books with four central books of which he is the protagonist. Two victories of the light—the battle in heaven and the creation—are juxtaposed at the centre of this central part. The repentance of Adam and Eve is given a greater weight. This much said, it becomes important to add that the degree of corrective action is slight. It may be that no more could be done since the poem had been in print for seven years. It may also be that Milton did not wish to do more.

Barker rightly observes that the twelve-book version does not supersede the ten-book one, that one must read both poems and be aware of both patterns, and that the poem is suspended "between the horns of a paradox."[21] For such a paradox to exist, the poem's primary genres must be in contest with rather than concordant with each other. The

[21] A. E. Barker "Structural Pattern in *Paradise Lost*," reprinted in *Milton: Modern Essays in Criticism*, New York, Oxford Press, 1965, p. 154.

poem does not seek the assimilation of one genre by another or even, to quote Coleridge's famous phrase, "the balance or reconciliation of opposite or discordant qualities."[22] Rather, it seeks to navigate between genres, remaining responsive to the current of each without surrendering to the pull of either.

Such a hypothesis seems natural when we remind ourselves of the poem's antithetical world, the embattled contraries between which the choosing centre is suspended, as the poem itself is suspended creatively between competing claims on its identity. It is not simply a mixed-genre poem but a poem of which generic uncertainty may be a keynote. Critics may be understandably reluctant to admit uncertainty at the heart of a poem. A work of art thus divided is considered to be in a state of civil war. But creative indeterminacy can also be read as a sign of the authentic rather than the chaotic. Two powerful patterns of possibility contest with each other as they do in reality. The outcome will shift from moment to moment. The poem's obligation is to draw the field of force and not the local and possibly transient settlement.

Against this hypothesis it can be argued that Aristotle treats tragedy and epic as concordant genres.[23] The manner of presentation and the magnitude of the action are important but not fundamental differences and certainly not differences that might place either genre in potential conflict with the other. When Hobbes tells us that "the heroic poem, dramatic, is tragedy" he is carrying convergence a step further. He does so in proceeding to the masterfully sterile conclusion that "there can be no more or less than six kinds of poetry."[24] The Italian critics avoid Hobbes's

---

[22] *Biographia Literaria*, Ch. XIV.

[23] *Poetics*, 1459b.

[24] Hobbes, "The Answer of Mr. Hobbes to Sr. Will. D'Avenant's Preface before *Gondibert" Critical Essays of the Seventeenth Century*, ed. J. E. Spingarn, Oxford, Clarendon Press, 1908, Vol. II, pp. 54-55.

overwhelming simplicity but, as Steadman shows, they do not on the whole regard tragedy and epic as divergent.[25]

This objection has force. It can be partly countered by arguing that even though the Italian critics may not have seen tragedy and epic as divergent, they did recognize the creative potentiality of divergent genres. If the creation is the perfect poem, its mimesis may consist not only of simulating its variety (which includes generic variety), but also of simulating the manner in which the first poem triumphed over its own divisiveness. Creation, we must not forget, was won out of chaos, from equal energies implacably opposed. The best poem may be that in which the centre succeeds in holding against the maximum of centrifugal force. Like Milton's universe, such a poem is continually threatened by its contents. Tasso seems to be advocating a poetics of contrariety on this model when he argues, that "the art of composing a poem resembles the plan of the Universe which is composed of contraries." He goes on to maintain that "such a variety will be so much the more marvellous as it brings with it a measure of difficulty and almost impossibility."[26] Guarini is less given to the *tour de force* than Tasso. In defending tragicomedy he considers it as a third genre arising from two genres which are divergent but not so divergent that they cannot be creatively mingled. Each genre tempers the other so that the overall composition corresponds more fully "to the mixture of the human body which consists entirely in the tempering of the four humours."[27]

There is thus some sanction in Renaissance criticism for the curbing by divergent genres of each other's excesses or for the submission of their divergences to the cohesive force of the poem. Milton's poem can be seen from both

[25] *Epic and Tragic Structure in "Paradise Lost."*

[26] *Discourses on the Heroic Poem*, p. 78.

[27] "The Compendium of Tragicomic Poetry" in *Literary Criticism: Plato to Dryden*, ed. Allan H. Gilbert, New York, American Book Company, 1940, p. 512.

viewpoints but, like any deeply creative achievement, it has to go beyond the gestures towards it that are made by critical theory.

As has been indicated, Milton equivocates mildly about the kind of song he is singing when he links the poem to that particular word. The varying epithets are not difficult to bring together but the variations remind us to be cautious in our classification of the poem. No more than a reminder is needed, since the poem at its very outset, in announcing the compass of its subject, is also conveying that announcement through a vivid drama of contesting genres. The opening lines of *Paradise Lost* have been commented on in great detail and from what may seem every possible angle[28] but their status as a generic manifesto still remains to be examined. In attempting the unattempted Milton may have been attempting an unattempted mixture.

Milton's virtuosity in stating the subject of the whole poem before the predicate of its initial sentence spectacularly isolates the first five lines from the narrative flow. The mini-drama of these lines is therefore all the more effective in counselling us not only on what the poem is to be about but also on how it is to be experienced. From the beginning the tragic weight accumulates, reinforced by the alliterative joinings and by the alternative scansions of the first line. If the dominant stress falls on "man's," we are reading a poem sombrely homocentric in its allocation of destructiveness. If it falls on "first" we are reading a poem of the gestation of evil, with the alliterative movement through "first," "fruit," and "forbidden" compounding the inex-

---

[28] Among the examinations are "The opening of *Paradise Lost*" by David Daiches in *The Living Milton*, ed. Frank Kermode, London, Routledge and Kegan Paul, 1960, pp. 55-69 and Joseph Summers, *The Muse's Method*, London, Chatto and Windus, 1962, pp. 11-31. Book-length studies of the invocations include Anne D. Ferry, *Milton's Epic Voice*, Cambridge, Mass., Harvard University Press, 1963, and William Riggs, *The Christian Poet in "Paradise Lost,"* Berkeley, University of California Press, 1972.

orable growth.[29] "Tree," "tast," and "mortal" are the origin of this growth though, dramatically, they are arrived at as its climax, the tragic centre of the darkening song. "World" and "woe" sound the dimensions of a universe of tragedy. Nothing so far has restrained the onward movement, the accumulation of sorrow. The prospective genre of the poem has been uncomprisingly and it would seem, irrevocably stated. Yet on the basis of a text from Romans: V, 19, a counter-movement launches itself, generating itself from the previous movements by virtue of the coupling between man and "greater man." There is even a counter-alliteration, responding to the massed alliterative linkages of destructiveness, affirming the victory of the light in "restore" and "regain." This is what we might say on a superficial reading. A reading more open to the poem's reality would recognize that the relationship between human tragedy and providential epic is more complex than the simple overcoming of one genre by another. It is possible to say, by adjusting our minds slightly to the impact of the opening, that the epic retrieval stands at the horizon of the poem, while the tragic gestation (to which the bulk of the first five lines are given) unavoidably dominates its stage. It is possible to reflect on the distancing force of "till" and ask if the deliverance at the horizon is more than potential. How far does the tragic actuality frustrate and even nullify the epic promise? It is certainly true, as the mind moves with the poem in its unfolding, that we cannot avoid passing through the tragic proliferation before arriving at the genre that might contain it. The two genres are in fact inexorably entangled by the powerfully staged drama of the poem's syntax. The poem does not choose between affiliations. It forms itself out of the contest between them.

[29] In asking some seventy students to read this line, I have found that 45 percent put the dominant stress on "man's" and 45 percent put it on "first." The remainder put it on the third syllable of "disobedience." Of those stressing "man's," the great majority were men. Of those stressing "first" the great majority were women.

Paradise Lost presents itself as not only a mixed-genre poem but as a mixed-genre poem of deep generic uncertainty. It has to be uncertain because the very history that it seeks to understand has perhaps fortunately, not yet found its genre. The poem seeks its identity between contesting possibilities as does that human community which is both the poem's subject and its audience.

Though the contest of primary genres in the opening lines of *Paradise Lost* has been examined, not every genre in those first five lines has been identified. Between the accumulating onslaught of the tragic, "under her own waight groaning" as the twelfth book says of history (539), and the restorative encirclement of the providential, there is the muted phrase "With loss of Eden." The residual alliteration with "world" and "woe" attaches the half-line to the tragic momentum. The loss can be taken as the sum of our sadness, the distillation of everything that has gone before it in the sentence. But the half-line is also an entry into a possibly triumphant future, that Ithaca which the highest of heroes may regain. The phrase stands between two worlds, distanced from itself by the poem's initial onslaught of destructiveness and distanced again from itself by the postponing force of "till." The curiously nondescript language suggests the absence or rather the residual and unavoidably veiled presence of what the phrase invokes. It can no longer be known in its own right but only through the ways of loss and seeking.

In the days when it was fashionable to distinguish between the real and nominal subjects of *Paradise Lost*, Paul Elmer More observed that the real subject of the poem was paradise.[30] The remark is neither naive nor tautological. The strong affinities of Eden with Arcadia, the golden age and the pastoral strain in the Bible, not only establish it in the landscape of memory, including literary memory, but

[30] *Shelburne Essays*, as quoted by E.M.W. Tillyard, *Milton*, London, Chatto and Windus, 1930, p. 283.

also affiliate it to a third genre, the pastoral. The three genres in turn affiliate themselves to the three main locales of the poem so that we can think with caution, but without injustice, of a tragic hell (including human fallenness), an epic heaven, and a pastoral paradise. Since the forces in the universe of *Paradise Lost* converge so powerfully upon its centre of decision we can argue that the pastoral understanding plays a crucial part in the poem's declaration of itself.

Knott skilfully underlines the *otium* of Paradise, its "grateful vicissitude," the harmony of man with nature and the harmony of nature with itself.[31] Cities in *Paradise Lost* are not statements of civilization. Babel and Pandemonium tell of their pride. The world is likened once to a metropolis "With glistening spires and pinnacles adorned" (III, 549) but it is viewed thus by Satan in the image of the desirable. Little is said of the metropolitan amenities of heaven except that its shape is "undetermined," that it is adorned with opal towers and battlements of sapphire (II, 1047-50) and that the dust of its main road is gold (VII, 577). It is Satan not God who lives in what might metaphorically be called a palace, a superstructure built on a structure of pyramids and towers "From diamond quarries hewn and rocks of gold" (V, 754-61). Heaven is most frequently spoken of in pastoral language, possibly as an accommodation to Adam, who is unfamiliar with city life, but more probably to indicate the continuity between the celestial and the unfallen.

Yet though the ideal order of *Paradise Lost* has extensive pastoral elements, and though the poem can be poignantly pastoral in its nostalgia, the "happy rural seat of various view" (IV, 247) does not always open out into pastoral

[31] John R. Knott, Jr., *Milton's Pastoral Vision*, Chicago, University of Chicago Press, 1971. The phrase "grateful vicissitude" (*P.L.* VI, 8) describes the alternation of light and darkness issuing from a cave within the mount of God. It is used by Summers (*The Muse's Method*, pp. 71-86) as emblematic of Paradise.

prospects. The weeping trees that are spoken of in the next line suggest a place haunted by tragedy as well as by creative plenitude. There is much foreboding in the language of Paradise—in the wantonness of its energies, the "mazy error" of its brooks, and in its surpassing of that "fair field" where the "fairer flower," Prosespina, was gathered (V, 294-97; IV, 268-72; IV, 237-40). More important, Paradise is not a place of tranquility, of fragile but deep peace before the gathering storm. In its nature it is free from the burden of the past but in its nature it is also singularly subject to the anxieties of the unprecedented. Nearly everything that happens in Paradise happens for the first time, so if one's response to life is not the result of a pre-existent, celestially implanted programme, it can only come together and manifest a pattern through a series of related improvisations Baffling dreams, angelic visitations, and discussions with the author of one's being on the need of the self for an otherness seem part of the normalities of Paradise.

"Is there no change of death in Paradise?" Wallace Stevens asks. "Does ripe fruit never fall? Or do the boughs/ Hang always heavy in that perfect sky?"[32] In the stasis of perfection all change is the death of perfection. Yet not to change is to perpetuate the permanence of lifelessness. Milton provides for change in Paradise that is quite other than the "change of death," thereby adroitly satisfying the second of Stevens' desiderata for a supreme fiction: "It must change."[33] In his repeated use of the figure of the dance in describing ideal order, he advises us of a perfection consummated in motion rather than memorialized in stillness.[34] Motion must include alteration in one's state of being as well as alteration in one's place, and this alteration takes place as Raphael suggests by the working of body

---

[32] Wallace Stevens, "Sunday Morning," *Harmonium*, New York, Alfred A. Knopf, 1923, p. 92.

[33] Stevens, *Notes Toward a Supreme Fiction*, Cummington, The Cummington Press, 1942, p. 21.

[34] Summers, *The Muse's Method*, pp. 85-86.

up to spirit "in bounds/Proportion'd to each kind" (V, 478-79). Such evolution cannot take place by standing still on an ontological escalator. In a world in which the perfection of the human species includes the power of free choice—a power whose importance is underlined by the enormous cosmic price the divine is prepared to pay to keep it in being—there must be a steady succession of opportunities for self-formative choosing. It is hard to believe that Adam and Eve, if they had not eaten of the apple, would have lived happily ever after as creative gardeners.[35]

The Appleton estate, in Marvell's poem, subversively mimeticizes the world from which it withdraws. Milton's garden, in its crises, makes itself continuous with that future which is to become its tragic legacy. It is no accident that the images Michael uses to characterize progress in history correspond to the images Raphael uses to characterize upward evolution on the ontological scale (V, 996-98; V, 575-77; XII, 300-304). In the first place, the equivalence makes evident the restoration of the *status quo ante*. By making himself eligible for the continuing intervention of "supernal grace" man is able to stand as he once did "on eev'n ground against his mortal foe" (III, 179). In the second place, the statement of equivalence made through figures of progress with which we are not unfamiliar, joins the pre-lapsarian and post-lapsarian worlds. The status of man in a fallen world is radically different and his commitment to destructiveness requires the steady application of a counter-force that no longer lies within his natural capacity. But if the conditions for that counter-force are brought into being, the two worlds can reflect each other in their opportunities and challenges.[36] The pastoral idyll

[35] For the challenges of Edenic life see for example, Barbara Lewalski, "Innocence and Experience in Milton's Eden," *New Essays on "Paradise Lost,"* ed. T. Kranidas, Berkeley, University of California Press, 1969, pp. 86-117.

[36] The continuity between the pre- and post-lapsarian worlds has been noted by Louis Martz. *Poet of Exile: A Study of Milton's Poetry*, New Haven,

never quite existed. The garden was fully itself only in creative dependence on a shaping principle beyond itself. It was a place not of withdrawal, but of change and growth built on evolving inter-relationships with the entire structure of reality which surrounded it. What was lost was not the garden but that creative possibility which the garden embodied and promised.

This excursion into the poem suggests how it responds to those stresses and balances which the first five lines urge so compellingly on our reading of what follows. The pastoral statement does not exist by itself. It is annexed in the first place to a tragic unfolding through which we are obliged to make our way in order to measure what is meant by "loss of Eden." It is attached in the second place to a providential counter-poem through which the lost possibilities can be recovered and fulfilled. In fact its location and attachments are suggestive of the created world in *Paradise Lost*, suspended from heaven by a golden chain and connected to hell by a causeway. What the pastoral centre comes to mean depends on how it is oriented. As a generic claim it must yield to those more powerful claimants which seek possession of the structure of things.[37] The drama of genres the first five lines enact is thus singularly accurate in prefiguring not only the generic character of the poem, but the disposition of real forces which that character represents.

One of the unusual strengths of *Paradise Lost* is the poem's capacity to reconsider itself. It can indulge in "tedious havoc" and then excoriate it (IX, 27-33). It can describe the fall of Mulciber in language of limpid beauty and then pull us back from our involvement with a "Thus they relate/Erring" (I, 738-48), leaving us to wonder whether the event

---

Yale University Press, 1980, p. 140. But the continuity is not inherent and is possible in a fallen world only by the continuing application of grace to an agent responding through creative choices.

[37] Knott observes (*Milton's Pastoral Vision*, p. xiv) that "the very conflict of modes, epic against pastoral, seems to doom Eden in advance."

is being questioned or whether language itself is being rebuked as falsification. It propounds huge structures of elaboration and ornament to arrive at the "upright heart" in its unadorned authenticity. It uses the past with lavish erudition and overgoes it with competitive zest, largely to underline the obsolescence of what it invokes. It appoints Michael, the leader of the angelic battalions, to preach the politics of non-violence and the primacy of the interior victory. Some of these dismissals are designed to educate the reader and to instruct him in discriminating truth from its cunning resemblance.[38] Others arise because the poem in charting the progress from shadowy types to truth, endows itself with a history that to some degree mirrors the history it interprets. But we are also looking at a poem that is endeavouring to achieve its identity and that, as the opening lines have promised, will form itself among contesting generic possibilities. It must not only make itself but justify what it makes against the challenges of an era of deep change. Since its attitude to the inheritance is so powerfully revisionary, honesty demands that it also be self-revising.

In the fifth book of *Paradise Lost* Adam and Eve, after a troubled night, do not simply address the almighty in prayer. Rather they participate in a prayer which the whole creation offers to its maker out of the way in which it moves and lives. The prayer is Vaughan's "great hymn/And Symphony of nature," the ardent music of "the world in tune." It is also Herbert's "something understood," a structure of relationships which the mind experiences as the ground of its being.[39] "Firm peace" and "wonted calm" are its consequences (V, 209-10). We are told that Adam and Eve have previously made their "unisons" in "various style" (145-

[38] The thought is from *Areopagitica*. See *Complete Prose* II, p. 514.

[39] Vaughan, *The Morning-watch*, in *The Complete Poetry of Henry Vaughan*, ed. French Fogle, New York, Doubleday, 1964, pp. 176-77. Herbert, *Prayer* (1), *The Works of George Herbert*, ed. F. E. Hutchinson, Oxford, The Clarendon Press, 1941, p. 51.

46). The plenitude of innocence offers more than one way of access and relationship. The "unmediated" art of the person praying (148-49)[40] may even find the opportunity to invent a genre.

At the end of the tenth book Adam and Eve pray again. The first prayer preceded the descent of Raphael. The second precedes the descent of Michael. The world has changed and a lost structure of possibility, borne away as in the real world, on the flood of history's disappointments, has also taken with it its proper language. The new desolation calls for the unadorned, the concentration on what is primary. Many poems have an energy of destitution within them, waving their leaves and flowers in the sun so that they may wither into the truth of themselves.[41] In *Paradise Lost* that destitutive energy is launched by an immense act of original destructiveness. From the moment that Adam and Eve eat the apple, much in the poem is rendered obsolete, including some of its literary genres. In these stern dismissals lies a great deal of the poem's authenticity as well as its weight of sadness. But the world remains before us and remains capable of yielding us its language. If *Paradise Lost* is an uncertain epic it is uncertain not because it is confused or vacillating, but because it is clear about how it must form itself.

It is apparent, as we consider the problem, that the poem cannot form itself with finality. It can only activate further and attempt to bring under its organizing momentum the evolving cross-play of its stresses and strains. The contest of genres is only one register of that cross-play. When

[40] Since the poet cannot attain a pre-lapsarian oneness with creation, his verse in IX, 24 is "unpremeditated' rather than "unmediated." The word has specific and interesting echoes in the "unpremeditated art" of Shelley's skylark and in the "unpremeditated, joyous energy" Yeats finds in the statues of Mausolus and Artemisia at the British Museum. *Autobiographies*, London, Macmillan, 1955, p. 150.

[41] The thought is from Yeats, *The Coming of Wisdom with Time*, in *Collected Poems*, p. 105.

Jameson puts forward the proposition that "genre theory must always in one way or another project a model of the coexistence or tension between generic modes or strands," the "methodological axiom,"[42] as he terms it, supports the evidence of this chapter and also invites us to consider the extent to which generic tensions in *Paradise Lost* can be brought into relationship with other tensions which animate rather than rupture the poem. The degree to which all these tensions can be read as symptomatic of a political unconscious is not a matter Jameson studies, though *Paradise Lost* is indeed a crucial text (and test) for such a hypothesis. We can initiate such a study by pointing to the disjunction both strongly creative and troublingly problematic, between a cosmic status quo that is unchallengeable in its nature and a human status quo that exists to be challenged. That individualism which confronts and interrogates institutionality may find itself in subversion on one level; it must find itself in submission on another. Whether at any given point we are to subvert or submit, whether we are to be conservative or revolutionary, whether specific choices before us are self-serving or self-making are not matters on which the poem provides us with an unambiguous guidance system that will exempt us from the responsibilities of reading. Instructions on how to read *Paradise Lost* are certainly not lacking in the poem, but those instructions must themselves be subject to the vigilances of interpretation.

The most favoured strategy for unifying these sometimes

---

[42] Fredric Jameson, *The Political Unconscious*, Ithaca, Cornell University Press, 1981. This chapter was written before Jameson's book was published.

The "methodological axiom" invites elaboration. Apart from states of peaceful coexistence and of coexistence with tension, states of cold war, containment, and of open hostility can also be treated as having their literary equivalents.

Both the co-existence of genres and their co-existence with tension are charted as they apply to Milton's last poems, in *Composite Orders*. The title, as the editors point out, derives from Wordsworth.

sharp disjunctions is to argue that there is a true and a false version of everything in the poem and that the poem commits to the reader, rather than to any of its participating forces, the responsibility of separating the truth from its cunning resemblance. The strategy may succeed in unifying the poem, but it does so largely by setting up unification as an imperative and by then proposing that every element in the poem be read so as to achieve maximum compliance with that imperative. There are events such as the separation of Adam from Eve in the ninth book of *Paradise Lost* which may be too densely complex in their admissions and recognitions to allow any clear-cut discrimination of the wheat from the chaff. More comprehensively, the strategy ignores the disjunction between what it dismisses and the literary impact of that which is dismissed. Despite intelligent and impressive scholarly attempts to overcome the fissure, readers of the poem continue to see a difference between what the poem actually does and what it exhorts us to see it as having done. Attempts to eliminate these differences by postulating a reading horizon in relation to which the differences disappear can call upon considerable historical evidence, but the potential circularity of the argument cannot but trouble those who enlist its support. In saying this I do not seek to renounce that historically situated reading of which I myself have been a principal advocate. I merely argue that such a reading should not be dominated by the need to sustain a unifying imperative.

To abandon this imperative is not easy in the face of a poem that is perhaps the most militantly organized in the language. Even adverse judgements about *Paradise Lost* take advantage of the imperative's requirements, arguing that the requirements do not work and that they are incapable of holding together the poem's obduracies and autonomies. The Romantic critics can be seen as pioneers in suggesting that the poem may well be more significant and more capable of imparting its real complexities to us when it is laid open not to a disjunctive reading but to one that inhabits rather than overrides the poem's crucial dissensions. This fundamental perception is probably more important than the views of Milton's Satan and of Milton's God with which the perception is associated and which have encouraged the simplistic conclusion that the Romantic response to *Paradise Lost* is no more than a matter of turning the poem upside down. The consequences and rewards of a reading strategy which accepts the poem's difference with itself as an unavoidable and perhaps sustaining element in its movement of self-comprehension have still to be worked out by the scholar-critic. The next chapter in Milton commentary might not be amiss if it were to proceed on these lines.

❦

Interchapter: The Hollow Rent

TOWARDS THE END of September 1943 Thomas Mann was working on Chapter II of *Doctor Faustus*. He was however by no means satisfied with his existing version of Chapter VIII, Kretschmar's lecture on Beethoven's unfinished Opus 111. A month or two earlier he had read Theodor Wiesengrund Adorno's manuscript, "Zur Philosophie der Modernen Musik." The manuscript illuminated for Mann certain aspects of his hero's predicament. Early in October he spent an evening with the Adornos. After a discussion of humaneness as romantic resistance to society and convention (Rousseau) and as rebellion (the prose scene in Goethe's *Faust*), Adorno played Opus 111 in its incomplete entirety. For the next three days, Mann continues, he immersed himself "in a thorough-going revision and extension of the lecture on the sonata, which became a significant enrichment and embellishment of the chapter and indeed of the whole book."[1]

Kretschmar's momentous lecture is undermined by the circumstances of its delivery. He stutters frustratingly at crucial moments in the formulation of his argument. The stentorian playing of Opus 111 by the lecturer even as he lectures threatens to obliterate what it is supposed to illustrate. But the proposition lingers on and broods over the rest of the book. It cannot be dismissed by the surrounding comedy. It is summed up in the report of Kretschmar's final sentences.

[1] Thomas Mann, *The Genesis of a Novel*, London, Secker and Warburg, 1961, pp. 35-42.

It had happened that the Sonata had come, in the second enormous movement, to an end, an end without any return. . . .

And when he said "the sonata," he meant not only this one in C minor, but the sonata in general, as a species, as traditional art form; it itself was here at an end, brought to its end, it had fulfilled its destiny, reached its goal, beyond which there was no going, it cancelled and resolved itself, it took leave.[2]

That perfection extinguishes what it perfects is not a proposition peculiar to Mann. It has a strong sanction in Aristotle's finding that after many changes, including Sophocles' introduction of the third actor, tragedy reached the perfection of its form and so ceased to develop (*Poetics* 1449a). Critics observe, and not without relish, that Milton's achievement in the epic was so overwhelming that it could only survive thereafter, metamorphosed into the novel, or internalized as the heroic poem of consciousness. Wagner made music drama all but impossible. The anxieties of coming after Shakespeare have precipitated apprehensive debates (in which Eliot was a notable participant) on the possibility of a poetic drama.[3] More fundamentally, the *telos*-oriented models of change we have studied in Spenser and in Milton, move towards a time when "no more change shall be." History, like art, will make itself unnecessary when it achieves coincidence with its final form. The difference is that the death of art is within time.

The threat of closure, not simply of the poem but of the genre and even of the medium, can be regarded as leading to responses which have already been outlined, such as the mixed-genre poem and the internalizing of the heroic.

[2] Thomas Mann, *Dr. Faustus*, New York, Alfred A. Knopf, 1948, p. 55.
[3] Yeats turns to the *Noh* form, as Mann's hero turns to the new possibilities of atonality because modern poetic drama "always dominated by the example of Shakespeare," sought to "restore an irrevocable past."

We must however question the assumption that these two powerful trends in the history of the unfinished are no more than a strategy for preserving life on the margins, attempts to deliver us from the burden of the past and its pre-emption of creative possibilities. Such a pattern of cause and effect is uncritically formalist, preoccupied with the momentum of the genre (or with the predecessor who embodies that momentum) and insensitive to the manner in which affiliations with the world affect the filiations of the text. Mixed genres can respond to a genre's impending exhaustion; but they can also be a literary reflection of a society questioning its stratifications, or a discourse uneasy about its ideology. The internalization of the heroic goes hand in hand with meditative traditions both Protestant and Ignatian. In a larger context, it reflects a religious experientialism which itself responds to the triumphant empiricism of a new science by which the physical world is increasingly appropriated. The imagination must maintain its tenancy in a realm both vulnerable to invasion and repeatedly called on to justify itself. Interiority in such circumstances is the beginning of the art of exile and perhaps of the proposition that there is no art but in exile. Even if we set aside social linkages, limiting ourselves fastidiously to the literary succession, we have to take account of arguments such as that of Joan Webber who finds the movement of the epic to be inward from the beginning or that of Joseph Wittreich for whom interiority is a function of the prophetic mode and is therefore embedded in the history of literature. In Milton's overall statement, the destruction of Paradise (*P.L.* XI, 829-38), the subsequent affirmation of the paradise within, and the presentation of *Paradise Regained* as the forming/finding of that interior paradise establish a narrative for internalization within the movement of the œuvre itself. The importance of *Paradise Regained* for the Romantics arises from its advanced position in this narrative and from a multiple structure of temptation, used for the first time in Milton's œuvre, that anticipates some of the complexities of subsequent poems of self-formation.[4]

When we look more closely at Kretschmar's paradox of the unfinished as decisively finished, the terminal statement that in utter honesty to itself terminates itself even in mid-career, its factual basis must be regarded as doubtful. Mann's view is in contrast to Derrida's view of classical non-closure as brought about by the magnitude rather than the exhaustion of the field. It is Derrida's proposition that responds better to the evidence. In both *The Faerie Queene* and *The Cantos*, the movement is not to extinction but to openness even though the designed diminuendos of both poems offer themselves as evocative of extinction. Closure is abandoned in order to invoke a larger whole where the dissenting forces that have resisted closure will be brought together in a stable harmony or known as aspects of a single voice. The unfinished justifies its status not because nothing remains to be said, but because more remains to be said than it can accommodate.

The alternative model of the unfinished invokes not the magnitude of the field but its resistant character, its capacity to subvert the unifying fictions that are brought to bear upon it. It retreats from purposiveness in order to valorize mutability. It moves away from the incorporative power of the whole to the resistance and givenness of the fragment. We may be tempted to designate this model as Romantic but the truth is that the earlier Romantics still cling to the holistic commitment, admitting its impossibility

[4] Joan Webber, *Milton and his Epic Tradition*, Seattle, University of Washington Press, 1979. Joseph Wittreich, "Epic Convention and Prophetic Interiority," *Composite Orders*, pp. 43-74. *Visionary Poetics: Milton's Tradition and his Legacy*, Huntington Library Publications, San Marino, 1979. For a thoughtful exploration of the importance of *Paradise Regained* to the Romantics, see Stuart Curran, "The Mental Pinnacle: *Paradise Regained* and the Romantic Four-Book Epic" in *Calm of Mind*, ed. Joseph A. Wittreich, Jr., Cleveland, The Press of Case Western Reserve University, 1971, pp. 133-62.

only reluctantly in the undertow of the language of their loyalties. The unachievable œuvres laid down by Wordsworth and Coleridge valorize the whole and promise its progressive occupancy in a secularized version of the Areopagitican paradigm. When Wordsworth, in a moment of elation, says of *The Recluse*, "Indeed I know not anything which will not come within the scope of my plan,"[5] he invokes an inclusiveness similar to that invoked by Spenser and Milton, formulated not as the conclusive reconciliations of a higher and sacred authorship, but as the imagined yet unattainable human integration. The whole is both monumentalized and placed further out of reach by the author's notes towards it, the fragments of fragments to which Wordsworth's great works are reduced by the dimensions of the totality in which he himself locates them. *The Recluse* was never completed and the prelude to that incompleteness was rewritten repeatedly in Wordsworth's lifetime to be published only after his death and under a title he never gave it. Barthes, in writing of Fourier, speaks of the meta-book as a perpetual preface.[6] With Wordsworth we seem relegated to remaining in the ante-chambers of a central structure known only by its precincts. Nevertheless we can still maintain that it is the central structure which determines the character of the precincts.

The whole can be humanised and yet remain privileged but the search for the whole, already interiorised, will then be directed by a human teleology. The fictions which announce that teleology must question themselves in offering themselves. The secularization of the sacred does not simply deprive us of a transcendental referent; it also deprives a community of a shared language. If the poet is to be a man speaking to other men he must show, in Keats's words,

---

[5] *The Letters of Dorothy Wordsworth: The Early Years, 1787-1805*, ed. Ernest de Selincourt, revised Chester L. Shaver, Oxford, The Clarendon Press, 1967, p. 212.

[6] Roland Barthes, *Sade, Fourier, Loyola*, trans. Richard Miller, New York, Hill and Wang, 1976, pp. 88-90.

that his dream is not that of a fanatic or a savage. To do that he must doubt his own dream. These destabilizing possibilities are latent from the beginning in the Romantic affirmation. Their pervasiveness is apparent from their presence even in the Prospectus to *The Recluse*, the strong manifesto to the heroic poem of consciousness.

> Not Chaos, not
> The darkest pit of lowest Erebus,
> Nor aught of blinder vacancy, scooped out
> By help of dreams—can breed such fear and awe
> As fall upon us often when we look
> Into our Minds, into the mind of Man—
> My haunt and the main region of my song.
>
> (35-41)

In a text so saturated with references to *Paradise Lost*, every filiation must be weighed by the reader. The invocation to Book III defines the "Muses' haunt" as "Clear spring, or shady grove, or sunny hill." It is there that the poet, even in blindness, can never cease to wander, "Smit with the love of sacred song." In Wordsworth's lines, blindness is associated not with illumination, but with vacancy, and the "hard and rare" ascent of the earlier poet's journey is contrasted with the almost precipitate momentum of descent in "darkest," "pit," and "lowest." More striking still is Wordsworth's use of the dream as a means of disinterment, an instrument to scoop out the "blinder vacancy." The passage recalls Satan's excavations of self-discovery as every deep discloses a lower deep (IV, 75-78). Yet the abyss of the mind offers more than even these grim exhumations can yield. Its darkness is not simply the "haunt" but is boldly claimed as the "main region" of the poet's song.

The Prospectus retreats subsequently from this powerful recognition, pointing to "beauty" as a "living Presence," promising to "chant" the "spousal verse" of the "great consummation" between man and Nature, and dwelling on the exquisite fitting of the individual mind to the external world and on the even more exquisite fitting of the latter to the former. This emphasis on fully reciprocal, carefully dovetailed relationships perhaps indicates some uneasiness with the disruptive energy of the previous lines. Nevertheless the lines stand and their effect is not simply that of an impediment to be overcome by poetry's affirmative power. We can say that the darkness is en route to the light. We can also suggest, as Shelley was to do, that it is part of the light's nature.

The unifying imperative is prominent in Wordsworth and is often part of the advice on how we should read his landscapes. Discordant elements are reconciled by an "Invisible workmanship which makes them move/In one society" (*Prelude* I, 350-55). This is the 1805 language. In 1850 the workmanship is "Inscrutable" not "Invisible"[7] and the discordant elements are made to "cling together." The implicit image of lovers separated and perhaps precariously reunited throws a fresh light on Coleridge's view of the imagination as bringing about "the balance or reconciliation of opposite or discordant qualities."[8] We are made more strongly aware of another aspect of the imagination which Coleridge also notes, "its struggle to idealize and to unify."[9] The clinging together can be a final state, or the anxious anticipation of yet another sundering, and the craft of that cosmic poem which makes the reunion possible is now unknowable rather than simply unseen. The 1850 language uncovers perils which are not evident in the earlier version. Its admissions are all the more significant, given the generally more prudent tones of Wordsworth's later text.

The nature of Wordsworth's *concordia discors* and the degree to which it threatens the unifying imperative are brought

---

[7] Quotations from *The Prelude* are from the edition by Ernest de Selincourt, Oxford, The Clarendon Press, 1926.

[8] *Biographia Literaria*, Chapter XIV.

[9] *Ibid.*, Chapter XIII.

out more boldly in the poet's account of his descent from
the Simplon pass.

> The immeasurable height
> Of woods decaying, never to be decay'd,
> The stationary blasts of water-falls,
> And every where along the hollow rent
> Winds thwarting winds, bewilder'd and forlorn,
> The torrents shooting from the clear blue sky,
> The rocks that mutter'd close upon our ears,
> Black drizzling crags that spake by the way-side
> As if a voice were in them, the sick sight
> And giddy prospect of the raving stream,
> The unfetter'd clouds, and region of the Heavens,
> Tumult and peace, the darkness and the light
> Were all like workings of one mind, the features
> Of the same face, blossoms upon one tree,
> Characters of the great Apocalypse,
> The types and symbols of Eternity,
> Of first and last, and midst, and without end.
>   (1805, VI, 556-72)[10]

The landscape is first delineated in paradox—the undecay-
ing yet decaying woods, the "stationary blasts" and the
"winds thwarting winds." Then the turbulent stasis gives
way to the feverishness of the muttering rocks and the
speaking crags, intensifying into the sick sight of the raving
stream—the reinforcement of vertigo by delirium. Even the
blue sky is the source of shooting torrents. The region of

---

[10] 1805 and 1850 are substantially in agreement on this passage except
that 1850 substitutes the "narrow" for the "hollow" rent. A basic problem
with this passage is that of relating it satisfactorily to a crucial statement
on the imagination (1805, 525-48; 1850, 592-616) with which it is juxta-
posed. The assertion there is that our destiny is harboured in "The in-
visible world" and that our home "Is with infinitude and only there." It
does not seem to me that the "hollow rent" passage denies this finding,
but its proximity to a passage in which the imagination finds part of itself
through its dismissal of nature undermines the finality of that dismissal.

135

the heavens is remote indeed from the "hollow rent" which is the poet's world and it is against the crushing immediacy of what is seen from the rent that the unifying statement must be made. The workings of the mind suggesting process, the features of the face suggesting change and constancy, the blossoms on the tree suggesting growth and vital relationships, the "characters" which suggest the obscure yet powerful inscriptions of being in becoming, and the types and symbols which in their bewildering tumult, are nevertheless to be absorbed and quietened in finality, are converging forces of unification mobilised against the disruptive power of the text. In contending against the intimidations of the actual the imagination emerges as the implied and essential reader, recuperating the fevered landscape and bringing together the shattered script of things.

The struggle to idealize and to unify lays itself open to continuing challenges as it makes its way along the hollow rent. It is not fanciful to associate that rent with the "blinder vacancy" scooped out of darkness which, in the Prospectus to *The Recluse*, is claimed as the main region of the poet's song. Confirming evidence comes appropriately when it might be least expected, in the account of the ascent of Snowdon, when the poet, no longer confined to the "hollow rent," looks across a "huge sea" of mist, the "meek and silent" floor of a still world, lit by a naked moon. We are encouraged to think of this changeless, lunar space as the true home of the ideal, shielded from the violating energy of the actual by a protective screen so extensive that even the "real sea" gives up its majesty to it, "Usurp'd upon as far as sight could reach" (1805, XIV, 51). The arrestingly distinctive word "usurp'd," appropriated from the Simplon experience, reiterates the previous violation of a habitual order of understanding, a violation that may be imperatively called for if the imagination is to penetrate a part of its nature that has hitherto been hidden from itself. Yet the imagination's deeper self-knowledge, as in the Simplon experience, lies in its re-engagement with what it has usurped. Placed with extraordinary particularity, "At distance not the third part of a mile" from the "shore" on which the poet stands is

> . . . a fracture in the vapour,
> A deep and gloomy breathing-place through which
> Mounted the roar of waters, torrents, streams
> Innumerable, roaring with one voice
> . . . .
> . . . . in that breach
> Through which the homeless voice of waters rose,
> That dark deep thoroughfare had Nature lodg'd
> The Soul, the Imagination of the whole.
>
> (1805, 56-65)

The vapour recalls both the vapours rising from the cleft of the oracle at Delphi and the "unfather'd vapour" (1805, VI, 527; 1850, 595) to which the imagination is likened in the Simplon experience. That the imagination should reside both in the vapour itself and in a fracture in the vapour, described as a "breathing-place," is a significant admission of its duality. That it should be "exalted" in its pursuit of infinity, not by an overall understanding, but by the seeking force of an "underpresence" (1805, XIII,69-72) seems a further recognition of the creative rights of the "blinder vacancy." In 1850, these understandings are blurred by a stronger and more explicit filiation to Milton. The mind now broods

> Over the dark abyss, intent to hear
> Its voices issuing forth to silent light
> In one continuous stream.
>
> (72-74)

The connection with *Paradise Lost* reminds us not only of the spirit of creation in Book I, brooding over the "vast abyss," but also of the light in Book III, investing "as with a mantle," "the rising world of waters dark and deep." In

Wordsworth's scene the mantle is one of mist and not of light. It makes possible an illusory segregation ruptured only by the "blue chasm" drawn by that crucial fracture across the otherwise seamless text of a fictive unity. Yet it is precisely in that "dark deep thoroughfare," amid the "homeless voice" of innumerable waters that the "Imagination of the whole" must be lodged. The surrender to Milton in the 1850 version, the transference of the mind out of the fracture to the omniscience above it, strips the 1805 text of its audacity, its commitment to live within its own disruptiveness.[11] Nevertheless that recognition re-

---

[11] A number of significant divergences between 1805 and 1850 need to be noted. The 1850 version makes no reference to the "Imagination of the whole" or to the "dark, deep, thoroughfare" to which the capacity to seek the whole is confined and above which it must endeavour to raise itself. The distance between overall understanding and labyrinthine seeking is emblematized in 1805 by the "image of a mighty mind" raised above itself by an "underpresence" (69ff.). These particularities disappear in 1850. The 1805 description is of a "blue chasm" and a "fracture" less than "the third part of a mile" from the shore. In 1850 the poem speaks merely of a "rift," "Not distant from the shore." In 1805, the waters in the chasm are "homeless"; the epithet vanishes in 1850. The cumulative de-emphasis shifts attention from the disruptive fracture to the lunar and Olympian world above the mist. In accord with this hypothesis, 1850 adds language (50-52) freeing the "ethereal vault" from the mist's encroachment. Under these circumstances the chasm described in 1805 as "deep and gloomy" can safely be described as "abysmal, gloomy"; the new epithet with its Miltonic overtones (reinforced by the "dark abyss" of 72) does not add to the intensity of perception of the passage but rather strengthens its dismissive force.

The fracture and the rent image a whole that has been violently sundered. The dark deep thoroughfare associates the rent with the traffic of the mind. Thus the fracture is not to be escaped from but inhabited as one of the formative *loci* of consciousness. My view differs or wanders from Hartman's deeply persuasive reading (*Wordsworth's Poetry*, esp. pp. 33-69) in my strong sense of the text's disruptiveness and in my suggestion that Wordsworth finds the imagination called on not simply to address that disruptiveness, but to do so by agreeing to live within it. I do not seek to argue that the fracture rather than the world above the mist is the imagination's primary habitat. Both realms must obviously be inhabited if the extremities of the broken text are to be adequately possessed.

mains nascent in the Simplon narrative and in the Prospectus to *The Recluse*. The rich synonymization of the chasm, the fracture, the breach, the dark deep thoroughfare, the hollow rent, and the blinder vacancy point cumulatively to the imagination as not the redeemer but the reader of darkness and as unavoidably a citizen of the darkness which it reads.

This book does not attempt the formidable task of reading Wordsworth's poetry against the stresses and disjunctions of the Prospectus. Nevertheless it does make an attempt to show how the poetry is consistent with the poetics, how it anticipates and even deepens the sombre commitments of the manifesto. It is apparent that the dark, deep thoroughfare can have no conclusive termination, that the poet must always stand on the brink of a further subversiveness which the darkness flings against the light that penetrates it. When we align the Wordsworthian with the Miltonic œuvre, *The Prelude* parallels Milton's Nativity poem, a work which it otherwise does not resemble. It certifies the poet's coming of age, the growth of his mind to the point where it is "in order serviceable" for the greater work ahead. But the growth may only mean that the mind has been brought to a threshold where it is able to discern its own dissensions. The greater work ahead can then only be inconclusive, the continuing struggle to unify those dissensions.

In his recognition of the fragmentary status of poetic achievement Wordsworth is not entirely alone. Blake, a strenuously affirmative poet, writes in a visionary mode which can hardly be regarded as intrinsically sceptical. Indeed the extent and confidence with which Blake's language of naming takes his myth for granted enrolls the reader not simply as a participant but virtually as a disciple

It may be the reality of this double citizenship which brings about interpenetration of the Simplon and the Snowdon experiences and enables them to be thought of as calling for each other even while they are worked through as contending.

139

in that myth. The suddennesses and discontinuities of Blake's narrative present themselves similarly as outcomes of a fundamental myth which the reader is presumed to possess.[12] Yet the reader's difficulties in arriving at the causative myth may replicate those of an author who seeks literature as system only to find literature as fragments. The journey of self-retrieval engenders its own impediments on a scale which has to be described as epic. The fallen nature, not simply of discourse but of unscrutinized creativeness, is a proposition within consciousness which must make that consciousness pervasively uncertain of its claims. These observations are made to suggest what can be elicited from Blake's work from a vantage point open to its instabilities and to the problems any substantial achievement bequeaths. Blake himself emphatically valorizes the whole and the fragment can only be for him the sign of a destructive divisiveness, proliferating from the primary divisiveness of the fall. It is not only desirable but essential that the fragment be incorporated in the whole and be transformed in its incorporation. Nevertheless there can be a

---

[12] Helen T. McNeil emphasizes the "violent, absolute confrontations" of *The Four Zoas* and its abandonment of "the associative obligations of major poetry" to an extent that "threatens the mimetic mode itself." "The Formal Art of *The Four Zoas*" in *Blake's Visionary Forms Dramatic*, ed. David V. Erdman and John E. Grant, Princeton, Princeton University Press, 1970, pp. 373, 379, 390. As Joseph Wittreich observes, these characteristics do not result in *The Four Zoas* "isolating itself by innovation from *Milton* and *Jerusalem*." The poem "anticipates the innovations that are subdued into the structure of Blake's later epics." "Opening the Seals" in *Blake's Sublime Allegory*, ed. Stuart Curran and Joseph A. Wittreich, Madison, The University of Wisconsin Press, 1973, pp. 42-43. Wittreich sees the poem as "an epic of contending, but complementary perspectives," reminiscent of "the repeated confrontations within and between perspectives in Revelation." The question I am raising concerns the extent to which even a mode as self-confident as the prophetic may be beset with uncertainty and the extent to which that uncertainty may be implicit in the "contending perspectives" the prophetic voice struggles to establish as "complementary." Note 11 to this chapter studies a similar issue in relation to Wordsworth.

disjunction between an œuvre's primary pursuit and the problems which may be engendered by the very strategy and assumptions of that pursuit. Significantly, *The Four Zoas* remains unfinished, both because its manuscript text is open to revision and indecisively organized and because the manuscript is unengraved. We must remember that for Blake, the making of the book was part of the utterance. Lying at the chronological beginning of Blake's mythical narrative, the inchoate epic with its insolubly tangled layers of revision, arches across the maximum possible distance, from the blotting out of origin to its ultimate reinscription. Physically as well as symbolically the manuscript is indeed that palimpsest which images the capacity of the Romantic poem to create itself out of its own erasure. This incompleteness of the causative and foundational myth concedes much to the severance of consciousness from its source. The beginning is known not as itself, but in the consequences it is alleged to generate, the poems which are built on the poem that is not quite written and that become the only means of tapping that unwrittenness. Blake's narratives are significantly discontinuous not only within themselves but among themselves. While announcing themselves as proceeding from a foundational narrative, they can illuminate only intermittently that which is claimed to lie behind them. They thus enroll not simply the reader but the author in the effort to overcome their cleavages and to place on a unified plane of vision the different levels on which the narratives unfold. This primary indeterminacy returns us to a troubling proposition. We cannot know our origins except as our origins are inscribed in the effort to know them. Moreover, we cannot be certain that the inscriptions which result from our effort to know are really disclosures of our origins.

These underlinings have been offered because the movement from the fragment as less than complete to the fragment as other than complete is brought about in the brief space of transition between earlier and later Romanticism.

141

Events in that space are complicated by Blake's limited audience and by the fact that *The Prelude* was known only to members of the Wordsworth circle. Since the lines of literary transmission are disputable and tenuous, we must restrict ourselves to charting positions in a field, putting them into relationships which are conceptual rather than historical. The effect of later Romanticism seems to be to move closer to the centre elements which we have already detected as claiming autonomy in an earlier discourse but which have been treated by that discourse as capable of absorption, or of a transformation which would make them eligible for spontaneous membership of the unity they once resisted. The relationship between these two layers of Romanticism can be read as not one of antithesis but of difference, seeking not an inversion of privileges but rather a redistribution, an acknowledgement of the fragment's otherness and of the rights of negotiation arising out of that otherness.

In leaning to this view we need to note that from Chaucer onwards, errancy and its associated figure, the labyrinth, were seen as testifying to rather than denying the whole.[13] Among images of truth, the hill and the labyrinth are not opposed to each other. The maze is simply the experiential tracing and discovery of that which is discerned synchronically from the hill. Errancy is entertained, not as Mutability's dangerous daughter, but rather as labyrinthine purposiveness, the rendering of pattern within and through the entanglements of the actual. Thomas Browne finds it entirely consistent that the course of things should be both linear and serpentine though his preference is, predictably, for the latter.[14] Herbert's principal thematic paradox is the relationship between the simplicity of truth and the laby-

---

[13] Eugene Vinaver, *The Rise of Romance*, New York, Oxford University Press, 1971, Chapter V. Donald L. Howard, "Flying through space: Chaucer and Milton," *Milton and the Line of Vision*, ed. J. A. Wittreich, Jr., Madison, The University of Wisconsin Press, 1975, pp. 3-23.

[14] Thomas Browne, *Religio Medici*, I, 16-17.

rinth of its discovery, a relationship which dominates the
rhetorical drama of "The Collar," and the providential be-
nignities of "The Pulley."[15] The legitimization of errancy
by way of romance, the association of errancy with deferral,
and the conception of the unfinished as a relinquishment
of the poem's plenitude to the greater plenitude of the vast
design not only give status to that partial inscription of the
whole which is the fragment, but offer the fragment as the
natural means of knowing. Yet from this reassurance that
the fragment intimates the whole it is only a small step to
the disturbing knowledge that the fragment may intimate
no more than its possible relationship with other frag-
ments. That small step may be unavoidable in any dis-
course that cannot assume its own fictions.

Blake's confident requirement that we take his fiction for
granted is, in the first place, an attempt to universalize a
private myth, to state that its fundamental articulations are
latent in every reader's consciousness. But the strategy also
seeks to insulate the fiction from scrutiny, since the dis-
course which might otherwise investigate the myth is made
to depend upon the myth for its survival. The fragment is
devalued in that discourse as it is not in Spenser and in
Milton, since it is treated as the expression not of a limited
but of a divided consciousness. The combination of an in-
vulnerable fiction and of a view of the fragment which
overcomes its potential autonomy through a transforma-
tional reinstatement by which that autonomy is obliterated
can be taken together as powerfully conservationist. But

---

[15] *Jordan II* can be regarded as applying the proposition to poetic lan-
guage. The labyrinth of "inventiveness" is discarded in favour of a "ready
penned" simplicity that is only found by passing through the labyrinth.
In *The Pearl* the labyrinthine figure is explicit and climactic; it is the "silk
twist" of heavenly guidance which makes purposiveness possible in the
maze. The pattern of Herbert's œuvre, *The Temple*, in which the penitent
returns repeatedly, though with gathering self-awareness, to crucial points
on the map of understanding (signified by the repeated titles) can be
viewed as the tracing of a "purposive labyrinth."

the price paid is the admission of the otherness of the fragment and the literature of undecidability duly takes advantage of that opening. *The Triumph of Life* seems to offer a view of the fragment as divided rather than limited and as other than the whole rather than potentially part of it because of that ineradicable self-division.

Blake, by assuming the otherness of the fragment, ironically brings the day of the fragment nearer. Wordsworth contributes to the same outcome by monumentalizing the fragment so that the whole recedes into a background which the great endeavours of the foreground dominate. The whole may be invoked as the imagination's ordering principle but that invocation does not lead to admissions of the poem's manifest insufficiency, its need to surrender to a more inclusive ordering. To yield to the divine poem is the Renaissance artist's prudent self-effacement from the problems his work may have raised. But the individual cannot yield to his œuvre. He remains under some obligation to achieve it. Shelley disposes of this difficulty by freeing the œuvre from individual ownership and exalting it into the macro-poem of ongoing human consciousness.[16] In doing this, however, he reduces the individual œuvre to a fragment and the individual poem to a fragment within that fragment.

Shelley's understanding is anticipated by Schlegel, who in the *Athenaeum Fragments* (a seminal work published in the same year as the *Lyrical Ballads*), affirms, echoing Winckelmann, that "all the classical poems of the ancients are coherent, inseparable; they form an organic whole, they constitute, properly viewed, only a single poem."[17] Schlegel does not fully share Winckelmann's view of the non-identity between the classical and the contemporary. "In

[16] "A Defence of Poetry," *English Critical Essays. Nineteenth Century*, ed. Edmund D. Jones, London, Oxford University Press, 1940, p. 41.

[17] "Athenaeum Fragments," *Lucinde and the Fragments*, trans. Peter Firchow, Minneapolis, University of Minnesota Press, 1971. Fragment no. 96.

a perfect literature," he argues, "all books should be only a single book."[18] Having postulated this ideal, however, Schlegel then proceeds to erase it by a necessity which, in the end, seems more desirable than the ideal it replaces. It is the essence of Romantic poetry that it should "forever be becoming and never be perfected."[19] The fragment

---

[18] *Ibid.*

[19] "Athenaeum Fragments," 116. Wordsworth's "something evermore about to be (*Prelude*, 1805, VI,542; 1850, 608), seems almost a translation of Schlegel's phrasing.

René Wellek observes that this fragment "has been quoted over and over again and has been made the key for the interpretation of the whole of Romanticism." He cautions us that Schlegel is using the term "romantic" not as a contrast to "classical" but in preference to "modern" or "interesting." This "highly idiosyncratic" usage was "very soon abandoned" by Schlegel himself. *A History of Modern Criticism 1750-1950. Vol. II. The Romantic Age*, New Haven, Yale University Press, 1955, pp. 12-13. Wellek's warnings still leave intact the relationship between fragment 116, Shelley's view of the poem of consciousness, and Eliot's statement on the "simultaneous presence" and "simultaneous order" of "the whole of the literature of Europe from Homer." "Tradition and the Individual Talent," *Selected Essays*, p. 14.

Wellek indicates (p. 7) that Eliot's view is "substantially the same" as Schlegel's. It is probably so when one is dealing (as Winckelmann does) with a fixed canon such as that of classical art and literature. When the canon is continually changing, problems arise for which fragment 116 provides an answer that Eliot is indisposed to accept. There may be an important difference to be explored. Apart from the chauvinistic restriction to the "literature of Europe," Eliot's view seems dominated by the assumption that the macro-poem of that literature is, in its nature, closed. The existing "monuments" form not simply an order, but an "ideal order." That order is "complete before the new work arrives." For order to persist after "the really new" work of art has been admitted, "the relations, proportions, values of each work of art toward the whole are readjusted." The museum of art remains unviolated except for these tactful accommodations which uncomfortably acknowledge each new entry into the monumental array. The crucial difference between this language and that of fragment 116 is surely that Schlegel's perception and Shelley's are grounded on the unfinished nature of the macro-poem. The "really new" work of art can call for fundamental reconsideration rather than polite readjustment. The deep shifts of understanding to which it can conceivably persuade us bear witness to and justify the macro-poem's openness.

therefore is the empirical if not the ideal form of poetry as well as the "real form of universal philosophy."[20] If Schlegel admits the inevitability of the fragment, he also lays the ground for claims of its self-sufficiency. "In poetry too, every whole can be a part and every part really a whole."[21] Since every integration broaches the possibility of a larger integration, the whole proclaims itself as a fragment even in arriving at its wholeness. But the fragment can also be quintessential, the nucleus of a larger totality rather than simply one of its many members. The aphorisms in which Schlegel writes are the traditional form of the quintessential fragment, and the fragments which make up Pound's *Cantos* can well be treated as an imagistic version of the aphorism.[22] This quality of the fragment is most strikingly revealed by its isolation. By removing it from the field it might normally occupy, its creative density is thrown into relief. But the removal can have consequences quite other than the suggesting of potential connections inherent in the compression of the fragment. In a particularly vivid simile Schlegel tells us that "a fragment, like a miniature work of art, has to be entirely isolated from the surrounding world and be complete in itself like a porcupine."[23] The image is noteworthy because it suggests not only the self-contained nature of the fragment but also its resistance to investigation, its refusal to enter prospective fields of relationship. That property of the fragment can also become important in the great chain of literature's dismantling.

The shift to the fragment may seem to revise sharply the

---

[20] No. 259.

[21] "Critical Fragments," *Lucinde and the Fragments*. Fragment no. 14.

[22] On Pound and the aphorism, see Hugh Kenner, *The Poetry of Ezra Pound*, London, Faber and Faber, 1951, pp. 44-45. Despite Pound's adverse statements, his connections with the Romantics are sufficiently substantial to be the subject of a monograph by George Bornstein. "The Post-Romantic Consciousness of Ezra Pound," *English Literary Studies Monograph Series*, no. 8, University of Victoria, 1977.

[23] "Athenaeum Fragments," no. 297.

commitment to the whole of the earlier Romantics but, as our examination shows, there is a basis for the shift even in the work of those who seek the whole with fervour. We can look forward (or onward) to the autonomy of the fragment, to the dissociation of change from its final cause, and to the oblique attainment by Mutability of nearly all the status Spenser denied her. As we consider the poetics of the unfinished we might say that its implicit and evolving formulations are not discontinuous in their problematics, in their raising of a further interrogation by the manner in which the previous question was closed. The line of change responds to the inheritance; it also turns on the inheritance in ways which the pun is needed to suggest.

Don Juan: The Sea and St. Peter's

I

IN THE FOURTH CANTO of *Childe Harold*, the wanderer en route from Venice to Rome pauses before "a matchless cataract." The scene is one of "endless torture" and of "agony" wrung out between the darkened rocks "That guard the gulf around, in pitiless horror set." The "fierce footsteps" of the deliriously bounding waters crush the cliffs, forcing them to yield, "a fearful vent" to the torrent's straining passage (LXIX-LXXI).[1] Byron's language vividly recalls the descent in *The Prelude* to Domodossala from the Simplon pass with the "muttering crags" looming over the "raving stream," as it fights its way along the "hollow rent." Indeed the successor poet proceeds even further in re-inventing a text he probably had not read. Wordsworth's landscape is notable for the contrast between the turbulence below and the tranquility above, as the "unfettered clouds," indifferent to the "giddy prospect" beneath them, float serenely in their transit through the heavens. In Byron's landscape, a rainbow arches over the scene of anguish, like "Love watching Madness with unalterable mien." Both writers confront us with a scene of brute force, an enormous fissure tearing apart contrasted possibilities, a text of things that seems devastatingly fractured. But there is one crucial dif-

---

[1] Quotations from *Childe Harold* follow the text of *Byron: Poetical Works*, ed. Frederick Page, 3rd edn., Oxford, Oxford University Press, 1970. Quotations from *Don Juan* follow the text in *Lord Byron: Don Juan*, ed. T. G. Steffan, E. Steffan and W. W. Pratt, Harmondsworth, Penguin Books, 1973.

ference: the cataract at Velino is an artificial cataract.[2] Wordsworth announces the rupture and intensifies our sense of it so that he may advise us that the closing of the rupture is the imagination's privilege. He offers us not one but five unifying strategies, five ways of healing the dissociated text as the pursuit of the whole encounters that necessary subversion by which its own endurance is to be challenged and educated. Byron has no such remedies to propose. Instead he confronts us with the startling possibility that the fractured text may be a work of art rather than nature, that the imagination may originate the very fissure that it endeavours to heal.

Thirty-six stanzas later, the traveller approaches Diana's grave at Aricia, south-east of Rome, the grave of which Egeria is the nymph. Fern, flowers, and ivy are "Fantastically tangled" in a gentle plenitude, quietly emulative of the "enormous bliss" (V, 297) of Milton's paradise. In one of the several connections between the final Canto and its predecessor, the landscape also reflects the invocation of Clarens, "birthplace of deep love," an invocation which formed the climax of the third Canto. The solitude around Clarens was love's recess, the refuge into which he had been driven by the "world's waste." Linked to the reforming force of Rousseau's philosophy, love could have been thought of as a social force and not simply a personal emotion, capable of some share in the making of history. But it was its nature to "advance or die," to shrivel away if it did not grow into a "boundless blessing" (C11-C111). The direction taken is evident in Canto IV. The "venom" in the mind is not expelled. "Weeds of dark luxuriance" flourish in its fertility. "Dark at the core, though tempting to the

---

[2] *Poetical Works*, p. 891. Byron's note refers us to his note on *Manfred* II, 11, 1ff. where the "sunbow" arches over a torrent, the foaming light of which resembles the pale courser's tail/The Giant steed, to be bestrode by Death/As told in the Apocalypse." Wordsworth's reference to the "Characters of the Great Apocalypse" is recalled, though the import is sharply and significantly different.

eyes," they call to mind the forbidden "fruit" of Paradise. The associations become more specific with "flowers whose wild odours breathe but agonies" and "trees whose gums are poisons" replacing Milton's "rich trees" weeping "odorous gums and balm" (IV, 268). Milton's trees weep both in their natural plenitude and in anticipation of the world into which that plenitude is to be metamorphosed. Byron's trees provide that metamorphosis. As "Passion flies/O'er the world's wilderness" in *Childe Harold* we are reminded of "*Joshua* whom the Gentiles *Jesus* call" who will bring back "long-wander'd man" through "the world's wilderness," "safe to eternal Paradise of rest" (XII, 310-14). It is not rest which is offered in Byron's poem but the vain seeking of a "celestial fruit" craved for and yet "forbidden," dispensed by a love which has lost even its precarious refuge in reality.

> The mind hath made thee, as it peopled heaven,
> Even with its own desiring phantasy,
> And to a thought such shape and image given,
> As haunts the unquench'd soul. . . .
>
> (XXI)

The stanza which follows may be the grimmest in Byron's poetry.

> Of its own beauty is the mind diseased,
> And fevers into false creation:—Where,
> Where are the forms the sculptor's soul hath seized?
> In him alone. Can Nature show so fair?
> Where are the charms and virtues which we dare
> Conceive in boyhood and pursue as men,
> The unreach'd Paradise of our despair
> Which o'er informs the pencil and the pen
> And overpowers the page where it would bloom again?
>
> (XXII)

That the imagination is open to betrayal by its own creative momentum is not an unusual conclusion by 1818.

Byron's achievement lies in the conviction and explicitness with which he delineates that betrayal. The clanguorous commitment to "What Mind can make, when Nature's self would fail" (XLIX) is turned, in the fourth line, savagely against itself. The golden world, far from ennobling us by our resolute pursuit of it, dooms us by its ineradicable segregation from the actual. The mind is sundered by an alienation out of which Paradise can be constituted only by constituting the despair which cannot reach it. Desire validates itself by positing the unattainable, by finding its authenticity interred in its defeat. The page of the poem is obliterated by the very intensity needed to form its characters.

In the year after this passage was composed, Shelley's Demogorgon once more proclaimed the enthronement of that love which Byron found a fiction of the subverted consciousness. Poised on the "slippery steep" and "crag-like agony" of a landscape reminiscent of the cataract at Velino, love is no longer the rainbow of an unreachable promise. Instead, it "springs" into action, spreading its "healing wings" over the world's tumult. Hope creates "from its own wreck the thing it contemplates" in a Phoenix-like resurrection from its ashes.[3] In the exchange of understandings between poetic colleagues this may well be Shelley's rejoinder to Byron. But to counter what Byron has said is not to erase it.

In our own century, a sixty-year-old man among school children contemplates the waste and the purposelessness ingrained in the nature of life. It is a prosaic situation for the high Romantic argument but great affirmations are, by now, made in familiar places. Beauty, Yeats tells us, is "born out of its own despair." We might conclude that Yeats is taking Shelley's side against Byron but there is a reference in the previous stanza to the "self-born mockers of man's enterprise" which appears to give Byron his due

[3] *Prometheus Unbound*, IV, 554-78.

rights.[4] Yeats takes into account both subversion and the genesis of creativeness from the betrayal that cannot quite undermine it. He is the poet who completes the circle, the Yin and Yang that are necessary for the full statement.

To consider the repercussions of Byron's stanza is to reflect on its status in his own work. One would like to say that Byron also draws the circle and Childe Harold's varied responses to the voices of many places make the proposition not impossible to defend. Restorative movements can be traced in the poetry and can be justly characterised as movements rather than gestures. The difficulty is to estimate correctly their real as distinct from their rhetorical weight. The assaying becomes more complex when the rhetoric seems divided against itself. Thus, following the outburst against the mind's subversiveness, we are advised to "ponder boldly" and to refuse to resign our right of thought. We are assured that

> Though from our birth the faculty divine
> Is chain'd and tortured—cabin'd, cribb'd, confined,
> And bred in darkness lest the truth should shine
> Too brightly on the unprepared mind,
> The beam pours in for time and skill will couch the
> blind. . . .

"Cabin'd, cribb'd, confin'd" are Macbeth's words when he learns of Banquo's murder and Fleance's escape.[5] Macbeth is bred in darkness, not because he is unprepared for the shining of the light, but in order to become fully the agent of the darkness which breeds him. The allusion works against the counter-affirmation the argument of the stanza carries forward, affiliating the poetry to the negative understandings which it nominally seeks to resist. On the other hand, the "first created beam" of God's restorative power can be said to pour in on blind Samson and Samson

---

[4] *Among School Children*, in *Collected Poems*, p. 214.

[5] *Macbeth* III, IV, 24-5. The phrase is used again (within quotation marks) in *Don Juan* IV, 75 where Juan is literally confined to a cabin.

is accurately described as "chain'd and tortured." In an overall estimate, the Samson allusion probably prevails, but it is not permitted to do so decisively and one stanza is scarcely sufficient to stand in the scale against seven.[6]

The tannen tree in the twentieth stanza is another restorative image on which a dubious light is shed. It is "rooted in barrenness," grows to its greatest height on the loftiest rocks and "mocks/The howling tempest," until its stature makes it worthy of the granite mountains from which it wrings its strength. "The mind," we are told, "may grow the same." As Michael Cooke points out, the landscape is that of the forty-fifth stanza of the preceding Canto where "He who surpasses or subdues mankind/Must look down on the hate of those below." "Contending tempests" blow on his naked head as a reward for the toil that has led him to the summit.[7] It is Manfred's world and its defensive consolation is that of the mind as its own place, most fully itself in the most hostile of circumstances. That limited promise is restrained by the subjunctive, an earnest of frustrations that have yet to come into being. The approach of those frustrations may be indicated by the much less vigorous tree of the ninety-eighth stanza, with its blossoms lost and its rind put to the axe. The sap lasts in hope of a better spring, but in the season to come, another tree flourishes

> This boundless upas, this all blasting tree
> Whose root is earth, whose leaves and branches be
> The skies which rain their plagues on men like dew
>
> (CXXVI)

It is this monstrous growth, supplanting the tannen as the tree of the mind, which looms dominant and threatening, over the rest of the Canto. The tannen's endurance

---

[6] Byron's note (*Poetical Works*, p. 892) distinguishes reason from prejudice but the previous stanzas can scarcely be read as an offering of prejudice. The attempt to devalue them only acknowledges their weight.

[7] Michael Cooke, *The Blind Man Traces the Circle*, Princeton, Princeton University Press, 1969, pp. 103-05.

is not eradicated. But we are made strongly sensible of the destructive energy of the "dark luxuriance" arrayed against it.

It is plain that the momentum of self-defeat in this final Canto is not easily to be contained or diverted. We can take note of this momentum by agreeing that if the third Canto belongs to Rousseau, the fourth belongs to Calvin. But to say this is not to say enough. Nor is it quite enough to admit that Calvin is probably the better poet, though Bostetter is not unjust in describing the "Wordsworthian and Shelleyan" pronouncements in Canto III as "philosophically shallow."[8] The question to be asked is how far the idea of the ruin is to be pressed, particularly in the declamations of a figure who is self-confessedly, "a ruin amidst ruins" (XXV). Are we contemplating merely the ruins of Rome? Or are we contemplating something more basic, the ruin of previous ways of understanding?

Byron's awareness of time's power of erasure is extraordinary. Other celebrations of time take sufficient note of survivals to preach predictable sermons on the vanity or meaning of human endeavour. "How fallen, how changed, how defaced" are Poggio's words, at any rate in Gibbons' rendering of them, as he looks down upon the ruins of Rome. They are also Satan's first words to Beelzebub in hell, and behind them stand the words of Aeneas as he confronts the ghost of Hector in the ruins of Troy.[9] The end of an era is sounded in these comments even when the beginning of another era is prophesied and even when the new era, as in *Paradise Lost*, is demonically ushered in by the fall of man. Beginnings in their turn, while born and built in expectancy, can suffer the same fate as the

[8] E. G. Bostetter, *The Romantic Ventriloquists*, Revised edn., Seattle, University of Washington Press, 1975, pp. 267-68.

[9] *Aen*. II, 274-75. *P.L.* I, 84-87. *The Decline and Fall of the Roman Empire*, Chapter LXXI. If "how fallen, how changed" is a phrase taken from Satan's first words to the fallen Beelzebub, "defaced" is taken from Adam's first words to the fallen Eve (IX, 901).

endings on which they were erected. In *Paradise Lost* that saving reversal is offered as the main ground of our hopes. When we move outside Milton's encompassing inversions, the rhythm of self-defeat of the diabolic, a circle seems to be closed with melancholy elegance as the ruins of Rome are reflected upon in language that remembers the poem of Rome's founding. The delusiveness of ends and of beginnings is the natural stuff of orations upon history and Byron seems about to venture on this oration when he tells us that the true triumphal arch is not that of Titus or Trajan but of Time (CX). But elsewhere he doubts whether history may have even this much to impart to us. Rome is a desert, more unnavigable than the ocean, where we stumble over recollections, the remnants of a past too fragmented and vestigial to offer us any "lesson" (LXXI). Yet Time is not simply the last inheritor, Mutability's voracious male counterpart. He is also the "beautifier of the dead" and the "adorner of the ruin" (XXX), the restorer of a violated normality where the ruin blends into the rhythms it has outraged. Time's creative function may be to give the text back to its innocence, purging it from the destructive human emendation.

The sentimental distinction between ravaging man and unsullied nature is never far from the centre of the fourth Canto but it too may be one of those ruined propositions, those weather-beaten and time-tempered half-truths around which the poetry is made to circulate. Time teaches us that the shapes of understanding are fragmentary and provisional. Perhaps it does so by eradicating the structures of domination which are annexed to, and fortify, those shapes. There is in this process, the fulfillment of the sceptical wish for the annulment of ideological tyrannies. There is also attention to the Baconian warning not to propitiate those idols of the theatre which the rhetoric and drama of philosophies can erect.[10]

---

[10] *Novum Organum*, LXII-LXVII.

Byron advises us of the relativity of judgement, not by haphazardly providing us with various judgements fitted to the ambience of various places, but by engaging those judgements with each other, through overstatement, counterstatement, and the implication of statement in counterstatement.[11] These provisionalities have to be borne in mind as we approach St. Peter's and the possible consecration of the Canto.

> Thou seest not all; but piecemeal thou must break,
> To separate contemplation, the great whole;
> And as the ocean many bays will make
> That ask the eye—so here condense thy soul
> To more immediate objects, and control
> Thy thoughts until thy mind hath got by heart
> Its eloquent proportions, and unroll
> In mighty graduations, part by part,
> The story which at once upon thee did not dart
>
> (CLVII)

McGann finds that the experience of St. Peter's "finally exposes the teleology of the poem and of the life of man as well."[12] But the poem so far has not given the impression of gathering itself for the announcement of a final cause, and the announcement itself is not the kind of "omnific word" that might advise warring elements of their deeper relationships. McGann seems to put his own claim in perspective when he observes

[11] Michael Cooke observes that Byron's mind "appears to have worked by incessant qualifications" and that he was more given than any of his contemporaries to "the use of qualifying connectives." *The Blind Man traces the Circle*, pp. 44-45n. George Bornstein finds Wallace Stevens manipulating "negatives, subjunctives, interrogatives, and direct statements to mimic mental action while maintaining provisionality." *Transformations of Romanticism*, Chicago, University of Chicago Press, 1976, pp. 205ff. The point is made since Stevens is used later in this chapter to characterize Byron's response to facticity.

[12] Jerome McGann, *Fiery Dust: Byron's Poetic Development*, Chicago, University of Chicago Press, 1969, p. 38.

> This idea of "piecemeal" apprehension amounts to an
> analysis of poetic method in the poem itself. . . . The
> narrator . . . has continually to reformulate his un-
> derstanding of the significance of what he sees. Thus
> it is in the poem.[13]

This is indeed true, except that there is no reason why the
understanding achieved at St. Peter's should alone be ex-
empt from having to be reformulated. We do not make this
point to indulge in a type of ingenuity which most philos-
ophers have come to consider barren, but rather to note
that if St. Peter's is a work of art exemplifying harmony,
Velino is a work exemplifying division. That art is capable
of offering, and perhaps obliged to offer, both views of
itself may be more important in our overall reading than
either of the views offered. The poem both illustrates this
recognition by the specific occasions it chooses and mi-
meticizes the recognition by the way in which it moves
through its chosen occasions. It is only appropriate that a
little later—both as a recapitulation and as an insistence on
the necessary co-presence of divergent understandings—
the anguish of the Laocoön should be juxtaposed with the
ideal beauty of the statue of Apollo. Lastly, the image of
the ocean is itself destined to be reformulated: it will not
be the ocean to which the final stanzas turn.

It would be surprising if at this point in literary history
Byron's aim were to be, naively, the revalidation of the
Areopagitican model. The model is situated in the poem,
not to be hailed but to be interrogated. At issue is not the
fragmentary nature of understanding—that can hardly be
contested by a ruined self meditating among ruins—but
the proposition that the association of fragments leads to
progressively wider and more cohesive fields of compre-
hension, self-revisionary only to the extent dictated by the
greater magnitude and complexity of the field. Is the whole
more and more fully inscribed in the endeavour to reach
it or are we to think, as well, of a self-revisionary move-

---

[13] *Ibid.*, p. 39.

ment, with no final cause beyond its own continuance? The second possibility seems a better preface to a long poem yet to come, which McGann rightly describes as "radically, aggressively episodic and meandering."[14]

As the traveller prepares to face the ocean in the poem's final stanzas, he announces various connections with and revisions of his past. The slightly resentful "I have not loved the world, nor the world me" (III, CXIII-IV) is changed to the more conciliatory "I love not Man the less, but Nature more" (IV, CLXXVII). Mingling with the universe, a theme worn nearly to tatters in the third Canto, is reiterated as the wanderer's objective. Nature is coyly presented as the other partner to a series of trysts, "interviews" from which limited happinesses are stolen. Characteristically, the tongue-tied lover can neither adequately state nor effectively conceal his devotion. He is left as the custodian of "piecemeal" perceptions, awaiting the "great whole" in which they are to merge.

It is difficult to avoid the impression that these reassurances are offered to be overturned. The traveller had once preferred "clear placid Leman" to the "torn" ocean whose "stern delights" had moved him unduly (III, LXXXV). He now turns to face an ocean no longer torn but irresistibly inviolable. The repeated "roll" seems to take up and mock the unrolling of the whole at St. Peter's in "graduations" there described as "mighty" but now laid perilously open to the unending onslaught of the ocean's power. The "many bays" which, in Byron's earlier reflections, invited the eye and trained the soul to "condense" its aspirations to that which it was immediately capable of apprehending, are now the last refuge and the petty hope of those whose presumption marked the earth with ruin (CCLXXX). Bostetter is too mild in observing that the ocean represents that "impersonal power of nature"[15] which often symbol-

[14] McGann, *Don Juan in Context*, Chicago, University of Chicago Press, 1976, p. 3.

[15] Bostetter, *The Romantic Ventriloquists*, pp. 267-68.

izes Byron's fundamental vision. Nature is a gentler force, self-healing, as in the landscape of Thrasimene, unchanged in its deep self by the intrusions it accommodates. The ocean accepts no intrusion. It is overwhelming in its capacity for erasure. It tolerates no text but that of its "wild waves' play," a text that is preserved only by being continuously rewritten even as it is erased (CLXXXII). Byron's exultation in obliteration is evident everywhere in his apostrophe and his deification of the ocean's inviolability is made with a fervour not found in his consideration of St. Peter's. The ocean is exempt from the ravages of time. It is primal in its purity: "Such as creation's dawn beheld thou rollest now." It is the "glorious mirror" of the Almighty, the "image of eternity," the "throne/Of the invisible," the embodiment of omnipotence and solitude, dread, fathomless, alone, boundless, and endless (CLXXII-XXXIII). Educated by the poem, we look for a corrective movement which will question, or at least restrain, this torrent of superlatives. Stanza CLXXXIV may seem to offer this corrective but, as in a previous situation, it is only one stanza confronting several. Significantly it is coupled to its predecessors by an *and* rather than a *yet* or a *but*. It is less the modification of a previous thought than the poet's claim for exemption from the cleansing wrath he celebrates. The main affirmation remains dominant and perhaps excessively so. Yet there is a logic in arguing that if a work of art is poised on the engagement between unifying and divisive forces it is equally poised on the engagement between composition and eradication. The ocean may have another face but it is a face to be considered in another poem. The end of this poem is the *tabula rasa* before which it stands in worship.

II

Byron began the composition of *Don Juan* in July 1819, six months after completing the fourth Canto of *Childe Harold*. In the same year, in a reiterated incompleteness, the first and second *Hyperions* not only broke off, but broke off in mid-sentence. Three years later Beethoven wrote Opus 111, the unfinished nature of which was the subject of Kretschmar's momentous lecture. Eighteen twenty-two was also the year in which Schubert wrote the Symphony in E Minor, widely known as the Unfinished Symphony. In May of the same year Shelley began composition of *The Triumph of Life*. His final voyage was two months later, on July 8. The ship on which he went down was named the *Don Juan*. A year later Byron ceased writing his poem.

Bostetter notes that in the unfinished poems of the Romantics, each poet makes "his most determined attempt to solve the aesthetic and philosophical problems which confronted him." He adds that "each poem breaks off at a memorably dramatic point—as if a motion picture were abruptly frozen at the moment of critical action."[16] The drama of the unfinished, the carefully chosen point of arrest, rich in unravished possibilities or unnegotiable problems, obliges us to consider the forces in each venture that are inseparably part of the poem's self-acknowledgement but that have also placed completion beyond its reach. The diminuendo of *The Faerie Queene*'s exit is arranged with a virtuoso's skill as the poem relinquishes itself to a greater poem which calls in its nature for a higher than human authorship. Keats terminates the first *Hyperion* at the transformation of Apollo, marking a boundary which the poem is unable to cross at this point in its self-formation. He stops for a second time with the transit of *Hyperion* as the offered sign of a poem that is always in transit. Shelley proceeds for some four lines beyond his question mark as if to tell us that we must proceed even if we cannot progress. Nevertheless it is that haunting question mark which searches the nature of the Romantic inquiry and admits the impossibility of bringing it to a settlement other

---

[16] *The Romantic Ventriloquists, Intro.*, p. 6.

than that self-constituting, self-erasing dialogue which is the ongoing justification of the inquiry's right to life.

Don Juan is written in this climate and thus takes place in a succession of poems which steadily press forward the question of whether the long poem can properly be finished. In a world which lacks a world-view it is difficult to know where Ithaca is, or when and how Rome is to be founded. Even *Paradise Lost*, the most conclusive of long poems, is conclusive only because it seeks to expound definitively the forces at play in the theatre of history and because the exposition links a narrated beginning behind which it is impossible to go, to a prophesied end, beyond which all is "abyss/Eternity whose end no eye can reach" (XII, 555-56). Within the theatre of history itself, the forces can be precisely charted, but the outcome of their engagement depends upon a centre of free choice which leaves the poem structurally closed, yet open-ended in its implications. The world is "all before them where to choose" when Adam and Eve leave Paradise. Wordsworth uses the line and Byron mocks himself with it (XIV, 9). It is a line calling for a sequel, the successor poem which Blake writes when he has Milton undertake the journey of self-renewal to enter contemporaneity as Blake's colleague. Wordsworth in his turn writes the successor poem when he contemplates the revolution betrayed as Milton did, and climbs a hill as Adam did, to find his answer not in the reform of external institutions, but once again as Milton did in the remaking of the self. Byron's response to the invitation for a successor poem is *Don Juan*. It does not, like Blake's poem, propound a new mythology of which the literary past is a component, and it is not, like Wordsworth's, a heroic poem of the mind. But it may be closer to our time than either.

Milton mobilizes an antithetical world of time and space around a precarious centre, raising to their maximum dimensions the peril and opportunity which surround the gift of freedom. Byron's hero acquiesces in events, creative or catastrophic, which he has not made and is offered no prospect of changing. He falls from innocence, is ship-wrecked into paradise, is sold into slavery after the obliteration of that paradise, survives harem intrigues, war, the lusts of an empress, and the manners of English society. In these adventures he displays his share of decency and his share of weakness. The decency can be a matter of drawing the line and refusing to resort to cannibalism (II, 78-79) or of befriending a threatened child in a savage battle (VIII, 91-96). The "weakness" is a matter of acquiescence, preferable perhaps to the sexual egoism of other Don Juans. These qualities are not sufficiently engaged with each other for us to speak of Juan's development, and it seems proper that they should not be engaged since the poem of self-formation is not what Byron seeks. When the hero is not strongly characterized, attention shifts naturally to the action. Indeed it can be argued that it is easier to read the action philosophically or morally when it is carried forward by its impersonal momentum, independently of the co-operation or interference of the hero. The fall from innocence and the destruction of Haidée's paradise seem to promise such a momentum, a recurrent rhythm that could be cumulatively powerful, but its possibilities have already been discounted by a "fall" that is on the boundary of bedroom farce, by a paradise that is built upon slave labour, and by Haidée's inextricable mingling of innocence with self-indulgence. If any expectations are set up they seem set up in order to be undermined, to suggest that life is not purposeful but stubbornly miscellaneous. The question then raised is whether art should re-enact life to this extent.

This is not an easy question to answer and anyone who answered it successfully would have a vantage point from which to view *Don Juan*. To come closer to an answer it is necessary to look at the poem in more detail. The improvisatory element in *Don Juan* is striking to many readers. It is mentioned by the author in the course of these critical statements about the poem which draw attention to nearly everything else.

I rattle on exactly as I'd talk
With anybody on a ride or walk
(XV, 19)

Men should know why
They write and for what end; but note or text
I never know the word which will come next
(IX, 41)

"You ask me for the plan of Donny Johnny," Byron writes
to Murray on August 12, 1819 after completing two Cantos
of the poem. "I *have* no plan; I *had* no plan; but I had or
have materials."[17] Ten Cantos later he is even less prepared
to be definite, drawing attention to the inexhaustibility of
his "materials" and mocking the large-scale plans which
Wordsworth announces in the preface to *The Excursion*.

Here the twelfth canto of my introduction
Ends. When the body of the book's begun
You'll find it of a different construction

. . . .

The plan at present's simply in concoction. . . .
(XII, 87)

One advantage of an improvisatory poem is that it can
accept and indeed welcome the unexpected. It is not called
on by its structure to insist upon exclusions. It is free to
digress and when, as in the case of Byron's poem, it is
further opened up by its varieties of style and manner, its
hospitality can begin to seem inexhaustible. "I want a form
that's large enough to swim in/And talk on any subject that
I choose," is Auden's emulatory wish in his "Letter to Lord
Byron."[18] Virginia Woolf comments that *Don Juan* is "what
one has looked for in vain—an elastic shape that will hold

[17] *Byron's Letters and Journals*, ed. Leslie A. Marchand, Cambridge, Mass.,
Belknap Press of Harvard University, 1973.
[18] *Letter to Lord Byron*, in *W. H. Auden: Collected Poems*, ed. Edward
Mendelson, New York, Random House, 1976, p. 79.

whatever you choose to put into it."[19] The title of John D. Jump's essay, "Poem or Hold-all" indicates some justified uneasiness with this view.[20] *Paradise Lost* has also been spoken of as an infinite receptacle; but it is a receptacle distinguished by an ordering capability which can place and value everything it accepts. A picaresque poem such as *Don Juan* cannot achieve this capability, but it does not follow that it should resign itself to becoming a means of containment rather than of organization. Though the justification of God's ways may not be its objective it can still seek to arrive at understandings which are emergent rather than demonstrated. Even if it denies itself a narrative teleology it should still be able to devise a narrative rhetoric. Such a rhetoric, if it is sufficiently vigorous and if its relationships of situation, imagery, and authorial interjection are sufficiently cohesive, should be able to insinuate the design of the real behind the waywardness of the fictive flow and its digressive eddies.

"Design" is the word recommended by McGann in the best book so far written on *Don Juan*.[21] In suggesting that it is better to speak of the design of *Don Juan* rather than of its structure or form, McGann reminds us of Alpers' statement that it is better to speak of the organization of *The Faerie Queene* rather than of its structure.[22] Despite the apparent similarities, the directions of rectification are notably different. Alpers is trying to reclaim the autonomy of Spenser's epic against the thoroughgoing spatialization of the poem by some of its more gifted interpreters. McGann is endeavouring to state those principles of coherence in *Don Juan* which prevent it from being devoured by its au-

[19] Virginia Woolf, *A Writer's Diary*, London, The Hogarth Press, 1953, p. 3.

[20] John D. Jump, "Byron's *Don Juan*: Poem or Hold-all?" in *"Childe Harold's Pilgrimage" and "Don Juan,"* ed. John D. Jump, London, Macmillan (casebook series), 1973, pp. 226-43.

[21] McGann, *Don Juan in Context*, p. 4.

[22] Paul T. Alpers, *The Poetry of the Faerie Queene*, Princeton, Princeton University Press, 1967, pp. 107-33.

tonomy and enable it to stand above its own miscellaneity. The extreme of McGann's effort will be found in Ridenour's claim that "if *Don Juan* has any one serious defect as a work of art it is that in spite of its insistent casualness it makes its point with such single-minded perseverance."[23] Not everyone will agree with this instructive overstatement but the anxieties behind it will be evident. The poem must either conquer or abandon itself to its casualness. If it is not to be a hold-all, it must be something like Milton's infinite receptacle. Its improvisatory nature must be restated as its principal virtue rather than as its characteristic weakness. A powerful philosophical argument can then be made by a work of art which is able to arrive at the structure or even the design of the real behind the apparent randomness of the actual.

Ridenour's characterization of the design of *Don Juan* is strongly perceived and attractive as well as influential. According to him "the underlying principle of Byron's universe seems to be that its elements are, in their different ways, both means of grace and occasions of sin."[24] He continues,

> The universe, as Byron sees it, is not merely inconveniently arranged or not arranged at all and so humanly neutral. There is, from man's viewpoint at least, something profoundly wrong about it and about his place in it. But at the same time there is generous provision of means and opportunities of dealing with this wrongness and making it humanly right. But these means and opportunities have a way of being closely allied with the primary causes and manifestations of the wrongness. All this is not what *Don Juan* is about. It is about coming to terms with such a world.[25]

[23] George M. Ridenour, *The Style of "Don Juan,"* New Haven, Yale University Press, 1960, p. ix.

[24] *Ibid.,* pp. 9, 49.

[25] *Ibid.,* p. 49.

Perhaps unconsciously, Ridenour's language remembers Michael's words to Adam in *Paradise Lost* as he begins his lesson on the nature of history

> Good with bad
> Expect to hear, supernal grace contending
> With sinfulness of men;
>
> (XI, 358-60)

In Michael's stern teaching, the self is the primary locus of sinfulness. The world can be confirmed in its fallen destructiveness or brought back to order by that centre of choice around which it continues to be mobilized. It is capable of one course or another, but it is not ambivalent in the sense that it can simultaneously enter into both chemistries. Such deep-rooted ambivalence transfers uncertainty from that choosing centre where Milton places it to a world which can respond in more than one way (and perhaps in more than one way at the same time) to whatever choice is exercised at that centre. The compound indeterminacy which ensues is not what Milton intended but the threatening yet beneficent universe which it delineates can still be a fit subject for poetic study. Its narrative sign might well consist of the recurrent frustration of goodness by the very qualities which bring about that goodness.

Ridenour makes clear his firm subscription to the sign when he tells us that in *Don Juan* "charm and beauty are inextricably involved in violence and death." Elsewhere he finds that "the most powerful force undermining the paradisal relationship is the very force that made it a paradise in the first place." The myth of the Fall thus adapted, is according to him, one of the "main unifying devices in *Don Juan*."[26] Gleckner endorses this finding and carries it further in observing that *Don Juan* is concerned "not with morality or immorality but with nothingness, with a world devoid of value and humanity, a world in which even the

[26] *Ibid.*, pp. 81, 85, 122.

166

'good' (in any sense) quickly destroys itself in the effort to be what it is."[27] Such grim seriousness seems in excess of what Virginia Woolf calls "the springy, random, haphazard, galloping" nature of the poem[28] but it can be argued that it is precisely this discrepancy which enables the poem to contemplate its abyss.

Ridenour's view undoubtedly has its attractions and, up to the Haidée episode, the poem does seem to be proceeding from the universe he depicts, setting up a potential recurrence which could conceivably become its master rhythm. But the harem adventure, the Russian affair, and the English Cantos do not offer us a world in which the creative is undermined by its own creativeness. The siege of Ismail may seem a different matter, but that savagery and nobility go together in war is a proposition somewhat older than Homer. Byron's interest, in any case, does not lie in documenting the proposition. His concern is not with the waste of virtue, or with the inseparable entanglement of courage and brutality, but with the "tedious havoc" of the heroic, its obsolescence in a world that is even moderately enlightened. But "Patience and heroic Martyrdom" are not, as with Milton, Byron's better fortitudes, and his references to the Fall are neither frequent nor far-reaching. It might even be said that he avoids the topic with a success extraordinary in so talkative a poem.

Recurrence has also been detected in the manner in which the women in *Don Juan* appear to reflect each other. The English trio in particular, is said to recapitulate Donna Julia, Gulbayez, and Haidée. Their rebirth may imply either a deeply significant rhythm of renewal or certain typical restrictions in the male view of femininity. In any case, Byron is careful to distinguish Aurora Raby from Haidée as the gem of society is distinguished from the flower of nature.

---

[27] Robert F. Gleckner, *Byron and the Ruins of Paradise*, Baltimore, The Johns Hopkins Press, 1967, p. 332.

[28] Virginia Woolf, *A Writer's Diary*, p. 3.

We might make something of the difference between innocence and cultivation but the experience of the poem so far indicates that such discriminations are offered to be modified. There is nothing in the evidence at this point to lead us to suppose that Byron, having established an expectation, would not have prevented it, as before, from settling down. Here as elsewhere, his commitment is probably to openness.

Reflection will suggest why this unsettling is desirable. Byron completed *Manfred* in the year before he began the composition of *Don Juan*. He wrote *Cain* in the year between his two main bouts of preoccupation with the poem. Defiance, rebellion, withdrawal, exile, the religion of art, and Yeatsian rejoicing in the midst of tragedy are classic responses to a mocking or vindictive universe. It is more difficult to engage the self with a world which does not seem to consider the human situation sufficiently momentous to be worth the complexity of a relationship with it. Insult and humiliation are negative recognitions which can provoke dignified rejoinders such as the strengthening of the life of reason in the midst of a world which seems constituted to deny it. Indifference is a phenomenon more difficult to resist. Yet, as Camus suggests, there are consolations in a facticity that remains sheerly itself even if the consequence of that inviolability is the intermittent irrelevance of the human. For a world that intimates such specifications, the comic response may be more appropriate than the heroic gesture. In *Cain* and *Manfred* Byron had given his attention to the heroic possibilities. In *Don Juan* he sought to explore the comedy. While doing so he advanced the possibility of a universe that is not malignant or ambivalent but stubbornly heterogeneous, offering no purchase except to the combination of the voluble narrator and the acquiescent hero.

Openness and the reluctance to consolidate world-views have other virtues besides preservation of the comic spirit. A long poem, it has been argued earlier, has to sustain its magnitude by cultural omnivorousness as much as by narrative complication. *The Faerie Queene* sustains itself in both ways. Pound's *Cantos* rely exclusively on the first way. *Paradise Lost* does what is possible to complicate a narrative whose outlines have already been prescribed. On the other hand, its claim to an overall reading of human affairs not only justifies but demands cultural omnivorousness. *Don Juan's* episodic plot may seem at first to provide ample opportunities for proliferation, but the concentration on a single hero rules out the cross-connections which multiple narratives might make available and permits only the accumulation of episodes. It might still be possible to move the hero through a variety of situations which the authorial voice could then connect to a suitably wide range of cultural contexts. Unfortunately Juan's adventures must be predominantly amorous, though the siege of Ismail can be introduced to show Byron's much advertised adhesion to epic requirements while questioning, by its pointless brutality, the traditional association of love and war in the composition of the heroic. The narrative restrictions are in fact severe, and digression emerges as the major strategy for sustaining a poem of this length. However, digression is based on the right to some degree of irrelevance and therefore cannot attach itself to a world-view to which everything in the poem must be made relevant. The possibilities of the poem must be kept open and the most open of these possibilities is the relationship of the author himself to his literary experiment. When McGann describes *Don Juan* as "not a poem that develops" but "a poem that is added to," he puts his finger on Byron's problem. When he describes the poem as "radically, aggressively episodic and meandering,"[29] he indicates a solution to the problem,

---

[29] *Don Juan in Context*, p. 60, p. 3. Brian Willkie similarly observes that Byron wanted to create a poem "that was deliberately and in every sense inconclusive" though he adds that this was because Byron "wanted to show life itself as ultimately without meaning." *Romantic Poets and Epic Tradition*, Madison and Milwaukee, University of Wisconsin Press, 1965, p. 211.

but a solution which raises the question of how the poem can properly be finished.

The possibility of viewing *Don Juan* as a literary experiment was first suggested by Helen Gardner[30] and has been developed instructively by McGann. The term rightly suggests an accommodation to facticity and a strong sense of the provisionality of literary specifications. The rules of engagement between the author and his experiment are crucial; and it is the experiment rather than the author that should be called on to confirm or rearrange those rules. The desirability becomes all the stronger because a long poem, if only by virtue of its magnitude, is likely to accumulate rights of its own. The author should find himself in negotiation with an otherness certified as authentic by its very unpredictability, rather than with a controllable rhetorical construct. This double indeterminacy—designed, but also asserting its autonomy from the very mandate which bestowed that autonomy—is important in *Don Juan*. As the poem moves on, these compounded autonomies are likely to shift the centre of attention from the narration itself to the author's response to the narration.

It is impossible in a brief chapter to chart the changing content of the poet's response to his work, particularly when that response makes growing use of a privilege of disgressiveness that increasingly dissociates the response from the narration. It is, however, possible to consider not the poet's response to the entire content of his poem but, more restrictively, his changing view of the kind of poem he takes himself to be writing.

Byron's indications on this subject are profuse and contradictory to an extent that would be exasperating if we did not assume that we are being taught something by the contradictions. An example which may be of primary importance in delineating the author's view of his poem will

[30] Helen Gardner, *"Don Juan"* in *Byron: A Collection of Critical Essays*, ed. Paul West, Englewood Cliffs, Prentice-Hall, 1963.

help to outline the problem. In the eighth stanza of the "Dedication" Byron addresses Southey as follows

> For me, who, wandering with pedestrian Muses,
> Contend not with you on the winged steed,
> I wish your fate may yield ye, when she chooses,
> The fame you envy and the skill you need.

The immediate suggestion is that the author of *Don Juan* in his prosaic progress may well be more a poet than Southey on the winged steed with his epic pretensions. But the first line also associates Byron with the *musa pedestris* of Horace (*Serm.* II, vi, 17) and thus advises us that the poem is to be in a plain style historically defined by both precept and cumulative practice. The fourth line, with its epigrammatic balances, recalls Byron's lifelong commitment to Pope, an elegant practitioner of the plain style. However, the choice is not simply a matter of disavowing the soaring flight in favour of the pedestrian progress. Byron's muses wander and the word suggests Ariostan errancy, particularly because of the implicit contrast between the wandering muses' journeying on foot and tempted by every blandishment of the landscape and the undistracted movement of the winged steed to its destiny.

We are dealing then, we might suppose, with a digressive poem in the plain style. Unfortunately for our stability of perception, Byron advises us otherwise towards the end of the first Canto

> My poem's epic and is meant to be
> Divided in twelve books . . . .
> . . . .
> After the style of Virgil and of Homer
> . . . .
> With strict regard to Aristotle's rules
> The vade mecum of the true sublime.

In the stanza that follows Byron condemns the tedious embellishments and the "labyrinth of fables" favoured by his "epic brethren gone before." In the seventh stanza he had already said

> The regularity of my design
> Forbids all wandering as the worst of sinning. . . .

We now seem to be looking at a poem of the "true sublime," one which will not fall victim to digression and in which the winged steed pursues its resolute course. But to begin at the beginning is not "the style of Virgil and of Homer." The strategy licences a chronicle form in which wandering is not necessarily sinning, placing the emphasis on the unfolding of the tale rather than on its structuring. It is true that the tone is jesting and that Byron even suggests "Longinus o'er a bottle" as a description of his poem (204), but this is clearly one more of those dismissive statements that, even in their formulation, invite us to examine the partial validity of what they ostensibly dismiss. It is indeed "Longinus o'er a bottle" and not a responsible poet facing the problems of the real world who would write heroic poems according to mechanical formulae. A responsible poem must achieve the naturalizing of the heroic. After the rise of the novel and the Preface to the *Lyrical Ballads* an antique hero is no longer possible. Spenser and Milton achieve contemporaneity paradoxically by removal, by distancing their poems in highly organized, fictive universes to which the contemporary world is then engaged. The style in each case acts to maintain the requisite distance from what Yeats was later to call the "pushing world"[31] of the actual. The plain style, on the other hand, situates the poem in the everyday and the problem is one of achieving the higher stature within a location which the modern poet must accept. The disjunction in critical statements obliges us to realize that the pedestrian muses must do what the winged steed once did, that errancy must undertake what

[31] W. B. Yeats, "Certain Noble Plays of Japan," *Essays and Introductions*, London, Macmillan, 1961, p. 224.

purposiveness once achieved, that the work must instruct us, that the song must be moralized, that the poem may remain loyal to various desiderata, but that the desiderata in turn must adapt themselves to the creative needs and restrictions of the day.

In the seventh Canto, prefacing the siege of Ismail, Byron proposes to sing of "Fierce loves and faithless wars."

> I am not sure
> If this be the right reading—'tis no matter
> The fact's about the same, I am secure.
>
> (VII, 8)

The right reading of the quotation is "Fierce warres and faithfull loves shall moralize my song." It is the last line of the opening stanza of Spenser's proem to the first book of *The Faerie Queene*. If Byron draws attention to the misprision it is because he is defining with some care the devaluation of Spenser's currency. We live in a world of destructive passions and wars fought without principle. As for moralizing his song, Byron in remembering Spenser is also remembering Pope. It is "one poet's praise"

> That not in fancy's maze he wandered long
> But stooped to truth and moralized his song.
> (*Epistle to Dr. Arbuthnot*, 340-41)

The falcon is disciplined by the use of the lure as it stoops (swoops) in order to seize it. The lure provides both nourishment and training. It is in this context that Browne speaks of teaching his "haggard and unreclaimed reason to stoope unto the lure of faith"[32] and Pope may not have been unaware of this usage. When a poem is formed by a secular force such as fact rather than by a religious one such as faith, it is made to inhabit a world not Spenser's or Milton's.

---

[32] *Religio Medici*, I, 10. "Haggard," "unreclaimed," "stoope" and "lure" are technical terms in falconry which Browne is using adeptly. The implied metaphor is of Christ as the falconer, using the lure of faith as a means of nourishing reason and of curbing its waywardness.

It can no longer constitute the fictive as a territory of mediation between the ultimate and the actual. It must moralize its song by pointing with the satirist's finger rather than by recourse to the illustrious example. Alternatively it must instruct us by declining to organize the actual into false semblances of order or of purpose and by raising the question even if it is unable to answer it, of how we are to live within that desolation which we cannot help seeing when we attempt to see clearly.

The moralizing of his song is uniformly insisted on by the author in the shifting claims he makes about his poem. "My politics as yet are all to educate" is an early announcement (1, 7). When reviewers protest about the immorality of *Don Juan*, Byron scathingly leaves them

> to the purer page
> Of Smollett, Prior, Ariosto, Fielding
> Who say strange things for so correct an age. . . .
>   (IV, 98)[33]

The next Canto (dealing with Gulbayez' passion) is prefaced ironically by a condemnation of "amorous writing" and a resolve to make the poem a "moral model," "formed rather for instruction than delighting." As the seventh Canto begins, Byron notes that he has been accused of

> A tendency to underrate and scoff
> At human power and virtue and all that.

He says no more than has been said by an array of writers, philosophers and moralists "who knew this life was not worth a potato." Suwarrow follows in his obsession with glory. "Human power and virtue" are laid waste in the siege of Ismail. It is not the writer but the leaders of men who underrate these qualities by dedicating them to objectives which are meaningless. In Canto XII Byron returns

[33] Ariosto's presence in the "correct" age of the eighteenth century is notable.

more conventionally to his didactic purpose: "My muse by exhortation means to mend" (XII,39). A little later there is more than one muse: " 'Tis a great moral lesson they are reading." These tongue-in-cheek observations are not to be wholly dismissed. Once again, Byron sets up the specification not so that we can apply it mindlessly, but so that we can ask ourselves how the song is to be moralized. To have an admonition "to each error tacked" (V,2) is a course unlikely to result in literature. To "sketch your world exactly as it goes" (VIII, 89), to purge it of cant, to strip away its self-delusions is to leave it to speak against itself but also unavoidably, for itself. To rectify one must also understand.

It is apparent that the instructive force of Byron's poem is bound up with its fidelity to fact. "Fact is truth, the grand desideratum" (VII, 82), the muse deals not in fiction but in gathering a "repertory of facts" (XIV, 13) and the "part of a true poet" is "to escape from fiction/Whene'er he can" (VII, 86). "But you want facts not sighs"[34] is Auden's apt acknowledgement to Byron. It is an acknowledgement which reflects not only Byron's freedom from sentimentality but also his readiness to write the poem of his climate. The ideal-antique-fictive world Spenser uses and the mythic-historical world Milton uses as frames of understanding are no longer accessible to the new poet. Paradise is not lost by an act of choice. It is given, taken, and obliterated by the arbitrarinesses of the story. The difference says farewell to a previous order of poetry and to a classic pattern of retrieval in which the diagnosis of what is lost provides the impetus for its recovery. The "waste and icy clime" over which the Aurora Borealis of the new poetry intermittently flashes (VII, 1-8) gives us no basis for millennial expectations. The poet's responsibility is to prevent the escape into fiction, to oblige us to face what Yeats was

34 "Letter to Lord Byron," p. 83.

later to call the desolation of reality.[35] We are instructed by what we cannot avoid. Even the causal casualness of Byron's story is educational, since it questions the possibility of education by events.

Despite his commitment to his pedestrian muses Byron occasionally mounts the winged steed. "If you cannot fly, yet flutter" (XV, 27) is one of his suggestions to his less than vigorous Pegasus. Though the plain style prescribes the normal elevation for the poem, the higher mood is not absent. But it is the bleak landscape of the Aurora Borealis, the ruined landscape of "an old temple dwindled to a column" (XIII, 1), the recklessness of a small skiff sailing "in the wind's eye" (X, 4), and the insignificance of human endeavour as it confronts the ocean of the real in its obliterating resistances (XV, 99) that provide the images of poetry at its most "serious." None of these images are promises of design. The temple image may seem at first to offer such a promise but on closer inspection it points to erosion rather than to the recovery of a heritage.

Byron's voluminous advice on the poetics of his poem is, as has been suggested, meant to be engaged with the work. "Fact is truth" also in this limited realm and poetic specifications, like large philosophical statements, must submit themselves to the revisionary force of the actual. But the poetic claims, jostling against each other, have the additional effect of preventing attachment to any one of them, of keeping the course of the poem open, and of allowing it to decide which of its possibilities are to be fulfilled or invalidated. Similarly the varying styles of the poem, notwithstanding its normal acceptance of the plain style, allow it to move in various directions and to enlarge its capacity for inclusiveness.[36]

---

[35] W. B. Yeats, *Meru*, in *Collected Poems*, London, Macmillan, 1950, p. 333.

[36] As McGann observes, Byron's style is "formed out of a balance of styles but the balance is sought not from a sense of the limitations of any of the styles he uses but from a sense of the options they open up when

So far, our examination of the poem shows its main resources as uniformly oriented towards openness. The loosely connected narrative inhibits the building-up of causal momentum. The lack of recurrence enables the poem not to succumb to any dominant rhythm. The multiple claims the poem makes about its status make it difficult to affiliate it to any particular claim or cluster of claims. The varieties of style allow significant deviation from the poem's normal tenure of the plain style. To the extent that the poem is a generic mixture or a generic medley, the strategic effect is to open up further its range of options. The substantive effect is to insist that literary pretensions must, in Bacon's phrase, "be buckled and bowed unto the showes of things," that organizational expectations must submit to the persisting revisionary force of the actual. The author's varying stances towards his narrative and in particular his increasing use of the privilege of digressiveness[37] insist, further, on the need for receptivity to "fact" by placing a loose form, which is capable at any point of moving in several directions, in a flexible relationship to a floating commentary with which it is sometimes only flimsily engaged. It does not seem unsafe to conclude that openness is an important feature of *Don Juan*.

Don Juan has been variously identified as an epic, a negative epic, a mock-epic, an anti-epic, a verse novel, and an epic satire.[38] Such divergent descriptions urge us to the feeble finding that *Don Juan* is indeed a mixed-genre poem.

---

used in a mixed or medley fashion . . . the whole point of the style of *Don Juan* is to explore the interfaces between different things, events and moods." *"Don Juan" in Context*, pp. 93, 95.

[37] After having described wandering "as the worst of sinning" (I, 7) Byron owns (III, 96) that if he has any fault it is digression

> Leaving my people to proceed alone
> While I soliloquize beyond expression.

He suggests that his digressions are "addresses from the throne." In XII, 39 the ends of digression are moral and it is compared to "grace before a feast." As the poem proceeds it becomes the feast itself.

[38] McGann, *"Don Juan" in Context*, p. 3.

But the purpose of the mixture, as has been indicated, is not to exhibit the concurrence or contestation of genres. It is rather to make irrelevant the claim of any single genre to dominance, to question the applicability of those rules of engagement which literary investigations proffer in the face of the actual. The equivalent in the world of ideas to this curbing of pretensions is to loosen the hold on the mind of those systems of thought which Bacon tellingly describes as the idols of the theatre. In the deflationary zest it exhibits on both of these levels, the poem reveals itself as a true sceptical epic, buoyantly resistant to tyrannies, whether of ideology, discourse, social mores, or literary form.

The term "sceptical epic" is offered not as yet another identification of the elusive shape of Byron's poem. It is offered rather as a means of designating that elusiveness. Though the proposition will at first sight seem only ingenious, the epic is a form well-suited for sceptical statement. Its opportunities for scepticism arise naturally from its magnitude and from the inclusiveness which is a historical consequence of that magnitude. It has time and space to establish its indifference to purposiveness, not as a concession to anarchy, but as a proper distrust of fixed characterizations of meaning. Its openness can be designed to prevent narrative rhythms from establishing themselves, while not eradicating the possibility of those rhythms. Its resistance to structural organization can be built up and yet made to fall short of being dogmatically anti-structural. In moderating its own subversiveness, it has room to put forward and to frustrate epic promises and, in doing so, to offer itself as both an anti-epic and as a counter-poem to that anti-epic. Its prolixity in describing itself is simply part of its recognition that the factual is always self-revising and protean.

The epic encyclopedia is cumulative, a compendium of knowledge that is organized structurally rather than alphabetically. The sceptical encyclopedia is instructively self-cancelling for its more talented or determined compilers. The elements of that enlightened ignorance which is the true form of knowledge are brought together to undermine rather than to support each other. But the blank page of scepticism which results is not necessarily the page of defeat, awaiting the inscription of faith.[39] For Pyrrho, the blank page (or the page on which nothing can be finally written) promises rest in its acceptance of inconclusiveness rather than that restlessness which, having exhausted all secular possibilities, must now turn to the religious resolution. Byron may well be of the Pyrrhonic persuasion thus defined, notwithstanding his adverse remarks upon Pyrrho (IX, 18). Fact, not faith, remains his desideratum. Significantly, the "moment of critical action" at which the last published Canto "freezes" is the point at which the supernatural turns into the familiar—as it does not with Mozart's Don, defiant in the manner of earlier Byronic heroes. Byron's aim is not to persuade us to a transcendental settlement amid the bafflements of a babel of prolix opinion. Juan is not a seeker and, in response to the temptations of

---

[39] Don Cameron Allen remarks that "Montaigne adorns the skeptical tenets of the Pyrrhonists . . . with the green wreaths of Christian approval. . . . Pyrrhonic man, naked in mind, confessing his weakness, humble, obedient, and hating heresy will be a blank page for God to write upon as he pleases." *Doubt's Boundless Sea: Skepticism and Faith in the Renaissance*, Baltimore, The Johns Hopkins Press, 1964, p. 86.

The blank page calls for the inscription of the text of faith only in the religious realm. In the secular realm, indifference in valuation between possibilities can lead to acceptance of the status quo, either inert or pragmatically intelligent; but it can also lead to resistance against the excessive privileging of any possibility.

The prevalence of scepticism at the end of the seventeenth century is measured by Louis Bredvold's comment that by that time "every reader of any pretensions to cultivation knew Montaigne and Charron intimately and almost every scholar had read Sextus Empiricus." *The Intellectual Milieu of John Dryden*, Ann Arbor, University of Michigan Press, 1934, rptd. 1956, p. 15. Pierre Charron's *De la Sagesse* was among the most widely read books of the age and Samson Lennard's English translation of it (1608) itself ran into several editions.

the other extreme, he is also not a survivor or an endurer. He maintains himself without asserting himself. To be possessed by an identity is to hammer out one's future in its image with a zeal inimical to what Michael Cooke helpfully identifies as counter-heroism.[40] The essence of counter-heroism is that it should decline to be dominated by those metaphysical gestures which to Byron are, by now, only postures—postures he arrayed against each other and passed through to leave behind him in the more colourful confrontations of *Childe Harold*.

In a letter of January 2, 1818, to Hobhouse, Byron dedicates *Childe Harold* to him "in its complete or at least concluded state." These are words written to order for a study such as this. The possibility they adumbrate is that of a poem between the sea and St. Peter's, a poem which, in its nature, can be neither completed nor concluded. To write it one must abandon the pursuit of that "great whole" which the imagination seeks in Wordsworth's hollow rent, amid the homeless voice of many waters.[41] Equally, one must stand away from the pleasures of the void, the exhilarations of obliteration. A sceptical epic must be safeguarded against is own intensity, must ensure that its resistance to dogma does not itself become a dogma. It is easy to be swept away by an ocean which the questioning mind must also learn to resist.[42] Perched upon a humbler

---

[40] *The Blind Man Traces the Circle*, Chapter VI.

[41] The "great whole" of *Childe Harold*, IV, CLVII and of the 1805 *Prelude* (III, 130-31; deleted in 1850) possibly reflect the "stupendous whole" of Pope's *Essay on Man*, I, 267-68.

[42] If we seek to place Byron in relation to dogmatic scepticism, which argues that knowledge is impossible, Pyrrhonic scepticism, which argues that it is uncertain, and scientific scepticism, which argues that it is provisional, he is probably closest to the second position. Distrust of the "abyss of thought" is expressed in both IX, 18 and XIV, 1. Philosophic systems devour their predecessors, leaving any system only momentarily in possession of the field (XIV, 1-2). The ultimate questions (framed by Byron as Shelley was to frame them in *The Triumph of Life*) are "answerless and yet incessant" (VI, 63). "A calm and shallow station/Well nigh the

promontory, reminiscent of Pope's "isthmus of a middle state,"[43] extended into but distinct from the boundless sea of doubt, Byron finds himself free of the majesties of illusion, of the claims that had dominated his own poetic life. The comic voice is the proper voice of fact and in particular of those "squamous" facts which, for Wallace Stevens and others, exceed and thus instruct the "squirming" mind.[44]

Byron's last work, in its acceptance of the actual and its indifference to the purposive, swings the balance of power from the whole to the fragment. It effectively counters our readiness to argue that poems which are balanced between the forces of closure and the forces of openness such as *Paradise Lost* and *The Faerie Queene* are, *prima facie*, superior to poems such as *Don Juan* and *The Cantos* in which the forces of closure are not often effectively present.

The desire to find such a proposition correct is difficult to escape from and is not restricted to Renaissance scholars.

---

shore" is best for "moderate bathers" (IX, 18), though the significance of the "pretty shell" one gathers in that station is characteristically questioned by the language, reminding us of the shell that Newton gathers by the ocean (VII, 5) and the pebbles by the shore in *Paradise Regained* (IV, 330), which wise men gather in the name of knowledge. The "humbler promontory" (XV, 19) on which one perches and which one presumably leaves for another perch when the perceptions it can offer have been exhausted, is an alternative to the "calm and shallow station." Both offer an openness of understanding based on the pervasive admission of possibilities other than the one being entertained. The sceptical mind should be fully receptive to doubt but safeguarded by it rather than possessed by it.

Cooke observes (pp. 176-77) that Byron is less than just to Pyrrho or Montaigne. However, as Willkie suggests, some irony at Pyrrho's expense may be necessary to maintain a position that is fully Pyrrhonic. *Romantic Poets and Epic Tradition*, p. 190.

[43] *Essay on Man*, II,3. Byron's substitution of "perched" for "plac'd" suggests not only that his station is changeable, but that it was chosen rather than allotted.

[44] "Connoisseur of Chaos," *Parts of a World*, New York, Alfred A. Knopf, 1942, p. 50.

Spenser's and Milton's main work are built over a deep cleavage between the real and the actual and in their structures seek to mobilize the hope and even the prospect that the actual can be reclaimed in the image of the real. The fictive power is the witness of this hope. Its locus in a religious world is the redeemed mind. Wordsworth's sense of the presence of the whole is sufficiently strong for him to argue that its signature is to be found and followed, even in the most disruptive of environments. If, in Blake's poetry, the fragment can be found resisting the whole, it is only because of its imprisonment in a fallen nature from which its deep self cries out for liberation. Byron is unusual and perhaps bleakly forward-looking in declining to segregate the real from the actual, in his reluctance to subscribe to a distance that would make possible even that imaginative redemption that is entertained, though not unreservedly, by other Romantic poets. We live in the world as we find it, and if the findings do not gather into a pattern we must learn to live with the lack of pattern. The ability of the imagination to conceive of a fictive otherness which is then authenticated as a sign of the real by the very desire that proclaims its unattainability was considered and left behind in *Childe Harold*. Haidée's paradise is presented not as a zone of reality, but as an event given and taken by two waves of the sea. Don Juan having lost it, is not heard bemoaning its loss, or found dedicating his life to its recovery. Such a view places the onus of coherence (if there is one) on the commenting self and its awareness of what will suffice, rather than on the poem's narrative occasions or the responses of a participant notably unconcerned with the significance or inconsequentiality of those occasions. In Byron's poem the commenting self is comic, satiric, indignant, blasé, self-mocking, and courageous. To be this self is one way of living in the world and of responding to the demands it makes upon us; it may not be less taxing than the tragic or nihilist way.

The right of the poem to remain unfinished is evident

in everything that it makes of itself. At one time Byron proposed to have his hero guillotined in the turmoil of the French Revolution. Such a conclusion would have been in keeping with the date of the siege of Ismail.[45] Byron sought consistency in such matters, thinking it to be conducive to the realism of his poem: "I like to be particular in dates" (I, 103). Consistency would have been the only merit of such a termination. It would have guillotined the poem as well as its hero. It was better to have the poem cease in mid-canto even though we are denied cantos on astronomy and political economy (XII, 88) and though an undertaking to provide "a panoramic view" of hell (I, 200) never materializes. If the poem ceases it is certainly not because of that exhaustion of options which in the opinion of Dr. Kretschmar, brought Opus 111 to its end.

> I meant to make this poem very short
> But now I can't tell where it may not run.
>
> (XV, 22)

[45] Letter of 16 February 1821, to Murray. Other possibilities considered in the letter incude Don Juan's incarceration in either hell or an unhappy marriage. See also Elizabeth French Boyd, *Byron's "Don Juan." A Critical Study*, New Brunswick, Rutgers University Press, 1962, pp. 31-32, 41-42.

The Triumph of Life:
The Unfinished and the
Question Mark

UNTIL RECENTLY the reader of *The Triumph of Life* would probably have found the poem cut short by a question mark. Thomas Hutchinson's text, edited for the Clarendon Press in 1904 and still in print in the Oxford Standard Authors series, maintains this ending. Though C. D. Locock's two-volume edition for Methuen (1910) proceeds beyond the question mark and though the Julian edition by Ingpen and Peck follows suit, the addition was not decisively influential.[1] It is Donald Reiman's text first published in 1965 and now available in the Norton Anthology which makes many of us aware of how the poem really ended.[2]

Accuracy is always to be admired, but on this occasion we have to ask ourselves whether an ending generally admitted to be corrupt is altered significantly by its rectification. After the poet has asked the question, "Then what is Life?" his instructor in the new *Commedia* watches the chariot pass into the distance and returns seven words of a prospective answer. Since the instructor has just been described as a cripple it seems unlikely that his answer, if completed, would dispose of the question. In any case his few words are not enough to dissipate the force of an inquiry which is a cry of protest as much as a question. Shelley had written "cried" in the manuscript before re-

[1] The Houghton Mifflin edition by Woodberry (1901) the text of which is still current ends with the question mark.

[2] All quotations are from the Norton text.

184

placing it by the more neutral "said," a word which does less than its share of work in this highly charged context. He probably did so, as Reiman conjectures, to avoid a rhyme which many of us would not find intrusive.[3]

The poem still ends as most of us have felt it to end, dominated if not overwhelmed by that question mark. It is a climax the searching force of which is made all the more disturbing because of the inescapable engagement between the poem's conclusion and its title. A poem which christens itself *The Triumph of Life* and ends with the question "Then what is life?" must be taken as inaugurating a new era in inconclusiveness. It earns its right to do so mainly because the fiction it constructs is powerfully anti-fictional, a waking dream of the desolation of reality.

The poem begins as if it intends to keep its promises and to celebrate ardently what its title proclaims. Shelley had trouble with the opening, as is shown by the three cancelled versions printed by G. M. Matthews.[4] In its final version the opening affirms, with deepened emphasis, that symphony of nature to which Vaughan responds in *The Morning Watch* and which Adam and Eve articulate in the fifth book of *Paradise Lost*, in the dawn prayer that follows Eve's disturbing dream. In Shelley's poem the sequence is inverted, with the narrator passing from external serenity into the dream's disquietude. He lies on "the step/Of a green Apennine" beneath an old chestnut tree (25-26). The interior landscape is carefully matched to the external one. We have the same dew, the same dawn, the same slope, the same bough and the same "Sweet talk in music through the enamoured air" (34-39). The "strange trance" into which the poet is lulled is in fact singular in its transparency (31). It is important that the landscape of actuality should not

[3] Donald H. Reiman, *Shelley's "The Triumph of Life": A Critical Study*, Urbana, University of Illinois Press, 1965, p. 211. "Cried" rather than "said" is the word almost universally printed by editors.

[4] G. M. Matthews, "On Shelley's 'The Triumph of Life,' " *Studia Neophilologica*, XXIV (1962), pp. 104-34.

be altered as it passes into the world of the dream. A "Vision" is then "rolled" upon the poet's brain (40), anticipating these waves of vision which burst upon Rousseau's mind in the Labrador simile (404-11). The poet now relates the "tenour" of his "waking dream" (42), using in the words "Vision" and "waking dream" the precise language of the questions which end Keats's *Ode to a Nightingale*. Once again the literary affiliation serves notice of decisive differences. In Keats the dream world is the locus of a fragile harmony. In Shelley the exterior world is harmonious and the dream is at least initially a force of demystification, a counter-fiction designed to strip away the illusions that can reside in our habitual apprehension of the actual.

The poet finds himself beside a "public way" (43) which is the way of the world. A crowd flows along it, not dissimilar to that crowd which, in Eliot's *The Waste Land*, flows over London Bridge. It grows more agitated as "the woods of June" do "When the South wind shakes the extinguished day" (76). The death imagery is intensified by a "cold glare" that obscures the sun (77-79). It precedes a chariot that moves forward on "the silent storm/Of its own rushing splendour" (86-87), contrasting with the sun "Rejoicing in his splendour" and hastening to his task "Of glory and of good" at the beginning of the poem (1-3). The word "splendour" is often used in Shelley's poem and always with discriminations that need to be carefully registered. In this particular usage the oxymoronic "silent storm" strengthens the aura of the unnatural and prepares us for the deformed shape in the chariot. Dusky-hooded and double-caped, it crouches within "the shadow of a tomb" with a "cloud like crape" bent over what seems its head. A Janus-visaged shadow guides the chariot from its rear. The "shapes" that draw the chariot are "lost" in "thick lightnings" (89-97). The shadows, the shapes, the "seeming," and the lightning flashes that conceal instead of revealing outline an authenticity that eludes definition yet cannot be avoided.

The demonic connotations of the chariot will be evident, most notably in that threatening use of light imagery which is so prominent a feature of this poem. Literary affiliations add to the weight of perversion. The resemblance between the *Triumph* and Lucifera's pageant in *The Faerie Queene* has been documented by Carlos Baker.[5] Harold Bloom draws attention to the parody of Milton's "chariot of paternal deity" involved in the four faces and "banded" eyes of the charioteer (99-100).[6] We might add that "the beams that quench the Sun" (102) put to diabolic use the supersession of the sun by a superior light of creativeness that is so important in Renaissance Christian poetry. Similarly, the four pairs of banded eyes nullify a potential omniscience on which the poet specifically insists (103-04). "Speed in the van and blindness in the rear" are the result (101), and it is a result which might well serve as an epitaph for progress in our own time.

Although the demonic associations of the "Triumph" are numerous and potent, it does not follow that the pageant is to be unreservedly construed in this fashion. To do so may be to attach the poem to a value-system which it does not seek to entertain. More specifically, the identification of the demonic-parodic normally calls for a repudiation the poem may not invite. The question "Then what is Life?" would be less disturbing if it could be argued that none of the nature of life is to be found in the pageant. The poem's strength is that though provoking this answer it does not finally allow the answer to triumph. Nor does it allow the triumph of the opposite view. Its double abstention should be seen not as prevaricating but as creatively uncertain. Placed between surrender and negation, its enterprise (which

[5] *Shelley's Major Poetry: The Fabric of a Vision*, Princeton, Princeton University Press, 1948, p. 260, n. 5. Baker notes several other affiliations with Spenser.

[6] *Paradise Lost*, VI, 750; Harold Bloom, *Shelley's Mythmaking*, Ithaca, Cornell University Press, 1969, pp. 231-42; *Poetry and Repression*, New Haven, Yale University Press, 1976, pp. 85-111.

must in its nature be unfinished) is to find a third way which partakes of neither.

With these cautions we can return to the chariot as it moves "With solemn speed majestically on" (106), providing the "true similitude/Of a triumphal pageant" (117-18). At the center of the pageant and chained to the car are those "mighty captives" (135) who have compromised with the world and been conquered by it. In the van are those bacchantic celebrants whose pursuit of pleasure ends in a self-destructiveness, obliterated by the passing chariot wheels. In the rear are the old, trying helplessly to keep up with the chariot, consumed by frost as those in the van are by fire (175). The poet asks half to himself what the spectacle represents and what the shape within the car is. He is about to ask why everything is "amiss" when a voice answers "Life" (176-81). This cryptic guidance proceeds from what appears to be a deformed root on a hillside. It is what remains of Rousseau, who is to become the less-than-omniscient instructor in the Romantic *commedia*.

The "grim Feature" speaks (190) and we recall that the phrase was used in *Paradise Lost*[7] and used no more than once. Death is so characterized when he turns "His nostril wide into the murky air," snuffing the scent "Of mortal change on earth" (X, 272-80). For a narration of the progress of life this is an appropriately demonic prelude. Rousseau, as might be expected, concentrates upon the "mighty captives," those who were granted "thought's empire over thought" but who could not repress "the mutiny within" (211-13). The poet then asks Rousseau a fourfold question covering the whence, the how, the whither, and the why of the event he is witnessing. The relationship to the four Aristotelian causes will be evident. A full answer would result in a definitive explanation. But the question has also to be associated with the four blind faces of the Janus-like charioteer. From one who has fallen victim to the chariot

[7] Harry Buxton Forman, ed., *The Poetical Works of Percy Bysshe Shelley*, London, Reeves and Turner, 1876, Vol. III, 337-338n.

the answers provided must be expected to obscure una-
voidably what they seek to reveal.

It is to be noted that Rousseau undertakes only to answer
the question "whence?" The answer to "how?" can be
inferred by the poet. The answer to "whither?" cannot be
provided. The poet had previously begun to ask "why?"
and was cut off before he could formulate the question. It
is no surpise to learn that it cannot be answered. We can
be instructed in the enigmas of origins and history but the
final cause cannot be excavated and presumably cannot be
inferred from origins and history however intensively read
(295-304).

The origin is in a cavern under a mountain. The land-
scape is sufficiently close to the opening lines of the poem[8]
to allow us to speculate that the mountain may be that
"green Apennine" on which the poet fell into his "trance."
In the cavern Rousseau encounters

A shape all light, which with one hand did fling
Dew on the earth, as if she were the Dawn
  Whose invisible rain forever seemed to sing

....

In her right hand she bore a chrystal glass
Mantling with bright Nepenthe;—the fierce splendour
  Fell from her as she moved under the mass

Of the deep cavern.

(352-61)

The light, the dawn, the dew, and the singing are all cre-
ative in their stock associations but the "fierce splendour"
of the shape, the unendurable brilliance which the dark-
ness of the cavern accommodates to our capacities, inex-
tricably involves the menace of understanding with its
promise. The "bright Nepenthe" which the shape offers

---

[8] F. Melian Stawell, "Shelley's 'Triumph of Life,' " *Essays and Studies
by Members of the English Association*, V, Oxford, Clarendon Press, 1914,
p. 112 and n. 1.

has been likened[9] to that "Orient liquor in a crystal glass" which Comus offers the Lady in Milton's masque and which he says is superior to nepenthe.[10] The common source in *The Odyssey*[11] may be more relevant. Helen offers Telemachus nepenthe to enable him to forget grief. That purpose has already been met by the music of the waters in the cavern which induces total obliviousness to pain and pleasure (315-24). The purpose of nepenthe is to cause forgetting of that forgetfulness and thus, paradoxically, to prepare one for grief. It is like that "honey of generation" which Yeats speaks of in *Among School Children*.[12]

The shape moves along the stream that leads out of the cavern to "wondrous music" (369), the sweetness of which is twice emphasized (378, 382). Once again the flow of assertion is strongly undercut and we are made disturbingly aware of the fierceness in the sweetness.

> All that was seemed as if it had been not,
>   As if the gazer's mind was strewn beneath
> Her feet like embers, and she, thought by thought,
>
>   Trampled its fires into the dust of death,
> As Day upon the threshold of the east,
>   Treads out the lamps of night. . . .
>
>   . . . . . . like day she came
> Making the night a dream.
>
> (385-93)

The Son tramples the lesser sun in Herbert's *Jordan II* but it is death in Shelley's *Adonais*, trampling to fragments the

---

[9] Reiman, *Shelley's "The Triumph of Life,"* pp. 64-65.

[10] *Comus*, 65, 671-77.

[11] *Odyssey* IV, 219-32.

[12] *The Collected Poems of W. B. Yeats*, London, Macmillan, 1950, p. 244. The phrase is from Porphyry. See F.A.C. Wilson, *W. B. Yeats and Tradition*, London, Victor Gollancz, 1958, p. 212. "In the Philosophy of Shelley's Poetry," the cup held by the "shape all light" is specifically associated with "Porphyry's account." Yeats, *Essays and Introductions*, London, Macmillan, 1961, p. 89. Yeats finds the cup "full of oblivion and love."

many-coloured glass dome of life of which the reader is most strongly aware.[13] The violence of the image, the thought-by-thought obliteration of the gazer's consciousness deeply question a movement which is nevertheless likened to the natural succession of day to night and of wakefulness to dreaming. Enamourment with the light is entangled with awareness of the menace of the light in an unavoidable relationship which persists, even as the narrator raises his lips to the "bright Nepenthe" offered him by the "Shape."

"Shew whence I came, and where I am, and why—
Pass not away upon the passing stream."

"Arise and quench thy thirst," was her reply.
And as a shut lily stricken by the wand
    Of dewy morning's vital alchemy

I rose; and bending at her sweet command
    Touched with faint lips the cup she raised.
                                                        (398-404)

The three questions anticipate the four which the poet is later to ask. The thirst for knowledge is the natural basis of the inescapable love affair with light. The command to drink is "sweet." The lily opens to the magic of the wand. The dew, the dawn, and the alchemy are all signs pointing to creative transformation. Yet in the midst of these associations, the word "stricken" is also before us as the dark centre of the opening flower. The fear it congeals bursts into actuality at the moment the cup is touched.

And suddenly my brain became as sand
                                                        (405)

This is the culmination of the thought-by-thought trampling of the gazer's consciousness into the dust of death.

[13] *The Works of George Herbert*, ed. F. E. Hutchinson, Oxford, The Clarendon Press, 1941, p. 102. The connection with *Adonais* is noted by Tilottama Rajan, *Dark Interpreter*, Ithaca, Cornell University Press, 1980, p. 64.

As a condition of total receptivity it is to be distinguished from that Lethean forgetfulness which commitment to the shape has fiercely erased. The mind is now vacant and ready for the stern imprint of life. A "new Vision never seen before" (411) bursts on the narrator's consciousness.

> And the fair shape waned in the coming light
> As veil by veil the silent splendour drops
> From Lucifer, amid the chrysolite
>
> Of sunrise ere it strike the mountain tops
> (412-15)

Light follows light, and in the movement of life one form of light must give way to another. But when the waning of the light is compared to the removal of veil after veil we are invited to wonder if the core of light is darkness. Even as it recedes, the "shape all light" seems to point forward to the chariot. The "silent splendour" of its waning urges relationship to that "silent storm/Of its own rushing splendour" on which the chariot moves inexorably forward.

These links are intimations of the fierce core of reality and advisements that those who seek the light must learn to live with its darkness. But there are other intimations of continuity which are less disquieting, which point to tranquil closure, and which are mobilized with some deliberation as if to qualify or even contain the reigning momentum of that darkness. The morning star, Lucifer, is also the evening star, Venus, and the "day's path" will end as it began "In that star's smile." The light of the star is like the scent of a jonquil "When evening breezes fan it." It resembles the soft notes of a Brescian shepherd's song or the caress that turns slumber to content (415-23). The promise here is not merely of fulfillment but of fulfillment declared to sight, smell, hearing, and touch. For all that must follow and must brutally follow, it is an element in our knowledge of the successor shape:

So knew I in that light's severe excess
The presence of that shape which on the stream
Moved, as I moved along the wilderness
(424-26)

The "severe excess" of the new light recalls the "fierce splendour" of the old one. But it also points forward to a world of excess and punishment of which the chariot is to be the emblem. These junction points of language Shelley repeatedly constructs direct our understandings along apparently divergent routes which are then seen as proceeding from the same verbal nuclei, as engaged unavoidably with each other in the poem's exposition of itself. The junction points also bridge the distance between pristine felicity and the brutal world of the chariot, presenting it not as a fall but as a continuous movement, unavoidable, deeply problematic, claiming from us a response free of the simplifications of surrender or transcendence.

There is a continuity then between the new shape and the old one but it is a continuity which the triumph of the new shape weakens.

More dimly than a day appearing dream
The ghost of a forgotten form of sleep
A light from Heaven whose half extinguished beam

Through the sick day in which we wake to weep
Glimmers, forever sought, forever lost.—
So did that shape its obscure tenour keep
(427-32)

"The sick day in which we wake to weep" echoes "this harsh world in which we wake to weep" (334) which the narrator contrasts with that pristine felicity he inhabited before the coming of the "shape all light." The dream, the sleep, the ghostly remembrance, and the waning source organize the language of nostalgia into a pattern which is familiar but not for that reason ineffective. The poem does not dismiss this seeking of what is lost and the measuring

193

of the loss by the intensity of seeking. On the other hand, the man who speaks these words also declines to be delayed by "the phantom of that early form," plunging either willingly or compulsively into the "living storm" and its "thickest billows" (461-68). The storm is the "tempest" of the chariot's "splendour," and of the "loud million," "fiercely" extolling the fortune of the new light (436-44). We are taken back by the fierceness and the splendour to the original vision of the "shape all light." Is she to be sought by involvement in the storm or by turning back to the "half-extinguished" light from heaven? Is the way forward capable of becoming the way back, or is it the road to nowhere, as the poet's first apprehension of the chariot suggested? Or are *why?* and *whither?* open questions to be settled by the continuing response of human capability rather than by enthronement of the *whence?* and *how?* of the past? The poem cannot answer these questions, and that is why it has to end with a question in which all subordinate questions are enrolled. But the interpenetrations of its imagery raise these issues with an intensity that strikes us as authentic precisely because it is so pervasively resistant to resolution.

These interpenetrations continue as the instructor comes to the end of his story. An extensive reference to Dante seems to affirm the safeguarding power of love and the possibility of deliverance from the inferno. Yet the rest of the poem is almost exclusively concerned with the growth of miscreation in the inferno. Dante's teaching is virtually forgotten as we are asked to behold a wonder worthy of his rhyme (471). The phrase "Behold a wonder" in *Paradise Lost* (I, 877) introduces an account of how the "throng numberless" of fallen angels contract themselves to fit into Pandemonium.[14] Here it prefaces an account, based upon Lucretius,[15] of the generation of phantoms from the disem-

---

[14] Reiman, Shelley's "The Triumph of Life," p. 78, 142n.
[15] Paul Turner, "Shelley and Lucretius," RES, N.S., X (1959), pp. 269-82.

bodied attributes of men and women. Warped by the mis-creative light of the chariot, these attributes seem to become the roles that people play in the world's pageant, while those divested of these attributes wither as their identities are surrendered to their roles. A remarkable amount of attention is given to this part of the narrative, and the purpose cannot be simply that the mist, flies, and gnats which surround "lawyer, statesman, priest, and theorist" (510) take us back to the beginning of the poet's waking dream (46). We might note that gnats, flies, and a thick fog surround a statesman in Vaughan's "The World"[16] and that his sorry state is contrasted with the great ring of pure and endless light which is eternity. The "shape all light" and the "pure and endless light" are evidently related to each other and, given Dante's counsel, we are probably being advised that the way up is also the way back. How-ever the advice rests on an approving reference to Dante which is not further developed and on an allusion to a poem by Vaughan the implications of which have to be teased out by the literary scholar. As a basis for deliverance this is neither extensive enough nor firm enough. It is one way, and an important way, of responding to the poem. But the limitations within which the response is maintained suggest that it is not meant to be final.

The complexities of this passage do not consist simply of the interplay between an implied means of deliverance and the actuality of ongoing miscreation. The forms produced by the car from disembodied attributes are three times described as "phantoms," as "shadows," and even as "shadows of shadows" (482, 487, 488, 528, 534). Reality may be elsewhere than in the pageant and these closing suggestions balance the opening awareness of the over-whelming reality of the pageant. Both possibilities, neither conclusively endorsed, surround the final question "Then

16 *Henry Vaughan. The Complete Poems*, ed. Alan Rudrum. Harmonds-worth, Penguin Books, 1976, p. 227.

what is life?" as if to advise us of the range of comprehension which any prospective answer must accommodate.

There is yet another element in the passage which can be even more subversive of any conjectured settlement. The production of phantoms comes about through a process of "shedding" in which the disembodied attributes that are shed are developed or combined into misshapen entities. We have to remember that the "shape all light" also divested itself of its "fierce splendour" as it moved into the cavern, and divested itself "veil by veil" of its "silent splendour" as it gave way to the new shape which it had itself introduced. Paradoxically, the veil-by-veil divesting resulted not in the exposing of the light's true nature but in its reduction to a "ghost" or "phantom" (428, 464). We have to ask whether the heart of light is darkness, whether light is to be regarded as the quintessence or the envelope, whether behind the attributes there is only emptiness. Is the chariot itself that dark core of reality made accessible only by the waning of the light? Equally we must ask ourselves whether destruction comes about through the dissociation of light from an unavoidable darkness by which it must always be accompanied and with which it must always remain in dialogue. Clearly, more is involved here than a simple inversion of the values associated with light and darkness. The imagery is consistently proposing an entanglement, though not one which it can make emergent at the level of organization.[17]

More indeterminacies are produced in our overall assessment of the *Triumph of Life* by the dubious status of the instructor. It may be better to be a chained captive than a deformed root, though on the other hand, the root is on a hillside, the outcrop of a landscape which provides an alternative to the way of the world. The humiliated teacher is at the beginning, on the defensive, blaming circum-

[17] For the complexities of the light-dark imagery see Rajan, *Dark Interpreter*, pp. 62-65; Harold Bloom, *Shelley's Mythmaking*, p. 270.

stances for his misfortune (201-02) and pointing repeatedly to his privileged status. A thousand beacons have been lit by the spark he kindled (206-07). In the battle with Life he has been overcome not by the conqueror, but by his own heart (239-43). Unlike the "great bards of old" who "inly quelled/The passions which they sung," he has suffered what he wrote (274-79). Nevertheless his own exposition shows that those who failed to "repress the mutiny within" (212-13)[18] and those who quelled their passions are equally victims of the chariot. Those who tempered their passions to their audience are as humiliated as those who could not temper them to their object (240-43; 275-78). If Rousseau's spark has lit a thousand beacons, his words, as he comes to admit, have also been seeds of misery (280-81). Finally he can only hold that he is one of those who have created "even/If it be but a world of agony" (294-95).

The divided mind of the instructor or to put it more accurately, the double understanding by which his mind is occupied, is crystallized in the passage in which he names himself:

> And if the spark with which Heaven lit my spirit
>   Earth had with purer nutriment supplied
> Corruption would not now thus much inherit
>   Of what was once Rousseau—nor this disguise
> Stain that within which still disdains to wear it.
> (201-05)

The last line can also be read (and is so read by Matthews) as "Stained that which ought to have disdained to wear it." The manuscript at this point is insolubly indecisive, and Reiman, whose reading has been quoted, has to admit the Matthews version as an alternative.[19] The consequences are substantial. One version suggests that Rousseau could

---

[18] Matthews was the first editor to correct "mystery" to "mutiny."
[19] Reiman, pp. 41-42, 162-63.

have refrained from joining the procession and did not. The other implies that he can do no more than disdain a course of action he was obliged to take. Later in the poem Rousseau says

> I among the multitude
> Was swept; me sweetest flowers delayed not long
> Me not the shadow nor the solitude
>
> Me not the falling stream's Lethean song
> Me, not the phantom of that early form
> Which moved upon its motion,—but among
>
> The thickest billows of the living storm
> I plunged. . . .
>
> (460-67)

Attached to one version of line 205, we can take these lines as implying that an alternative way existed and was not chosen. Attached to the other version, they imply that the alternative existed only in the mind and was not accessible to the will. Unattached to line 205, the passage is capable of being read in either or both ways. The speaker regards himself both as "swept" along passively by the multitude and as plunging actively into "the living storm." The "me," repeated four times in four lines, can suggest both the delusive frenzy of self-realization and the self striving vainly to protect its identity from the momentum of events. The "flower," the "shadow," the "solitude," the "phantom," and the contrast between the gently falling stream and the storm's "thickest billows," point to an alternative possibility, enfeebled either by deliberate self-deception or by a force of actuality which the will cannot resist. The double reading may seem a needless compounding of complexity but we must remember that Rousseau at one point warns the poet against joining "the dance which I had well forborne" (189) and that at another point (305-06) he seems to recognize that the dance must be joined and that one must be either an actor or a victim in it. The central indecisiveness of 205 lies not simply in what the text means,

198

but more fundamentally in what the text is, thus becoming symptomatic of a double understanding which pervades the poem. In its apprehension of an event the mind is held between or situated upon two views of the nature of possibility. To commit itself to either view would be to simplify the interrogative force of the event, the question mark with which it seeks to retaliate to any assessment that the understanding may make.

The poet, ironically, is more inclined than the instructor to instructing. The most openly didactic remark in the poem—about the irreconcilability of good and the means of good (230-31)—belongs to him. When the instructor points to "the heirs/Of Caesar's crime" (283-84) it is the poet, not he, who defines the crime and its consequences. The "sacred few" (128) are not named by the instructor, who concerns himself with what is in the cavalcade and not with those who succeeded in not joining it. It is the poet who names two of the few and advises us of the way taken by those who did not fall victim to the chariot. The latent didacticism is present again in 115-27, and in the one "dispute" between the poet and the instructor the poet expresses weariness with the figures cast on "the false and fragile glass" of the world, whereas the instructor's view more realistically is that no man can avoid casting his shadow (243-51).[20] The poet in fact functions as a naive reader of the poem, putting forward a view of it which is unfortunately still endorsed by more than one critic. When in the end he asks the question "Then, what is Life?" he is admitting that the simple reading is no longer possible. Rousseau's "And what thou wouldst be taught I then may learn/From thee" (307-08) is not, as it superficially seems to be, the defeated statement of a deficient teacher, but an indi-

---

[20] The "serious folly as of old" (73) of those who take part in the cavalcade differentiates the poet's moralizing from Rousseau's ambivalent view.

cation that one is instructed by experience and that only the victims of life can be colleagues in learning.

Given the poet's relatively fixed stance and the instructor's revisionary view of his status, we can expect Rousseau's autobiography—his new confession, as it were—to expose itself to a subversive reading. Subversion is all the more likely since the account—though this is not apparent on a first perusal—does establish a dominant tonality. The constituents of this tonality can be discerned in the attention given to the state of pristine consciousness, in the similes of reassurance that accompany the waning of the shape all light, in the similes of loss that immediately follow, and in the prospective means of retrieval that the digressive reference to Dante offers. To place at the horizon what was relinquished at the source is a familiar strategy in literature and one which will continue to console us by its transformation of absence into destiny. Yet the movement, even in declaring itself, discloses itself as other than it aspires to be. Retrieval is sought not of pristine felicity but of the undiminished presence of the "shape all light" and yet, as the narrative makes clear, it was commitment to that presence ("Pass not away upon the passing stream") which led inexorably to its waning. Recovery of the light might do no more than once again initiate the unavoidable course of its reduction.

The counter-tonality is established in the carefully charted declensions of "splendour" and of "music."[21] Shelley's

---

[21] The declensions of "splendour" have been brought out in the main text. There is "sweet talk in music" in the framing prologue (39). "Melodious dew" (67) springs from the fountains ignored by those who follow the chariot. There is "music" in the "ever moving wings" of the shapes that guide the chariot (98). The multitudes attending the chariot rejoice in "fierce song" (110). Those in the van dance to "savage music" (142). The pristine music in the cavern is described in 216-330. In 341 it is characterized as "oblivious melody, confusing sense." In 355 the dew cast by the "shape all light" sings a "silver music." In 369 the music is "wondrous." The shape's feet move in measure to the "ceaseless song/ Of leaves and winds" (275-76), described later (382) as a "sweet tune."

preoccupation with splendour may seem no more than a felicitous verbal obsession, but we have to remember that Plotinus (*Enneads* VI, 9,4; VI, 7,32; V, 9,1) uses the word in speaking of the one. Pound picks up that usage in his *Cantos* (notably Canto CXVI). If the allusion to Plotinus is intentional, it must be construed as fiercely revisionary since enamourment with the light leads us not back to but away from the source. Nevertheless, the movement of departure, however it is initiated, can be thought of (as in Plotinus) as generating a counter-force of return. As already indicated, there are elements in the poem which seem to incorporate such a counter-force. On the other hand, the onrush of the poem powerfully argues for a continuous and not necessarily reversible movement from origin to the dark present of the chariot, a movement to which no limited attachment is possible and in which to accept the beginning is to subscribe to the end. Yet the eyes of the charioteer are banded and not blinded. They are capable of piercing the sphere just as the beams from the chariot are capable of quenching the sun. The repossession of this potentiality is not excluded by the imagery, but the way to repossession, if it exists, is both indeterminate and radically threatened.

When we contemplate the state of pristine felicity with its remembrances of the Immortality Ode it becomes clear that that state cannot be sustained. To forget pain may be desirable but to be forgetful of "All pleasure and all pain,

---

In 421-23 there is a simile of reassurance involving the Brescian shepherd's lament. The chariot for Rousseau as in the poet's vision is accompanied by "savage music, stunning music" (435) with the multitude fiercely "extolling its advance" (438) in "exulting hymn" (456) that contrasts with the "Lethean song" (463) of an earlier psychic time. In the reference to Dante we are told that "The world can hear now the sweet notes that move/ The sphere whose light is melody to lovers" (478-79). One of the points to be noted is the continuity between the morning music on the "Pennine Steep," the Lethean music in the cavern, the music attending the "shape all light," and the Dantean music. The continuity prevents us from regarding the shape as no more than deceitful.

all hate and love" (315) is to intensify oblivion into mind-lessness. The initiation into knowledge is possible only within a framework of memory and desire, and that is why the shape in its considerate cruelty calls on the suppliant to arise and quench his thirst. The gesture ushers us into a world of woe. If we are blessed by the light it can only be in the form of the light's duplicity.

In attaining a full reading of *The Triumph of Life* it is important to pass through the exercise of considering the poem as a calculated insult to its title. As this chapter has indicated, there is ample sustenance for such a reading. The natural response, which is to reclaim the title from the poem, is supported not only from within the poem, but by the ambiguities of the title itself. It is not only possible but plausible to argue that there is a life other than that manifested in the chariot, and a triumph other than that which the infernal cavalcade represents. The purpose of demonic parody is to force us into commitment to its op-posite and into defining by rejection the content of alle-giance. Eliot speaks in *Ash-Wednesday* of redeeming the "unread vision" in the "higher dream" "While jewelled unicorns draw the gilded hearse." The pageant is more decorative than Shelley's but it is still a procession with death as its centrepiece calling for a vision that has yet to be deciphered within a dream which repudiation insti-gates. The view has its attractions but it pays no attention to the powerful continuities of Rousseau's story, to the insistent implication that the world of the chariot follows upon the world of the "shape all light" as June follows April in the advance of the year (308, 75). The forces sub-scribing to this continuity and the likelihood that any re-trieval of the light might simply reinitiate the movement into darkness have already been discussed. At this point it is sufficient to say that this strong strand in the imagery cannot be ignored.

The poem in the Shelley canon most notable for its en-ergy of repudiation is *Adonais* and yet even in *Adonais* the thrust away from the phenomenal to the real cannot be said to be wholly unqualified. Violent discontinuity is suggested by death's fragmentation of the many-coloured dome of life. The imperative force of "Die" is compounded by its positioning at the end of a line that gives way to another line which, in the gentle procession of its monosyllables, seems ardently expressive of fulfillment. Death joins together what life separates. Being is to becoming as steadfastness is to transience and the substance to the shadow. Yet "Flowers, ruins, statues, music, words" also transfuse, however imperfectly, the glory of the real. The phenomenal world is a sacrament of the ultimate, notwithstanding the gulf that divides it from the ultimate. "The soft sky smiles" and "the low wind whispers near" in phrases suggesting the allurement of the final voyage. "The massy earth and sphered skies are riven" and the poet is "borne darkly, fearfully afar" in phrases suggesting the menace of the same voyage. The soul of Adonais is a beacon that guides and beckons but it is also a flame "burning through the inmost veil of Heaven," destructive of the last protective illusion.[22] These comprehensive undercuttings fall well short of overthrowing the main movement but they restrain that movement notably even in affirming it. A poem such as the *Triumph of Life*, in which repudiation is distantly implied rather than ardently urged, is working against too heavy a weight of givenness for rejection to emerge as the poem's dominant or even concluding force.

Another way of reclaiming the title from the poem is to read the title resistively, not as repudiating the poem but as refusing to yield to it. That the soul should remain inviolate in Babylon is familiar Augustinian counsel which the poem supports with the examples of Socrates and Jesus. Support from outside the poem but within the œuvre comes mainly from *Prometheus Unbound*. "To hope till hope creates/From its own wreck the thing it contemplates" sounds

---

[22] All quotations from *Adonais* are from the last five stanzas.

like a clarion call to resistive triumph. The last line of *Prometheus Unbound*—"This is alone Life, Joy, Empire and Victory"—can be read as advising us how the ingredients of Shelley's final poem are to be delivered from the demonic world of their entrapment. But *Prometheus Unbound*, like *Adonais*, undercuts its dominant tonality. Demogorgon spoke as Eternity in the dethronement of Jupiter and was a serpent to that vulture which was once Jupiter's eagle. In the final lines he speaks of eternity not as himself, but as the "Mother of many acts and hours" who may one day free "the serpent that would clasp her."[23] The changes remind us that the millennial vision and the cyclic are psychic constants in Shelley's understanding, constants between which his poems must continually renegotiate their tenancy. Since even *Prometheus Unbound* is qualified in its vision of the victory of resistiveness it does not seem that in the more enigmatic *Triumph of Life* the resistive forces are strong enough to prevail. Significantly, it is the poet who notes that Christ and Socrates are not among the captives of the chariot. The instructor does not make anything of these examples.

If repudiation and resistance are means of coping with the poem that the poem defeats, the possibility remains of coming to terms with its givenness. The strongest basis for this view is offered by Harold Bloom and the essence of his evidence is provided in a footnote that is a remarkable compression of the essay it requires us to ponder.

> The world of the "Triumph" is a world deliberately emptied of myth, a world of *things*. In this world the myth is neither retracted (palinode), nor reversed (reaffirmation). The myth is simply absent, and the poem deals with the consequences of precisely that absence. The "myth" of the "Triumph" is thus seen

[23] Earl Wasserman, *Shelley: A Critical Reading*, Baltimore, The Johns Hopkins University Press, 1971, pp. 372-73.

to be an antimyth; the "Triumph" is a myth-*unmaking* poem, and is properly Shelley's last work.[24]

It should be emphasized that the reading which follows is by no means Bloom's view of the understanding to which we are brought by the poem.[25] It is merely one possible extension of the evidence. Nevertheless it is initially proposed that the poet's waking dream is of a demystified reality and that Rousseau's vision within the poet's vision is an interior history of that demystification. In this sense *The Triumph* is an anti-myth. The unveilings, unmaskings and divestings that are so characteristic a feature of its imagery are uniformly expressive of myth-unmaking. The mind is by its nature illusion-building. The triumph of life lies in its overthrowing of the fictive power and the privileged status which that power claims for its structures.

It can and possibly should be argued in rebuttal that the anti-myth is probably today's most influential myth and cannot claim privileged status simply by virtue of its comprehensive denial of the privileges of every other myth. Nevertheless the poem of the anti-myth has its rightful place in consciousness. Its unconsoling objectivity is something that the mind must prepare itself to engage. Perhaps the cardinal fact about *The Triumph* is that it will not yield to any hermeneutic redemption. There is always sufficient evidence in it to defeat any attempt to reorganize its facticity. That facticity must eventually stand in the obduracy of the poet's declaration of it.

It can be suggested that the anti-myth is by its nature the last word. This is not necessarily so or, to put it slightly differently, it is so only within an epistemological drama

---

[24] Harold Bloom, *Shelley's Mythmaking*, p. 220, n. 1.

[25] Bloom's view (which he italicizes) is that "The light of nature destroys the inner light of the poet only to be obliterated in turn by the real light of everyday life." *Shelley's Mythmaking*, p. 231. See also p. 227 and p. 270. See further *The Ringers in the Tower*, Chicago, University of Chicago Press, 1971, p. 114.

that may not be necessitated. Tilottama Rajan observed that "Shelley's final poem is not logocentric."[26] Nevertheless it "manages to triumph over its own deconstruction of a visionary poetics." This is yet another and an important probing of the poem's elusive title. It is not a matter of hope creating "from its own wreck the thing it contemplates" or in Yeats's successor language, of "beauty born out of its own despair." The resurrection of an unimpaired vision from its ashes emphasizes triumph through inviolability. In its nature, the claim resists negotiation. It is not equipped to enter that less spectacular but more difficult process in which the vision consents to be revised by its own inexorable emanation of self-questioning. The poem must successfully name that enemy which in the act of naming becomes no longer the enemy. The truce which can follow naming and recognition is at best unstable but despite its fragile duration and intermittent renewal it remains the only settlement worth securing. It is doubly undermined by the tendency of the fictive to re-mythologize the actual and by the tendency of the actual to deconstruct the fictive. Yet if it were divested of this double jeopardy it could not be the ground of the authentic.

Against this hope we might argue (taking counsel from the last sentence of Bloom's essay) that *The Triumph of Life* precludes any such settlement, internal or prospective, since the confrontation is not with the "thou" of otherness but with the "it" of facticity. Relationships with the "it" are non-negotiable. It will accept no change in its status or in

[26] *Dark Interpreter*, p. 95. Elsewhere (p. 67) Rajan observes that Shelley's poem is "not about a defeat but rather about the inner process by which the dreamer inspects the image of his defeat and seeks to know why it is so." Bloom (*The Ringers in the Tower*, p. 114) finds that the poem survives its own despair. The "why it is so," as Rajan recognizes, cannot be fully defined by a poem which in the end must teach us to respect its doubleness. The basis for surviving despair must also be tentative, putting forward not a solution, but an ongoing relationship with a reality that can no longer not be confronted.

the manner in which it is to be perceived. The triumph of life is thus the defeat of poetry. The poem certainly subscribes to such a view of the object, both by the manner in which it presents the object and by the manner in which it defeats the strategies it offers for dealing with the object. It is very much a climactic poem in the solar half of the Yeatsian cycle. But in the nature of life the gyre must turn. The basis for its turning remains present in that double awareness within the poem's self-disclosure which we have already discussed and by which the poem continues to be sustained. There is a different view of the nature of possibility implicit in the language of the view that is presented as dominant. The counter-view is not developed to the point where it can be fitted into a strategy for deliverance. It is however, mobilized sufficiently to suggest that any seeming finality, no matter how decisively it unveils itself, cannot divest itself of the potentiality to be otherwise. In a deconstructive world that which eludes deconstruction by concealing itself in the deconstructive statement has a status beyond that of survival and one which some of us may even wish to call privileged. To put it more prosaically, the last word is not spoken though a word may seem terminal at the point of its utterance. The relationship between the finality of *Adonais* and the antithetical finality of *The Triumph* suggests that the œuvre as Shelley works through it and perhaps as the Romantic understanding sees it is not capable of any real closure. This can be said despite the apparently terminal closure that seems brought about by the poem's self-unmaking.

Though the last words cannot be spoken, the words of *The Triumph* are the last that Shelley wrote. It is right that the poem should end with a question it is unable to answer and that the receding chariot should open a possible aperture on a dark horizon without indicating how that aperture is to be occupied. Rousseau's apparent liberation from the progress of the chariot is another sign among various indeterminacies. The question mark remains the most compelling of these signs.

Shelley's work is marked by a history of question marks. Three years before *The Triumph of Life*, the device had concluded the *Ode to the West Wind*, a poem which stands in dramatic contrast to Keats's *Ode to Autumn* written in the same year. In the first six lines of Shelley's *Ode* there is an assembling of ingredients which curiously anticipate those of *The Triumph of Life*. We have ghosts, pestilence-stricken multitudes, and, above all, a chariot. The "leaves dead" of the second line may seem more distant from Shelley's last poem, but the poet in *The Triumph* (54) refers to the multitude waiting on the chariot as "the million leaves of summer's bier" and the instructor (528-29) speaks of the phantoms created by the car as "numerous as the dead leaves blown/In Autumn evening from a poplar tree." The line of movement connecting the images is evident and significant. The leaves in the *Ode* are fleeing from enchantment. Those in *The Triumph* are fleeing into disenchantment. On this basis we can note that the concluding lines of the *Ode*, the understanding declared by the trumpet voice of prophecy, is in effect a claim for the triumph of life.

If winter comes, can spring be far behind?

Wasserman points out that Shelley had not originally framed the last line as a question. The question mark he observes, "accords with the half-skeptical note" on which Shelley ends "so many of his poems." Essentially it "reflects the fact that there is no inherent guarantee that man will continue to deflect the operations of the [cosmic] power by his own will."[27] The undercutting effect is certainly consistent with the effects already studied at the close of *Adonais* and of *Prometheus Unbound*. But the dominant tonality is more decisive here; the question almost asks us if we wish to deny the poem. Its psychic energy also proclaims a fun-

---

[27] Wasserman, *Shelley: A Critical Reading*, p. 261.

damental rhythm of the unfinished, the ceaseless renewal of the self-consuming. It is a rhythm different from the Renaissance view of an inclusive teleology in which the limited effort of the poem can only partially participate. Both understandings have a necessary place in the mind as shaping constants.

Three years before *The Ode to the West Wind* Shelley had composed *Mont Blanc.* There, the question mark had been the claim of the imagination flung almost tauntingly against the resistance of the mountain. If there was something unknowable in the mountain, to the mind and its acclimatizing metaphors there was also something in the mind unknowable to that otherness. One originating centre was made to confront another across a space for manifestation and negotiation. It was Shelley's first powerful encounter with facticity. The question mark it erected challenged the poem from which it was made to spring. That in the *Ode* invited corroboration of the poem from which it outflowed. In *The Triumph of Life* the question mark is the true sign of the unfinished since it movingly confesses the poem's inability to pronounce on its own nature. It would surely be an impoverishment of Shelley's œuvre to suggest that the later question mark supersedes the earlier ones. All three open the future to their interplay.

Though the question mark in *The Triumph* is questioned by other question marks, the force of destitution which it simultaneously recognizes and contests gives the poem a decisive place in the literary history of the unfinished. Platonic and Christian views of the fragment see it in relation to a whole before or beyond it. The many return to the one, having proceeded from it. The dismembered body of Osiris is reconstituted into the homogeneal and proportional form of truth. In Keats's more existential view as will be shown, the fragment takes its place in a process either cosmic as in the first *Hyperion,* or psychic as in the second. It is located and its meaning is defined by that which it supersedes and that to which it surrenders. In all three views of the fragment, the fragment either seeks or accepts connection. In *The Triumph of Life* it seems almost to resist it. We begin with givenness and we end with indeterminacy. The attempt to reach behind givenness and to establish a stable myth of origin results in only a fable of beginnings that is deeply divided within and against itself. Facing forward we are confronted with that question mark which may either repudiate causality or proclaim it as inherently subversive. Because the possibilities of retrieval are negotiated so largely through literary allusions, their redeeming force is established by indirection and has to be felt as penumbral rather than central. The central facticity remains densely enigmatic. It is the narrow disclosure within which we are educated and which ends cryptically at its boundaries. The fragment has not previously proclaimed its own ultimacy.[28] In *The Triumph of Life* it comes disturbingly close to doing so.

[28] According to Paul de Man, "*The Triumph of Life* warns us that nothing—whether deed, word, thought or text—ever happens in relation, positive or negative, to anything that precedes, follows, or exists elsewhere, but only as a random event whose power, like the power of death, is due to the randomness of its occurrence." "Shelley Disfigured," *Deconstruction and Criticism*, New York, Continuum, 1979, p. 69. This is a statement, if not of the ultimacy, at least of the finality, of the fragment. My view is similarly that the poem resists what I have called "hermeneutic redemption," confronting us with its givenness, after itself offering and exhausting a variety of strategies for dealing with that givenness. Nevertheless, a continuing response to the given seems possible, however strongly the given may resist the procedures for assimilation which the mind seems constituted to apply. The obstinacy of facticity is in fact necessary if thought is not to petrify, since thought proceeds most productively not by its extension, but rather by its erasure. Disfiguration, or "the repetitive erasures by which language performs the erasure of its own positions" (p. 65) is thus an ingredient in understanding but in the total movement of understanding it, in its turn, must be resisted by other ingredients with which it is unavoidably engaged.

❦

The Two *Hyperions*:
Compositions and Decompositions

ABOUT SEPTEMBER 1818 Keats began the writing of *Hyperion*. On September 21 of the following year he wrote to Reynolds stating that he was "giving up" *Hyperion*.[1] Which *Hyperion* he meant can be a question for dispute but that both were left unfinished is a matter of history. The year that is ushered in and out by these events and that is variously entitled the living year, the fertile year, and Keats's *annus mirabilis*, is described by Walter Jackson Bate as "the most productive in the life of any poet of the past three centuries."[2] As befits a poet, it is a year paradoxical in its structure. The brilliant core of achievement is surrounded by a poem twice abandoned. We might say that the fragmentary circumference directs our attention to the problematics of the centre, displaying its consolidations as unstable and provisional. The inquiry must go on and its continuing imperatives are testified to by the encirclement of the unfinished.

Incomplete poems are not uncommon even if we disregard Valéry's statement that apparently completed poems are not really completed but abandoned. But a poem twice abandoned is relatively rare. *Hyperion* moreover is not simply given up twice but given up twice in mid-sentence.

---

[1] The majority view is that Keats is referring to the second *Hyperion* or to the entire *Hyperion* effort. Aileen Ward is among those who argue that the reference is to the first *Hyperion*. *John Keats: The Making of a Poet*, London, Secker and Warburg, 1963, pp. 434-35n.

[2] Walter Jackson Bate, *John Keats*, Cambridge, Mass., Harvard University Press, 1963, p. 322.

Not finishing a sentence is normally a slovenly act. In the conveyances of a poem it can be an artistic withholding. When the withholding occurs twice something is being intimated. It is not a matter of saying that we have reached the margins of the inexpressible. Keats was fortunately not that kind of writer. Nor is it a matter of considerately handing over to the reader the pleasure of finishing what the poet has begun. The issues negotiated in the two *Hyperions* are too urgent and their sombre weight presses upon the poems too powerfully for such courtesies. It is more a matter of suggesting that the continuing poem of consciousness takes up and discards its vehicles in what Keats himself once called "the grand march of intellect."[3] The fragmentary nature of the individual disclosure and its openness to supersession, side by side with its participation in that revisionary movement to which its own incompleteness both contributes and testifies, are the elements which need to be underlined.

"The grand march of intellect" is too simple a phrase and too blatantly purposive in its connotations. Even Oceanus in the first *Hyperion* has more to say in his cosmic manifesto and his speech seems oblivious to its environment, the immensities of deprivation to which it is addressed. It is radically questioned by the manner in which Keats chooses to "station" his beginning. From the outset the weight of sadness and the possibility of subscription to an objective beyond sadness, the cost of change and its necessity, a necessity which presents itself as biologically demanded rather than creatively understood, seem enmeshed with each other in a manner the literary investigation can only explore and not conclude. Yet the poem twice unfinished makes something important and even haunting, of itself, precisely because it is twice unfinished.

---

[3] Letter of 3 May, 1818, to Reynolds. *The Letters of John Keats*, ed. Hyder Edward Rollins, Cambridge, Mass., Harvard University Press, 1958, vol. 1, p. 282. Hereafter referred to as Rollins.

An examination of Keats's œuvre is outside the scope of this study though given a writing span of less than six years, and the persistence of certain critical concerns in the letters, we might expect the œuvre to be tightly drawn together. The brief life, moving with feverish speed from the bucolic to the tragic, exhibits its continuities in accelerated development. Two of these continuities are interestingly characterized by Morris Dickstein, in his lucid book on Keats, as the Bower principle and the Bildung principle.[4] One should note that the Bower is not quite Spenser's Bower of Bliss. It is the embodiment of a naive rather than a decadent state, of oneness with nature, and of that unified sensibility whose loss was once ritually deplored. The Bildung principle is also not quite the principle of the Quest since its objective is not beyond itself but is rather coextensive with its own self-formation. Because the Bildung principle depends on the supersession or incorporation of a previous state by an emergent state, it entails the destruction of the Bower and is not ultimately compatible with a poetics of retrieval. It can of course be placed in engagement with such a poetics, with the poem itself as the mediating agent. It can also be similarly placed in engagement with a poetics of transcendence, seemingly as in *Endymion*, or with a poetics of historicity, seemingly as in the two *Hyperions*, on the basis of the conversion of the Bower state into the state prevailing in the golden age.

The previous paragraph has proceeded in directions which Dickstein might not endorse and, as will be shown later, the view taken of *Endymion* and the *Hyperions* is not one which can be finally sustained. Nevertheless, the implications of a helpful terminology need to be charted in the abstract. The relevance of the chart to Keats's work is clear. It is also clear that as early as *Sleep and Poetry*, the "nobler life" of the Bildung principle is associated with "the ago-

[4] Morris Dickstein, *Keats and his Poetry*, Chicago, University of Chicago Press, 1971, esp. pp. 30ff.

nies, the strife/Of human hearts" (124-25). The association at this point is unstable; it is undermined even as it is made. As the chariot of poetry enters the natural world it is attended by shapes of "mystery and fear" but also by shapes of "delight." Weeping may accompany the progress of the chariot but it is also accompanied by murmuring, smiling, and laughing. Finally "a lovely wreath of girls/Dancing their sleek hair into tangled curls" (149-50) indicates that the "nobler life" has yet to work itself free of the Bower's entanglements. When the chariot passes,

> A sense of real things comes doubly strong,
> And, like a muddy stream, would bear along
> My soul to nothingness.
>
> (157-59)

Endymion can talk correspondingly of "the journey homeward to habitual self" (II, 276) but the difference between the real and the habitual is a refinement in formulation that has yet to be achieved. The poetry of repudiation which Yeats writes when he converts the "muddy stream" of the ordinary into "the fury and the mire of human veins"[5] is also not as yet on Keats's horizon. We are still looking at latency, though the latency can form itself into statuesque life when Keats visualizes poetry as

> Might half slumb'ring on its own right arm. . . .
>
> (237)

The reluctance to leave the bower is apparent in the lines which immediately follow

> The very archings of her eye-lids charm
> A thousand willing agents to obey. . . .

As we look at the cluster of relationships, the "agonies and strife," the half-slumbering Apollo first in might and pre-

---

[5] Yeats, *Byzantium*, in *Collected Poems*, p. 280.

sumably first in beauty, and the finding that poetry "should be a friend/To soothe the cares and lift the thoughts of man" (246-47), all look forward to the two *Hyperions* but in ways that make evident the distance that must be travelled if these images are to be purged and their interior life intensified. Keats, characteristically, was fully aware of this distance.

> Oh for ten years, that I may overwhelm
> Myself in poesy; so I may do the deed
> That my own soul has to itself decreed.
> (96-98)

He was to receive less than four years, not ten, but tragically curtailed though the time was to be, its duration is less important than the idea that the mind must be overwhelmed in order to achieve its own imperatives. The thought strikingly delineates the interrelationship between the reluctantly eager self and the commitment which, paradoxically, promises destruction in that very purposiveness to which it asks us to subscribe.

Because of its inclusiveness and its elevation, the long poem is the natural vehicle of the "nobler life," that "higher mood" of resolute interrogation heard in Milton's poem before Apollo speaks to Lycidas. *Endymion* is Keats's first essay in this mood. It is tempting to treat it as an adventure in transcendence and even more intriguing to argue that the resurrection of the bower in Endymion's affair with Cynthia proclaims the impossibility of transcendence, the entanglements of a consciousness seeking its shaping principles and yet withheld from them by the very language of its seeking. The text most frequently cited in support of a transcendental reading is the "Fellowship with essence" passage:

> Wherein lies happiness? In that which becks
> Our ready minds to fellowship divine,

A fellowship with essence; till we shine
Full alchemiz'd, and free of space.

(I, 777-80)

Keats called for this revision in a letter to Taylor dated January 30, 1818. *Endymion* had been completed two months earlier. Thus the passage confers upon the poem a retrospective intention which can be treated either as corroborating the poem, or as imposing a stage direction upon it. The view of the poem as fundamentally at odds with a later insertion is not a view we would be eager to sustain unless it is called for by the sheer weight of evidence. If on the other hand, we treat the insertion as an endeavour to clarify rather than to re-orient the text, we have to note that according to the letter the intention of the new lines is not transcendental. Keats speaks of the passage as "a regular stepping of the Imagination towards Truth" and as setting before him the "gradations of happiness even like a kind of pleasure Thermometer." These are figures of continuity, not transcendence, and are fully consonant with Keats's letter of November 22, 1817 to Bailey in which he argues that a "Life of sensations rather than of Thoughts" is "a Shadow of reality to come." "Sensations" of course is to be read not as sensuality but as experiencing. Happiness in the hereafter, Keats continues, will consist of "Happiness on Earth repeated in a finer tone and so repeated." Adam's dream "seems to be a conviction that Imagination and its empyreal reflection are the same as human Life and its spiritual repetition." The language is uniformly that of continuity and invites us to note that fellowship is a human and social virtue, and that "Full alchemized" can be read as implying the maximum extraction of potentiality from the substance which is alchemized. Indeed the word "full" implies the possibility of partial alchemization even though that is foreign to the nature of the concept. "Essence" can be interpreted platonically but it can also be read as in the Glaucus episode

216

> *If he explores all forms and substances*
> *Straight homeward to their symbol essences;*
> *He shall not die.*
>
> (III, 699-701)

Here essence is viewed as kernel rather than as idea, a kernel made accessible to resolute exploration of a symbolic universe. The journey homeward of II, 276 is now the journey "straight homeward" but to a state more elemental than "habitual self."

The ascent to the finest tone is stated more erotically than in the "fellowship with essence" passage, in a passage which follows almost immediately upon it.

> But there are
> Richer entanglements, enthralments far
> More self-destroying, leading, by degrees,
> To the chief intensity: the crown of these
> Is made of love and friendship, and fits high
> Upon the forehead of humanity.
> All its more ponderous and bulky worth
> Is friendship, whence there ever issues forth
> A steady splendour; but at the tip-top
> There hangs by unseen film, an orbed drop
> Of light and that is love.
>
> (797-807)

The graduation "by degrees" to the "chief intensity" of love is once again a statement of continuity. But the evolution to a higher self now only seems possible by virtue of the destruction of a lower self. The melting, blending, mingling and inter-knitting with the climactic radiance (810-14) is, paradoxically, both maximum self-destruction and maximum self-attainment.

Self-destruction cannot always be ecstatic and it is difficult to contemplate without misgiving a pleasure thermometer rising by such degrees. Keats at this point may be too much like Crashaw, and Endymion's encounters

217

with his goddess show singularly little of the finer tone. But Endymion's quest is in more than one direction. It is submarine as well as celestial. The movement to the pinnacle is questioned by the movement to the core. Love as fulfillment confronts love as betrayal. Entanglements and enthralments can be threatening as well as liberating when one enlists in the service of La Belle Dame whose metaphysical sister is the shape all light.

The second book of *Endymion* ends with a startling line— "He saw the giant sea above his head"—that seems to usher us into the world of the interior and the primary. The Glaucus episode, which occupies most of the third book, is the most strongly presented in the poem. The freeing of Glaucus from bondage and of all those he has gathered from similar bondage is at best a rescue, not an exaltation. It assures us that we can overcome our enchantments but it cannot assure us that we will not endure enchantment. Indeed the requirement of endurance is carried further in Book IV where a centre of quietude is to be found in a dark region which is "the proper home/Of every ill":

> the man is yet to come
> Who hath not journeyed in this native hell
> (IV, 522-23)

Quietude is attained by wise passivity rather than by protest:

> Enter none
> Who strive therefore: on the sudden it is won
> Just when the sufferer begins to burn,
> Then it is free to him
>
> (531-34)

The relief makes a "Dark paradise" of the place. It is the other side of the light, not its demonic but its authentic image, a more convincing sisterhood than the identification of Cynthia with the Indian maid.

Endymion it becomes apparent is placed between two coordinates, one delineating, not altogether felicitously, the nature and end of attainment, and the other indicating the necessities which must be passed through to come upon attainment even in its dark mirror. The "suffocation of accidents," as Keats vividly puts it, calls for a recourse but "within the pale of the World."[6] Essence in this image is found not at the top of a ladder but in the grip of a stranglehold. Fellowship with it is companionship in its adversity.

Endymion is not a poem treated with much respect. Keats recognizes its "sentimental cast."[7] More tellingly, in the preface to the poem he affirms that its "foundations are too sandy." A "year's castigation" of it "would not benefit it."[8] He "leaped headlong into the sea" with it, he tells Hessey in October 1818.[9] According to a deleted preface he had "no inward feel of being able to finish" and as he proceeded his "steps were all uncertain."[10] Yet "that which is creative must create itself."[11] A poet makes rather than inherits his language of understanding. The less successful enterprise can be instructive to the critic because it formulates rather than overcomes the difficulties of achieving such a language. It thus can lay bare the problematics which a more fluent accomplishment might have concealed from even its author.

A week before making a crucial revision to *Endymion*, by then with his publisher, Keats had begun to think of his second long poem

   . . . the nature of *Hyperion* will lead me to treat it in a more naked and grecian Manner—and the march of

[6] Letter of 3 November, 1817, to Bailey. Rollins 1, p. 41.

[7] Letter of 23 January, 1818, to Haydon. Rollins 1, p. 207.

[8] Preface to *Endymion. The Poems of John Keats*, ed. Jack Stillinger, Cambridge, Mass., Belknap Press of Harvard University Press, 1978, p. 102. Quotations follow Stillinger's text.

[9] Letter of 8 October, 1818, to Hessey. Rollins 1, p. 374.

[10] *The Poems of John Keats*, ed. Miriam Allott, London, Longmans, 1970, p. 755.

[11] 9 October, 1818, to Hessey. Rollins 1, p. 374.

passion and endeavour will be undeviating—and one great contrast between them will be—that the Hero of the written tale Endymion being mortal is led on, like Buonaparte, by circumstance; whereas the Apollo in Hyperion being a fore-seeing God will shape his actions like one.[12]

Apollo, here presented as the central character in the coming poem, makes his appearance only in the last book of *Hyperion* and his orgasmic transformation brought about by his "knowledge enormous" (III, 113) scarcely corresponds with the calm choices which Keats implies in his letter. But some recoil from the ramblings of *Endymion* is justified and the undeviating march of passion and endeavour shifts the intention understandably in the direction of purposiveness. The march, moreover, has its echo elsewhere in Keats's correspondence. The famous letter to Reynolds on the chamber of maiden thought maintains that there is really a "grand march of intellect" and that Milton because of his earlier participation in this "general and gregarious advance," has been unable to see as far into the human heart as Wordsworth. His philosophy Keats suggests reassuringly "may be tolerably understood by one not much advanced in years."[13]

Keats owned an 1807 pocket edition of *Paradise Lost* which he read with a poet's eye, making extensive marginal notes on crucial passages. The comment that follows is on the opening of the third book

The management of the poem is Apollonian—Satan first '*throws round his baleful eyes*' [I, 56] the[n] awakes his legions, he consu[l]ts, he sets forward on his voyage—and just as he is getting to the end of it we see the Great God and our first parent, and that same satan all brough[t] in one's vision—we have the invocation

[12] 23 January, 1818, to Haydon. Rollins 1, p. 207.
[13] 3 May, 1818, to Reynolds. Rollins 1, pp. 281-82.

to light before we mount to heaven—we breathe more freely—we feel the great Author's consolations coming thick upon him at a time when he complains most— we are getting ripe for diversity—the immediate topic of the Poem opens with a grand Perspective of all concerned.[14]

Apollonian "management" seeks the overall view, the gathering of "diversity" into a "grand Perspective," as the "grand march of intellect" moves forward to a more inclusive understanding. We can enunciate this programme for a poem, founding it, as is done here, on Keats's views as expressed in his correspondence and yet realize that it is foreign to his temperament. The mind may be attracted to such a programme but in due course it must come to question its attraction. Keats is an exploratory, not a didactic, poet, justifiably hating poetry that "has a palpable design upon us."[15] He is also a poet of the truly exploratory, rather than of the exploratory staging of the didactic, as Donne is sometimes taken to be. Even this note on *Paradise Lost* based as it is on a firm line of thought in Keats's letters, is not without recollections of another view of the nature of poetry: we "breathe more freely" because the consolations come thick, because we are working ourselves free of the "suffocation of accidents." A "grand Perspective" is attained as quietude is attained in *Endymion* only after the darkness has been journeyed through.

If Keats seeks to be the poet of the finer tone and of the overall understanding he also seeks to be the poet of perplexity rather than pattern, of reality proved upon the pulses, of the agony and strife of human hearts, and of whatever labyrinths offer themselves beyond the darkening of the chamber of maiden thought. He may chide himself for looking too far into "the core/Of an eternal fierce destruc-

---

[14] Joseph A. Wittreich (ed.), *The Romantics on Milton*, Cleveland, The Press of Case Western Reserve University, 1970, p. 558.

[15] Letter of 3 February, 1818, to Reynolds. Rollins 1, p. 224.

tion,"[16] but a poet looks because he wishes to see, because he knows himself born to have the dream deconstructed. *Hyperion* cannot be simply a study in cosmic purposiveness though Oceanus' speech adheres to such a programme and proclaims, as Tilottama Rajan scathingly puts it, a *Bildungsroman* of consciousness.[17] But Oceanus' speech is subverted by the environment in which it is made, by Keats's "stationing" of it,[18] by the weight of woe it is unable to mitigate. Its status is further reduced by Clymene's vapid endorsement, and since Enceladus' bombastic militarism is no answer to the Titans' predicament, the general futility of the proceedings casts its pall over individual statements. As an argument Oceanus' speech is not demolished and is indeed not even countered, but it is a consolation that is made to struggle against considerably more than a suffocation of accidents.

The beginning *in medias res* works against the tendency of the epic to convert itself into panorama or chronicle, by locating the action in the clenched fist of causality. The hand opens out into future and past, prophecy and history or, more fundamentally, into destiny and origin. In *Hyperion* the beginning seems to initiate us into givenness. The history of dispossession is only dimly charted. There was a golden age "Of peaceful sway above man's harvesting" (I, 110). It has vanished. The enemy cannot be named (103-05) and the failure cannot be diagnosed (II, 129-36). Nevertheless the disinherited self is alienated from the real self (I, 112-114) and hopes of reinstating it are couched in a rhetoric which defines those hopes as fictive.

Since dispossession has no cause and since it is to be

---

[16] "Dear Reynolds, as last night I lay in bed," 95-99. *The Poems of John Keats*, p. 244.

[17] *Dark Interpreter*, p. 158.

[18] Keats, in his comments on *P.L.* VII, 420-23 (Wittreich, *The Romantics on Milton*, p. 559) finds Milton's "perseverance" in pursuing his "imagination to the utmost" most fully exemplified in his *"stationing or statu[a]ry*. He is not content with simple description, he must station."

justified, if at all, only by a future which has yet to be realized and which at this point cannot even be foreseen, we are left with the landscape of deprivation against which Keats assembles the statuary of the obsolete. If the past survives, it survives only as art. More pointedly, it survives as art in ruin. The Titans do not have the consolation of a policy, or even of the pseudo-policies advanced in Milton's hell of Belial's planned inconspicuousness or Mammon's seductive combination of the spirit of capitalism with the Protestant ethic. Acceptance of extinction as the price of a new consciousness may be wisdom but it is not a policy. Little remains but to turn for deliverance to the sole Titan who remains unvanquished and who conveniently manifests himself as soon as his name is spoken by an Enceladus approaching exhaustion of his rhetorical capabilities. Hyperion, however, is already doomed by the striking image which announces him to his fellows as "a vast shade/In midst of his own brightness" (II, 372-73). The resemblance to Shelley's "shape all light" is striking. As Hyperion confronts the Titans whose misery his own brightness exposes, he also paradoxically exposes his own future to his own depth. The view of light as an envelope surrounding a core of darkness is evidently conducive to a poetics of betrayal, but it would be simplifying the entanglements of the image to see it exclusively as supporting such a poetics. It is at the least also consonant with a poetry of self-formation in which a new self comes into being through its dismissal of a previous self.

Beginnings can sometimes be invested with finality. Hell in *Paradise Lost* is a state that cannot be changed, a demonic extreme that is necessary in cosmic logic. Keats has studied Milton's hell but his own sculptured sublime carves out a place that is irrevocably alienated from itself and not yet capable of attachment to a new self. Nowhere is this differentiation more apparent than in that intensity of dejection and inertness which Keats's opening lines so powerfully convey. They are to be compared to the beginning of the second book of *Paradise Lost* where Milton describes a "throne of royal state" on which

> Satan exalted sat, by merit raised
> To that bad eminence. . . .

In Keats's deprived world one is not allowed even the satisfactions of parody:

> Deep in the shady sadness of a vale
> Far sunken from the healthy breath of morn,
> Far from the fiery noon, and eve's one star,
> Sat grey-haired Saturn, quiet as a stone,
> Still as the silence round about his lair; . . .

Milton, a master of syntactic postponement, takes five lines to arrive at his predicate. Keats, emulating Milton's tactics, arrives in four lines at the same verb, "sat." The word "exalted" separates subject from predicate in Milton's verbal drama. The word "grey-haired" separates predicate from subject in Keats's answering inversion. One is a stationing of pride, the other of defeat. Milton begins his first line with "High" and his second with "Outshone," emphasizing the superlatives of Satan's exaltation. Keats begins his first line with "Deep" and his second and third lines with "Far," a word transplanted from Milton's opening line to suggest not the excess of glory, but the dimensions of its diminution. The careful modelling and the scrupulously regulated intertextuality do not end at this point. In opening Book II, Milton expects us to remember his opening to the whole poem in Book I where an even more imperious syntactic postponement had taken six lines to arrive at the predicate. Keats, withholding from us the promises of design which an invocation can be made to offer, plunges steadfastly into the dejection of things, as Endymion once did in his journey to the core. The denudation increases the force of destitution in Keats's beginning but it also compounds the problematics of that beginning. With the poem so decisively "situated" the risk it must negotiate is that of being trapped in its givenness.

In the "Saturn" movement of Gustav Holst's "The Planets," the brass cries out repeatedly in mounting protest against the mounting dismissal of the drumbeat. It is the claim of an old man's frenzy, of someone who will not go gentle into the night. This, as is obvious, is not at all the mood of the opening lines of *Hyperion*. Here the withdrawal from sustaining natural rhythms, the figure of the grey-haired ex-monarch of the world in its past infancy, the stone he resembles, which could very well be his tombstone, convey a sculpturally frozen numbness of destitution both in the still figure and its answering environment. "Lair" is a word almost cruelly chosen: the one-time ruler is now the hunted animal.[19] We see Chronos bewildered, unable to comprehend that his time is over on the clock of Kairos. A world of natural recurrence, of "peaceful sway above man's harvesting" must give way to a world which at this stage in the mind's elaborations seems to pitch a purposiveness all but crushing in its consequences against an innocence doomed by that unself-consciousness which seems unavoidably part of its nature. In the forward movement of consciousness this may be an important advance, but it is also one whose exactions are questioned by the very manner in which the advance is delineated.

The weight of dejection presses heavily, "forest upon forest," on the depths of the vale into which Saturn has withdrawn. The consolations of philosophy are obliged to struggle against that weight. Milton too begins in a world of defeat but it is the defeat of those who opposed the *status quo*. Keats studies the victims of a successful and necessary revolution who must learn to reconcile themselves to the indifference of history to its agents. "A mighty providence," Keats observes in language which, unlike Ar-

---

[19] The word may have seemed too cruel since Keats omitted three and a half lines containing it from the second *Hyperion*.

nold's, makes the man the prisoner as well as the spokes-man of the moment, "subdues the mightiest Minds to the service of the time being."[20] Translated into psychic politics the observation means that we must learn to accept dying into life, disinheritance beyond retrieval, the commitment to self-making rather than self-preservation.

Such a programme is not easy to carry into poetry, par-ticularly when the mind that carries it and that is now committed to the sorrow of the actual still clings to the proposition that beauty may be truth. A recent book on Keats suggests that aestheticism is Keats's solution to the problem posed by his scepticism.[21] The argument is per-suasive up to a point, but it leaves us with the feeling that aestheticism itself may be the problem or at least a solution which begets its problems. Hartman's essay on spectral symbolism in *Hyperion* helps us to maintain that the poem, for all its monumentality, is the writing large of an interior debate.[22] Indeed, the monumentality may be the means of adequately distancing a debate which it might otherwise be impossible to confront. Apollo's deification—or, more accurately, his transformation from a pastoral state similar to that which Saturn is significantly barred from retriev-ing—is emblematic of Keats's own willed progress from a pastoral to a purposive world. The change comes about in the third book of *Hyperion* and, not at all accidentally, it is in the third book of *Paradise Lost* that Keats sees the prin-ciples of Apollonian management announcing themselves within the world of that poem. His own poem urges itself towards such management while at the same time deeply questioning its possibility. The *Bildungsroman* of conscious-ness requires to be justified to the reader (if not to the unfortunate Titans) in ways beyond the mere allegation

[20] 3 May, 1818, to Reynolds. Rollins 1, p. 382.

[21] Ronald A. Sharp, *Keats, Scepticism, and the Religion of Beauty*, Athens, University of Georgia Press, 1979.

[22] *The Fate of Reading*, Chicago, University of Chicago Press, 1975, pp. 57-74.

that there is a *Bildungsroman*. The similarity of Apollo's original state to Saturn's and his passive openness to his metamorphosis leave us wondering what he has done to earn his privileges particularly when the Titans remain subjected to a deprivation for which it is hard to find a basis. If the basis is supersession by a superior state, the state must be shown and not claimed to be superior. Apollo's dying into life is named rather than lived through in a passage which is considerably below Keats's usual standard. It is possible that Keats could do no better but it may be more interesting to conjecture that he decided not to do better and that the poem at this point is entertaining but dismissing its own deliverance. It breaks off poised upon Apollo's shriek, the significantly inarticulate boundary between a superseded past and a future which cannot yet be brought into being, which the imagination can direct itself to but is unable to occupy. The inability admits, in effect, that the poem's actualities have revised its projected balance of forces, that it has contested all too successfully that view of the nature of coming consciousness which it nevertheless continues to underwrite. A real division of allegiance is involved here rather than that familiar undermining of didactic proclamation by imaginative accomplishment in which the authenticity of the latter is assumed and the repressive force of the former is taken to be exposed by it. Oceanus' manifesto is not devoid of eloquence. But it is positioned within a counter-eloquence that confronts it not as argument but, more effectively, as the givenness of deprivation. The result is to bring about a defensive segregation of the aesthetic from the existential. We are introduced to Apollo's realm by an invocation (significantly, the first in the poem) which twice dismisses the world of the Titans and even draws attention to the Muse's inadequacy to sing of such a world. The saving strategy that the poem thus offers itself, the insulation of the poetic from its challenges, is obviously a strategy attended by crucial impoverishments. As might be expected, it is not a

227

course which the main weight of the poem can finally en-
dorse. Oceanus may speak of first in beauty being first in
might, but the most haunting statement of beauty in the
poem belongs not to Apollo, but to Thea.

> But oh! how unlike marble was that face:
> How beautiful, if sorrow had not made
> Sorrow more beautiful than Beauty's self.
> (34-36)

In a journal letter to George and Georgiana Keats which
describes *Hyperion* as "scarce began," Keats says that he
can "never feel certain of any truth but from a clear per-
ception of its beauty."[23] In a letter two months earlier he
had expressed the hope that the "yearning passion" he
had for the beautiful would be "connected and made one
with the ambition" of his "intellect."[24] These statements
consort with a third one—"what the imagination seizes as
Beauty must be truth"—[25] and are quoted because the sta-
tus of the better-known lines at the end of "The Ode to a
Grecian Urn" is likely to remain permanently in doubt. In
these and other formulations the implied opposition which
is to be overcome (typically by an intensity of perception
which makes "all disagreeables evaporate")[26] is between
the imaginative and the intelligential, two contraries that
contest each other but with a restraint appropriately meas-
ured by the term, "disagreement." If the sadness of things
is to be admitted into the field of such a relationship its
undermining force cannot be indefinitely contained within
these moderating limits. Its presence must bring about some
revision of the relationship. The movement from Apollo-

---

[23] Journal Letter 16 December, 1818 to 4 January, 1819. Rollins 2, p. 19.

[24] Journal Letter of 14 to 31 October, 1818, to George and Georgiana Keats. Rollins 1, p. 404.

[25] 22 November, 1817, to Bailey. Rollins 1, p. 184.

[26] Letter of 21 December, 1817, to George and Thomas Keats. Rollins 1, p. 192.

nian to tragic beauty is necessary at some stage in Keats's development. It is possible that the first *Hyperion* initiates this movement. If so, the very poem which proclaims Apollo's triumph, is also subversively proclaiming his obsolescence.

In a letter of April 8, 1818 to Haydon written a few weeks before *Hyperion* was begun, Keats speaks of "the labyrinthian path to eminence in Art." He then goes on to draw attention to

> the innumerable compositions and decompositions which take place between the intellect and its thousand materials before it arrives at that trembling delicate and snail-horn perception of Beauty. I know not you[r] many havens of intenseness. . . .[27]

The allusion here is to Shakespeare's *Venus and Adonis*. Keats had quoted the passage in his letter of November 22, 1817 to Reynolds.[28] The love of a goddess for a mortal youth which is the dramatic context of the quotation is, of course, the subject of *Endymion*. When Endymion speaks of the rich, yet self-destroying entanglements and enthralments which lead by degrees to the chief intensity he is anticipating the language of Keats's letter and seeing the quest for beauty as mounting aesthetic excitement. *Endymion*, however, has been shown to lie between two co-ordinates. The view of beauty which has so far been outlined is the result of a pursuit along only one co-ordinate. Transferred to the other co-ordinate, the same view becomes the ancestor of the letter on soul-making which is perhaps Keats's most important critical statement.

In the passage just quoted from the letter to Haydon, the intellect seems to be presiding over its "thousand materials." Elsewhere, responsibilities can be differently distributed. Keats can talk of "hovering" between "an ex-

[27] Rollins 1, pp. 192-93.
[28] Rollins 1, p. 189.

quisite sense of the luxurious and a love for philosophy"[29] and as already mentioned, he can write of "passion" for the beautiful connected and made one with the "ambition" of the intellect. The first wording suggests a necessary vacillation between directed thought and unreflective openness of response. The second suggests an integration of two ways of willing or two directions of pursuit. In the letter on soul-making, the relationship proposed is not between intellect and the beautiful or the luxuriant, but between the mind and the heart. Moreover, it is the heart that is dominant in this relationship.

> I will call the *world* a School instituted for the purpose of teaching little children to read—I will call the *human heart* the *horn Book* used in that School—and I will call the *Child able to read, the Soul* made from that *School* and its *hornbook*. . . . Not merely is the Heart a Hornbook, it is the Minds Bible, it is the Minds experience, it is the teat from which the Mind or intelligence sucks its identity.[30]

The diminution of the mind's claims by likening it to a child who must be taught how to read is striking but is exceeded by that further and telling regression to a state of infancy that is implicitly mindless. The proposition that the mind is constituted exclusively by and through experience is of course respectable and of long standing, but Keats is speaking of the heart and not the senses, and again of the heart and not the imagination. The word is quite new in his lexicon and he did not live long enough to put it to sustained use. It is Yeats who writes of the heart as the soil in which the holy tree grows, the foul rag-and-bone shop from which the ladders reach upward, the sorrow-racked source in which the changeless work origi-

[29] Letter of 24 April, 1818, to Taylor. Rollins 1, p. 271.
[30] Journal Letter of 14 February to 3 May, 1819, to George and Georgiana Keats. Rollins 2, pp. 102-03.

nates, and the nourishment of the creative conflagration.[31] The heart, not the imagination, is the natural witness of the journey to the core; and the heart, not the intelligence, is the natural corrective of the journey to the apex. We do not accurately describe *Hyperion* when we describe it as a poem of the journey to the core. It is a poem of the self-achieving consciousness, monumentalized as mythic narrative. But again it is the heart which must authenticate the progress of such a poem, the "innumerable compositions and decompositions" that have to take place in that ongoing self-making to which the poem consents.

Some of the reasons why *Hyperion* cannot be finished will be evident. The Apollonian and Oceanic possibilities are put to school in a world of dejection. The brooding weight of that dejection ushers in the poem and continues to stand unnegotiably in its foreground. Thus the poem is subverted before it is under way and mythic narrative, as becomes apparent, is simply not a form able to absorb the undermining of its postulates. As the poem proceeds we recognize how close it is to conveying the opposite of what it argues and how, even in its segregation of realms, it raises the question of the possible irrelevance of the Apollonian. That a work should convey something other than its thesis in a way made possible only because of the protective blindness offered by that thesis is a proposition Paul de Man has made celebrated.[32] The blindness can sponsor a text that is fundamentally repressive, in which case the critic's task is to disinter and establish that sub-text which

---

[31] Yeats, "The Two Trees," *Collected Poems,* p. 54; "The Circus Animals' Desertion," *C.P.,* p. 391; "Meditations in Time of Civil War," *C.P.,* p. 228; "Two Songs From a Play," *C.P.,* p. 240. See also "Vacillation," *C.P.,* p. 285. James Jones (*Adam's Dream: Mythic Consciousness in Keats and Yeats,* Athens, University of Georgia Press, 1975, pp. 14-49) discusses soul-making in Keats and Yeats though not with reference to the connections cited above.

[32] *Blindness and Insight: Essays in the Rhetoric of Contemporary Criticism,* New York, Oxford University Press, 1971.

is the true text, through the cracks and gaps in the repressive structure.

Alternatively, the blindness can be a chosen fiction, a provocation that elicits in response a sub-text which otherwise would not come to life as vividly. The heart of the poem would then be taken to lie, not in the poem's unifying announcements or in its subversive recognitions, but in the interplay of provocation and retaliation. It is the second alternative which seems applicable to *Hyperion* and, as will be shown later, it also characterizes the poet's relationship to Moneta in the internalized world of the second *Hyperion*. The weight of woe which is the first *Hyperion*'s dominant reality, precedes and by its crushing presence diminishes whatever consolations can be urged against it. It is therefore not an interrogating force which is subversively generated while another understanding is being officially pursued. It would not be repressed if it were directly confronted. In fact it is placed in the poem and given its decisive positioning so that it can question through the immediacies of distress a remote though "mighty" providence which has set aside those whom it has used for the "service of the time being." The "justification" of the ways of that providence is that the setting aside is the unavoidable condition of a crucial advance in consciousness. But the actuality of that advance has yet to be established and must survive against our awareness of the cost. One looks unsuccessfully in the first *Hyperion* for that point of confessional self-disclosure—the magic moment of the deconstructionists—when the poem no longer silenced by its subterfuges,[33] no longer acquiescent in the treason of au-

---

[33] See Michael Ragussis, *The Subterfuge of Art*, Baltimore, The Johns Hopkins University Press, 1978, esp. pp. 35-69. For Ragussis the "skeptical underthought and the fragmentation of the Hyperion poems seem Keats's only defenses against the subterfuge of art" (p. 68). The fragmented work is the clearest illustration of the writer's "refusal to close the charmed circle of art around himself and his audience" (p. 9). My account differs in seeing Keats's fictions not as a means of excluding certain awareness,

thorship, betrays itself into its own reality. However if we are unsuccessful it is only because there is no specific "fissure," because it is the poem's entire environment which radically questions its philosophy and indeed the possibility of arriving at a philosophy. The grand march of intellect, a phrase which by now ought to seem reprehensible in its automated overtones, offers us certain blindnesses, or, to put it less starkly, certain Olympian indifferences. The poem resolutely refuses to allow those indifferences. Its very segregation of the realms of Apollo and the Titans underlines the necessity of a dialogue between them. Such a dialogue is all the more desirable because the stated purpose of the progress of intellect is to enable us to see deeper into the human heart. Yet the heart inherits that very dispossession which an advancing consciousness seeks to justify in the name of its advance. Apollonian management, whether viewed cosmically as the dominance of the teleological or psychically as the surrender of sensation to the stern chastenings of thought, must confront the privations which its claims inflict and educate itself into an exchange of understandings that is deeper than the mere appropriation of one term in a dialectic by another.

The deification of history is a widely shared commitment of nineteenth-century thought. *Hyperion* is a poem of deep engagement with that deification, resisting what it also entertains in a response sufficiently pervasive and complex to make the striking of a balance sheet not merely impossible but irrelevant. To understand the accuracy with which Keats identifies a problem which may permit no escape from its constraints it is instructive to turn to a writer of this century making his statement in a quite different con-

---

but as a means of confronting awareness which might otherwise be slurred over. The fiction itself undermines the protections it offers and thus makes it impossible not to acknowledge those awarenesses. The subterfuge seems to lie in the smuggling in of subversive forces under the cover of promises of order which cannot be maintained.

text. In 1930 we find the Frankfurt philosopher Horkheimer observing

> That history has realized a better society out of a worse one, that it can realize an even better one in its course, is a fact; but it is another fact that the path of history leads over the suffering and misery of individuals. Between these two facts there are a number of explanatory connections, but no justifying meaning.[34]

It is the fissure between "explanatory connections" and "justifying meaning" that Keats explores so probingly in *Hyperion*, and it is the impossibility of proceeding from one to the other which leaves the poem unfinished, poised on those interlaced yet divergent affiliations which must remain part of its problem, justly understood. If the exploration is to be carried further (and to carry it further is to be committed more fully to its essential inconclusiveness), it must be in a form more malleable and less sculptural, a form better suited to those compositions and decompositions which a later encounter with Moneta is to chart.

II

Keats's change of mind with respect to Milton is surely the swiftest disenchantment in the history of literature. The time at which he began to annotate his edition of *Paradise Lost* is conjectural, but Stuart Ende's suggestion of the winter of 1817-18 seems plausible.[35] If this date is accepted, the affair came to a climax some eighteen months later. "Shakespeare and the Paradise Lost every day become greater wonders to me," Keats wrote to Bailey on August 14, 1819.

---

[34] Max Horkheimer, *Anfange der bürgerlichen Geschichtsphilosophie*, Stuttgart, Kohlhammer, 1930, p. 44. As translated in *The Origin of Negative Dialectics* by Susan Buck-Morss, Hassocks, Sussex, The Harvester Press, 1977, p. 48.

[35] Stuart Ende, *Keats and the Sublime*, New Haven, Yale University Press, 1976, pp. 87-88.

"I look upon fine Phrases like a Lover" he continued.[36] He repeated himself ten days later to Reynolds: "I am convinced more and more day by day that fine writing is next to fine doing, the top thing in the world; the Paradise Lost becomes a greater wonder."[37] No more than four weeks later Reynolds received an altogether different letter: "I have given up Hyperion—there were too many Miltonic inversions in it—Miltonic verse can not be written but in an artful or rather artist's humour."[38] The entry three days later in a journal letter to George and Georgiana Keats is more emphatic

> The Paradise lost though so fine in itself is a curruption of our Language—it should be kept as it is unique—a curiosity—a beautiful and grand Curiosity. The most remarkable Production of the world. A northern dialect accommodating itself to Greek and Latin inversions and intonations. . . . I have but lately stood on my guard against Milton. Life to him would be death to me. Miltonic verse cannot be written but it [in] the vein of art—I wish to devote myself to another sensation—[39]

The grounds for dismissal at first seem to be stylistic. There is the adulatory reference to "fine writing" and the looking upon "fine phrases like a Lover," followed by the rejection of Milton's Latinity—a Latinity characterized in a manner that echoes the findings of Samuel Johnson. But the rejection of a style is sometimes symptomatic of the deeper rejection of what the style conveys. *Hyperion* is a Miltonic poem not simply in its cadences but in its attempt to assert the shape of order against the weight of woe. Both poems contemplate the defeats of history actual and mythic, and

[36] Rollins 2, p. 139.
[37] Rollins 2, p. 146.
[38] Letter of 21 September, 1819, to Reynolds. Rollins 2, p. 166.
[39] Letter to George and Georgiana Keats 17-27 September, 1819. Rollins 2, p. 212.

both seek understandings which will survive those defeats. Milton of course can justify God's ways by assigning to a freely choosing centre the entire onus of responsibility for destructiveness. Keats can entertain no such justification. Indeed, as he proceeds with his poem he raises before himself the inadequacies of purposiveness, of final causes or emergent claims. A poem which seeks to install or even to attain a "grand Perspective" at its centre may be able to do so only by betraying its own world. To be the poet of "another sensation" is to learn that one's business is to probe and not to justify.

On the half-title page of his edition of *Paradise Lost* Keats observes that Milton

> had an exquisite passion for what is properly in the sense of ease and pleasure, poetical Luxury—and with that it appears to me he would fain have been content if he could so doing have preserved his self-respect and feel of duty perform'd—but there was working in him as it were that same sort of thing as operates in the great world to the end of a Prophecy's being ac- complish'd—therefore he devoted himself rather to the Ardours than the pleasures of Song, solacing himself at intervals with cups of old wine—and those are with some exceptions the finest part of the Poem.[40]

Keats mirrors himself in this estimate of Milton. The "lux- ury" is reflected in his desire to die a death of luxury, the "ease" in his being "half in love with easeful death," the "feel of duty perform'd" in the commitment to a "nobler life," the acceptance of that "flaw in happiness" which cannot but be admitted into happiness and which "spoils the singing of the nightingale."[41] When Keats describes himself as "hovering between" an "exquisite sense of the

[40] Wittreich, *The Romantics on Milton*, p. 553.
[41] *Sleep and Poetry*, 58-159; *Ode to a Nightingale*, 52; "Dear Reynolds, as last night I lay in bed," 82-85.

luxurious and a love of philosophy" he reproduces the language of his comment on Milton. He admires the manner in which Milton's luxuriance is chastened and kept in place under the pressure of overall understandings to which the poetry should ideally subscribe rather than submit. In doing so he anticipates relationships later critics were to draw between the poet and the puritan, or the didactic and the imaginative, in Milton's accomplishment. The tempering thus achieved attracted Keats because it spoke deeply to him. It was abandoned because it did not speak deeply enough.

The only way out of the difficulties which the pressing concerns of the first *Hyperion* created was to internalize the conflict which it raised. The poem's increasing resistance to the understandings to which it was expected to testify, its inability to place the Apollonian within its boundaries, call for a different disposition, a fable that is psychological rather than dynastic. When this disposition is made one no longer has to think of the contest between Apollo and Hyperion

> As of a duel or the mortal wounds
> Of head or heel
> (*Paradise Lost* XII, 387-88)

The cruelties of supersession are overcome by an advancing self-understanding which by virtue of what it finds in itself, earns its progress and justifies its cost. We are made conscious of an inadequacy that has been passed through, not of a generation that has been cast aside. The mind does not avoid conversation or merely institute a conversation with the challenge to its structures that is urged upon it by the insistent heart. It is taught by the challenge to decipher itself. Its "strong identity" (*Hyperion* I, 114) is the condition of its future not the pastoral peace which it has left behind.

The second *Hyperion* is entitled "a dream" and it begins by suggesting that dreams are the aberration or privilege of those who stand at the fringes, of the "fanatic" on the circumference of society and the "savage" left behind by the march of progress. The dreaming of poetry is distinguished from the dreaming of dispossessed elites by poetry's ability to "tell" its dreams, its capacity to save imagination from "the sable charm/And dumb enchantment" with the counter-enchantment, the "fine spell" of words. At this point the poet too is a member of an elite the selectivity of which is underlined by "alone." But the potential brotherhood of poetry is now expanded by a reassurance offered to the reader as well as claimed by the author.

> Who alive can say
> "Thou art no poet; may'st not tell thy dreams?"

The emphasis here is not only upon utterance but on the right to utterance. The poet and the reader, recognized as prospective poet, are presumably to be distinguished from the non-poet by the kind of dream they liberate into language and thus expose to scrutiny. It is an emphasis which shifts subtly in the lines that follow

> Since every man whose soul is not a clod
> Hath visions and would speak, if he had lov'd,
> And been well nurtured in his mother tongue.

The poet here is, as with Wordsworth, a man speaking to men, sharing with all men the gift of vision and the desire for utterance, and differing from them in degree rather than kind. The ambiguous stationing of "lov'd" (it can be either intransitive or take "mother tongue" for its object, with the end-of-the-line position stressing the first possibility) leaves open the question of whether speech is made possible by love of language or by a love that is less particularized. "Nurtured" suggests that more than language is involved, that the mother tongue includes all that has reached expression in it. The text has brought us to the centrality indeed the universality of dreaming and to the vital nature of utterance which is the sustenance of the dream as well as the "fine spell" that liberates it. But the dream may not be the authentic dream which other men recognize in themselves and share with the writer. It may only be the sectarian dream of a fanatic, of a minor tribe the members of which have chosen to call themselves poets.

> Whether the dream now purposed to rehearse
> Be poet's or fanatic's will be known
> When this warm scribe my hand is in the grave.

The dream now depends on survival as well as utterance. Something in it, outlasting the "warm scribe" who reports it, must succeed in declaiming its authenticity.

This passage has been looked at in some slight detail because its tactics anticipate those of the poem's main encounter. The evolving adumbrations proceed as compositions and decompositions that bring us to a tentative understanding. It is not simply a matter of what is affirmed but of how we arrive at what is affirmed. Whatever knowledge we reach is shaped and led into by the history of attainment. The very process of coming to that attainment argues for the necessity of an attainment beyond it.

The poet stands in a place where trees of "every clime" (19) are present, suggesting that the place belongs to every country. He finds in an arbour the "refuge of a meal/By angel tasted, or our Mother Eve" (31). The discovery can be read as an affirmation of belatedness, of alienation from plenitude and from origins. Keats makes a quite explicit statement of belatedness in *Endymion* II, 723-32, but the march of intellect points in another direction. In any case there is still as much plenitude available as "the fabled horn/Thrice emptied could pour forth" (35-36). The poet eats liberally and then drinks "pledging all the mortals of the world" (44) in another affirmation of his desire for universality. Having swooned, he wakes before a sanctuary the antiquity of which exceeds even "The superannuations of sunk realms/Or nature's rocks toiled hard in waves and winds" (68-69). The ways north and south end in mists of nothingness. The way east is dominated by black gates "shut against the sunrise evermore." The way west is the only way available. It is also a way which must be taken since the poet is commanded either to ascend the sanctuary steps or to die on the marble where he stands. The dying into life that follows (126-27) reproduces Apollo's shriek of transformation in the first *Hyperion* but the survivor does not attain divinity. He merely dates on his doom (144-45) and secures a position where he can earn his enlightenment.[42]

The poet requests the "High Prophetess" of the sanctuary to "purge off/Benign, if it so please thee, my mind's film" (145-46). Michael in *Paradise Lost* is described as being of "regard benign" (XI, 336) and in a complex series of operations he removes the "film" from Adam's eyes, purges the "visual nerve" with euphrasy and rue and instills three drops of water from the well of life. In drawing attention to this connection Stuart Sperry persuasively shows us that the movement from the first Hyperion to the second is among other things a movement joining Milton to Dante.[43] Keats, at this time, was reading Cary's translation of the *Purgatorio* and Gittings finds traces of the translation in the second *Hyperion*.[44] Nevertheless Adam's education retains a relationship to the education of the poet by Moneta.

[42] The poet's and Apollo's dying into life are to be linked to Lamia's metamorphosis (1, 146-70) and to Satan's entry into the serpent (*P.L.* IX, 179-91), an account by which Keats was, perhaps unduly, impressed: "no passage of poetry ever can give a greater pain of suffocation" (Wittreich, *The Romantics on Milton*, p. 560). Keats can treat dying into life as ecstatic, as agonizing, as orgiastic, as the highest attainable intensity (*Why did I laugh Tonight?*), as progress to the "chief intensity" by successive enthralments (*Endymion*, 1, 797-807) and as the deathwards progress to "no death" (*The Fall of Hyperion*, 260-61). The antithetical relationship between ecstatic fulfillment and tragic discovery outlined by the last two references suggests not a prospective middle ground but rather a continuing engagement.

[43] Stuart Sperry, *Keats the Poet*, Princeton, Princeton University Press, 1973, pp. 310-35.

[44] Robert Gittings, *John Keats. The Living Year*, London, Heinemann (Mercury Books), 1962, pp. 178-79.

The dialogue with Moneta, a sterner Mnemosyne to the poet's Apollo, is a crucial event in the poetry of self-achieving. The debate within the self is fittingly shown as contentious rather than considerate, with the formative accusations, the understandings attained by defence against the searching over-statement, strongly and authentically conveyed. Twenty-four important lines (187-210) were, according to Woodhouse, intended to be erased, but editors have wisely let them stand. Their status as a draft within the text simply reminds us that all understanding has to be a draft, overlaid and partly superseded by the further understanding which the draft makes possible. This is the poem of the mind in the act of finding, not what will suffice, but what the frame of the present permits. Language, in the stages of registration of such a movement, is erased by that to which it gives way but reinscribed because that which succeeds it remains informed by a history it cannot efface.

Moneta's status in this dialogue needs to be considered. She is not Dante's Virgil, and though Adam's Michael is, as was pointed out, a distant likeness, Moneta faces a pupil who has survived a test and who will himself, in his contention with his teacher, define the nature of the responsible imagination. Her function is not to expound the vast design against the obscurations of adversity but to disclose the weight of sadness at the centre of things. Whatever understanding the poet achieves must be formed, rather than fractured, by that weight, and cannot be constituted in those evasions or transcendences of it that can at best only announce a preliminary gesture of the fictive capability. Moneta's apparent inconsistencies in performing this function deserve to be studied. She first makes the poet one of an elect minority, one who has the power "to die and live again" before his "fated hour" (142-43). Because the miseries of the world are misery to him and will not let him rest he has been permitted to "usurp this height" (167-69). But it is clear that the so-called usurpation was demanded and that the poet would have died if his attempt had failed (107-17). The initial presumption, the consequent ordeal, and the granting of a status which is nevertheless described as illegitimate, are consistent with the experience but not necessarily with the way in which it is spoken about. Moneta's function, it becomes apparent, is to provoke as much as to expound, to sting her pupil into acts of definition. Thus, having conceded him a position of privilege, she then twice contemptuously speaks of him as a "thing" (168, 178) and even more scathingly as a "Fever" of himself (169). His ailment is excessive responsiveness to the world's sorrow, an inability to keep pain and joy distinct. He is admitted to the "height" as a protection against his own self-destructiveness (171-80). It is a criticism the actual poet could urge against himself and which he does urge against himself in the "Epistle to Reynolds." But how then is the dream of the poet to be distinguished on the one hand from the fanatic's dream of paradise and of the bower's resurrection and on the other hand from the sensitive mind's nightmare of sorrow? Keeping a judicious balance is not the answer. When the poet describes his sickness as "not ignoble" (184) he is defending acceptance of the fever; when he describes the poet as "a sage/ A humanist, physician to all men" (189-90) he is implying that the poet himself must heal the fever he undertakes to endure. Apollo, we might remember, is a physician as well as a poet. Moneta's aggressive separation of the poet from the dreamer, thrust forward in no fewer than five variant stylings (199-202), and her previous association of visionaries with "dreamers weak" (161-62) seem to undermine these possibilities and even to betray the purpose of the dialogue, which is to arrive at the nature of the poetic dream. Yet, ironically, it establishes the quality of that dream, which is to be tormented by the world without and to be taunted by the voice within. That the poet should describe these observations as "courteous" (215) is perhaps indicative of a wry realism that answers from himself.

Moneta responds to the poet's recognition of her courtesy by undertaking to be kind to him for his "good will" (242). A change in relationship is taking place. The priestess is no longer the mentor, and even if she does not accept the poet as her colleague she seems ready to admit him as her audience. Indeed, the contrast between the "electral changing misery" of vision as experienced and the "wonder" of vision as disclosed strongly suggest the relationship between writer and audience. It is appropriate in these circumstances to note the extent to which Moneta embodies in herself what she has previously castigated the poet for being:

> My power, which to me is still a curse,
> Shall be to thee a wonder; for the scenes
> Still swooning vivid through my globed brain
> With an electral changing misery,
> Thou shall with those dull mortal eyes behold,
> Free from all pain, if wonder pain thee not.
>
> (243-48)

It is the poet's stubborn adherence to his calling and his progressive characterization of that calling under assault that entitles him to see Moneta's face unveiled:

> Then saw I a wan face
> Not pin'd by human sorrows, but bright blanch'd
> By an immortal sickness which kills not:
> It works a constant change, which happy death
> Can put no end to; deathwards progressing
> To no death was that visage; it had pass'd
> The lilly and the snow;
>
> (256-62)

The "constant change" is not seasonal recurrence, or even the natural movement of life to death, but an eternal onwardness, not caught in time like Thea's tragic dignity, but manifest as an immortal sickness. The poet's own "sickness not ignoble" which Moneta had rebuked in him is now seen to be implacably eternized in her. Yet the terror is not without tranquillity. The eyes "Half-closed, and visionless entire . . . Of all external things," their gaze concentrated on inwardness, beam "like the mild moon" in "blank Splendour" (264-69). The poet, at one time seized by fear, is not reassured by the "benignant light" of these eyes into avoiding flight while keeping a cautious and respectful distance. On the contrary he is consumed by curiosity.

> As I had found
> A grain of gold upon a mountain's side
> And twing'd with avarice strain'd out my eyes
> To search its sullen entrails rich with ore,
> So at the view of sad Moneta's brow,
> I ached to see what things the hollow brain
> Behind enwombed:
>
> (271-77)

It is important that the simile is in the first person. A greater distance could have been maintained between the miner's avarice and the poet's compulsive inquiry. But there is avarice, or to put it slightly differently, a creative and therefore exploitative greed, in the inquiry. The explorer is also the would-be possessor. Once again the relationship between priestess and poet is changing. Moneta previously the poet's mentor, is now on the verge of becoming his subject. He aches to see

> what high tragedy
> In the dark secret chambers of her skull
> Was acting, that could give so dread a stress
> To her cold lips, and fill with such a light
> Her planetary eyes;
>
> (277-81)

The concerns are literary, but the poet, avid to explore the deep dichotomies that lie behind the "stress" on those "cold lips," is a poet committed to search the mountain's "sullen entrails," to give himself to what the core of fierce destruction yields. Endymion's submarine voyage must be carried on with no assurance that there is quietude at the centre. A different self speaks from the one that first questioned Moneta and the attitude of this new self to Moneta is ambivalent. If the poet invokes the prophetess with "act adorant" he also summons her by his "conjuration" (283, 291). As "The pale omega of a withered race" (the language is expressive of the shifting relationship in aptly suggesting both reverence and belittlement), Moneta and all that she sees must be brought forward into the imagination's immediacy. The "fine spell of words" does more than simply tell the dream. It raises it into existence out of its darkness. And the poet does not simply search Moneta's consciousness. He appropriates some of her powers. He sees as a god sees, with his "enormous ken" matching Apollo's "knowledge enormous," comprehending the depth of things as the outer eye takes in their size and shape (302-06). But to see as a god sees is to endure as an immortal endures. It is to take on the unremitting burden of Moneta's deathward progress to no death (388-99). The poet's dream is certified by its cost.

With the conjuration of Moneta the first *Hyperion* begins again. There are changes in the turns of language, a reduction in the number of Miltonic inversions,[45] an abbreviated description of Thea and a deletion of Saturn's hope (I, 141-65) of forming another universe out of chaos. . . . More important for our purpose are Moneta's attempted guidances. At first she seeks to maintain her status as mentor by insisting on the figural character of what the poet sees:

[45] Bate (*John Keats*, p. 604n.) notes that inversions of noun and adjective decline in frequency from once in fourteen lines in *Hyperion* to once in thirty-three lines in *The Fall of Hyperion*. These figures however include 310 lines before *The Fall of Hyperion* reaches the point where *Hyperion* begins. Only 219 lines are actually shared by the two poems. It may be the difficulty of eliminating Miltonic resonances from these lines which led Keats to make the remarks discussed in the body of this chapter.

> "So Saturn sat
> When he had lost his realms"
> (301-02)

Later, she concedes more to the reliability of the representation

> "That Divinity
>
> ....
>
> Is Thea, softest-natur'd of our brood"
> (332-35)

At the beginning of the second Canto she shifts from vision to narrative much as Michael did in passing from the eleventh to the twelfth book of *Paradise Lost*

> "Mortal that thou may'st understand arights
> I humanize my sayings to thine ear,
> Making comparisons of earthly things,"
> (1-3)

The language also remembers the manner in which Raphael begins his account of the battle in heaven (*P.L.* V, 571-74). Yet after providing an account of Hyperion's palace, Moneta seems to abandon the pretense that the divine must be accommodated to the human, and with "Thither we tend," transports the poet to the scene of whatever action remains. Thirteen lines farther on the poem breaks off. Moneta's unstable, not to say defensive, view of her status, suggests the extent to which the balance of power has changed, and the extent to which the poet may be disinterring rather than witnessing the "high tragedy" being acted in the "secret chamber" of consciousness. The past is being repossessed but within the guiding interpretative power of a present already constituted by acts of self-formation.

Keats's success in composing the frame dream is authoritative. The internalization re-enacts the mythic-dynastic past, putting the supersessions of the fable into alignment with the self-formative growth of the mind that discovers the fable. A myth of transformational change is surrounded and interpreted by the pre-emptive transformation of the narrating consciousness. The past is obliged to enter contemporaneity. It is remembered and remade in the context of recognition every new author must create in himself.[46] That is why the gates of the temple are barred against the east and barred in that direction only. The point is not that the past must be rejected. Rather it is to be reappropriated on the ground of the present. This too is part of the poet's dream—a dream not of paradise but of the painful passage from paradise to reality.

Paradoxically, the very success of the frame-dream becomes the main reason why the poem must remain unfinished. The difficulties raised by the first *Hyperion* requires its problems to be internalized. The internalization gives access to refinements of composition and decomposition that simply cannot be worked through within the bolder dispositions of the original fable. But with the poetry of self-formation so authentically written into the context there is little for the fable left to do. This is in itself not a fatal objection. The revisionary reading of the fable brought about by its location in the frame might be a matter of interest even if the fable said nothing that was not in the frame. The difficulties lie in the frame and can be adumbrated by pointing out that "frame" is almost certainly the wrong word.

[46] In Blake's *Milton* a literary figure in the mythologized past has to remake himself in order to enter the creative present. In Keats, the myth involves revolutionary overthrow rather than remaking. The fable Keats chooses makes it extremely difficult to postulate a continuing mythic presence that maintains itself through revolutionary transformations. Internalization makes it possible to combine a transformational view of change with the continuance and constituting of the self through and even because of the transformations. At the same time, internalization preempts the fable not only by transferring it to a psychic theatre, but because self-formation can negotiate the problematics which dynastic supersession is able only to raise.

The poem of self-formation is, in its nature, open. The consolidations it brings about are achieved to be superseded. That which is creative must create itself, but in doing so creates its own obsolescence. Placed in its real time of consciousness, such a poem can slight itself by looking forward even to imaginative closures, to the ultimate retrieval or the final attainment. It establishes its objectives out of its onward movement and the objectives are likely to change as the movement proceeds. It is difficult for such a poem to collect itself around a myth of victory and of deification unless, as in Milton's approaches to the problem, that victory is both internalized and placed at the end of time. One might argue that Keats's myth, unlike Milton's, is revolutionary and that a revolutionary myth, if correctly placed and read, can and should be made to subscribe to the permanent revolution of the advancing consciousness. The argument might hold if psychic politics did not radically question the transformations to which it is made to adjust and if the politics themselves were not subject to revision by the continuing dialogue between the change and the cost.

Keats and Shelley might have written more of their unfinished poems if they had lived longer, but we have to ask ourselves what is achieved by their breaking off where they did. The second *Hyperion* does not even proceed as far as the first did. It stops short of the council of fallen Titans, not to mention the deification of Apollo. Significantly it is entitled *The Fall of Hyperion*. Its emphasis is on the environment of defeat with which the world confronts the cry of the heart. It forces the mind to question that vast shade under the brittle surface of its brightness. As the questioning proceeds, the dream changes and the dream that once was can be seen as the dream of the fanatic or the savage. But the deeper dream survives. Hyperion flares on and the brief glory of his transit, a movement which inscribes its own effacement, is one more event in a poem that can only be written, not concluded. The poem, like the encounter with Moneta it depicts, is that individuation of the common utterance by which the utterance is found and named, at once protected and interrogated. But it is also a poem of self-making, erasing itself even as it inscribes itself. It accepts its own nature by breaking off in mid-sentence.

The dignity of a fragment in a poetry of self-formation lies in its finding its place in a process, in its being justified by its own extinction. It makes the truth instead of returning to it. It contributes to a whole which is neither beginning nor end but only history. The unfinished, in such a view, carries with it no natural citizenship, no whole from which it was disinherited, or from which its incompleteness has been made to proceed. Spenser and Milton can situate their poems on generic contests that lead back to real dichotomies surrendered to settlement at the end of time. Byron writes a poem which is additive and which is cumulative only in its openness. Shelley's question mark is the self-definition of a poem unable to pronounce on its own nature. Keats's doubly unfinished effort, the myth of abandonment he himself abandons, is his testimony to the ongoing poem of the heart. The first *Hyperion* is described as a fragment. The second is described as a dream. It is as if the incomplete and the unreal, submitted to "the giant agony of the world," are provinces which the mind must agree to inhabit in search of whatever understanding it can acquire.

T. S. Eliot: *Mythos, Logos,* and the Design of Accident

LET US BEGIN with what we hope will be a useful simplification. The myth in Eliot is a myth of the search for the word. Having registered this simplification, let us ask ourselves about the probable dispositions of an œuvre in which *mythos* and *logos* are joined in this special manner.

It is apparent, to start with, that a search for the word can be initiated only when there is a premonition that the word exists, or a felt need for its presence, or a felt discontent with what can come to be known as the symptoms of its absence. This is perhaps the most distant periphery from which a search can proceed and it is a periphery on which Eliot's work begins. The œuvre does not launch iself to a clearly defined objective or probe, as Milton's œuvre does, into a constant centre through varying generic strategies.[1] Nevertheless it displays the variety fitting to that classical œuvre it dimly reproduces by proceeding not through genres but through the appropriately diminished presence of gestures evocative of genres. In this sense the ambience of *Prufrock* is comic, that of *Gerontion* tragic and that of *The Waste Land* epic-encyclopedic. The agents of the unfolding utterance are placed in middle age, in old age, and in the case of Tiresias, beyond age. Within the macro-poem it can even be said that the Sweeney poems function as a sub-plot accompanying in their insinuations and frustrations, the movement of the main plot of self-discovery.[2]

---

[1] The view of Milton's œuvre touched on here is more fully expounded in *The Lofty Rhyme*, London, Routledge and Kegan Paul, 1970.

[2] For elaboration of these propositions and for a fuller treatment of the

To suggest this much is already to imply a purposeful-
ness foreign to the tonalities of the first poem in the œuvre,
to its hesitancies and its volubly justified retreats from the
necessities it declines to formulate. Prufrock can begin the
love song which eventually must be sung to Beatrice with
a deflationary dismissal of all those sunsets into which
lovers walk to the accompaniment of sumptuous music.[3]
But the commitment to face reality cannot be long sus-
tained. A tentative effort to ascertain the nature of the
overwhelming question is waved off-stage before it mate-
rializes. The internal rhyme of "tedious" and "insidious"
makes it evident that the past alliance of levity and seri-
ousness is now to be the alliance of boredom and betrayal.[4]
The reproachfully impatient "do not ask 'what is it?' " of-
fers itself as a request not to seek underlining of the ob-
vious, rather than as a warning not to seek clarification of
what is as yet unknown. In its styling the dismissal defines
a discontent significantly short of that promised by the first
lines of the poem in which the magic lantern of a later
image had thrown the nerves of a sickness upon the screen
of the world. Alienation from the environment can be the
first indication that the environment itself is alienated only
if the protesting persona ceases to be a participant in what
he dismisses. Until this severance is made, protest is only
that self-indulgence of self-scrutiny which a civilized world
permits as the proof of its tolerance. Disgust could indeed
be creative if Prufrock were not too urbane for disgust. The
death of the estranged self, its surrender and reconstitution
within reality, could likewise be creative if Gerontion had
the metaphysical courage to advance to that surrender, if

---

interconnections of the Eliot œuvre than is possible here, see *The Over-
whelming Question,* Toronto, University of Toronto Press, 1976.

[3] The etherized patient to whom the sunset is compared reappears in
East Coker III. In *East Coker* IV, "The whole earth is our hospital." Thomas
Browne offers the same suggestion in *Religio Medici,* 11, 2.

[4] Eliot's influential observations on metaphysical wit which draw at-
tention to this alliance are to be found in his 1921 essay on Marvell. *Selected
Essays,* London, Faber and Faber, 1932, pp. 292-304.

he were not trapped in his status as the residual inheritor of beauty lost in terror and terror twisted into inquisition.

Human behaviour begins as mimesis. Falling away from creativeness, it deforms itself into parody. Parody can be, as in Milton, a demonic emulation of a lost world. It can also be a remembrance that has forgotten its origins, that lives on only in the severed and surrogate gesture. Eliot's early poetry is rich in the rituals of debasement: life measured with coffee spoons, the trivialised rhythms of Ecclesiastes and Hesiod, the sacrament dissolved in whispers of anxiety and aimlessness, prophecy devalued into fortune-telling, and love automated into lust. Even the concept of unified sensibility can be mocked. With Donne the intellect was at the tips of the senses. In "The Portrait of a Lady" a Pole playing Chopin to a titillated audience transmits the Preludes through his hair and finger tips. The style of debasement can vary from poem to poem and even within a given poem, but as the debasements gather themselves they begin to articulate a language of loss. A language of loss, however residual and disjointed, is the first step towards a language of reality.

The key turns in the door and turns once only as the mind acknowledges in responding to the thunder's voice in *The Waste Land*. The wording suggests not simply that there was a single turn of the key but, more significantly, that the sound of severance was heard no more than once. The memory of that sound is all that remains to tell us that the life we accept and endorse is imprisonment rather than life. We could call that memory Christian grace or neo-Platonic remembrance. Eliot wisely refrains from doing either. He is not propounding or even dramatizing a structure of beliefs, but inscribing a document of the human journey. The force of that document depends on its demonstration of the disinherited mind at work, achieving its liberation only out of the evidence available to it within the terms of its exile.

The key is a key in another sense. The self must learn to decode itself and in doing so must resist the "civilized" self-analysis which *The Waste Land* offers as a substitute for doubt and in which Eliot's early characters are so intelligently expert. The true decipherment calls for dying into life. To die resolutely away from an illusion accepted as reality by nearly everyone else demands a commitment which must be extracted from the data of a world peopled by those, including even the questioning self, who in their exiled natures will ignore and resist the very understandings that will free them. That Eliot moves with singular skill to the finding of this commitment, and that his definition of our predicament is scrupulously from the inside of that predicament and within the limitations that confinement in it imposes, are judgements which by now discourage questioning.

Since the search for the word has to be conducted in a language which must be increasingly recognized as an impediment to that search, there is a sense in which the poem's object is to find its way around its own betrayals. The formulation of inadequacies must be brought to a point where escape from them is possible because absorption in them is a danger that has been survived. Out of the œuvre's self-scrutiny or out of the ironies of its presentation, a movement of self-discovery must be generated which will sustain the movement of the œuvre to its *telos* and the advancement of its language from talk to speech. The attainment of a discourse replenished by reality establishes the œuvre's previous discourse not as irrelevant, but rather as decentered, as displaced and trivialized by its attachment to substitute centres. The passage through that discourse can therefore be seen as purifying rather than abandoning the tribe's dialect. It can justly remain part of the œuvre's ordering of itself, the achieving of its right to reinstatement.

What are euphemistically described as the difficulties of communication are evident from the beginning in Eliot's macro-poem. Prufrock's repeated "how should I begin?" and his "It is impossible to say just what I mean!," complemented by the conjectured mocking of "That is not what

I meant at all" define a separation of which Sweeney's "I've got to use words when I talk to you" is a more savage rendering. "The Word within a word, unable to speak a word" locates itself in these spaces of frustration. The incarnational paradox was once taken for a wonder. It is now a sign pointing, not to the "impossible union of spheres of existence," but rather to the gulf between the word and its auditors. *Ash-Wednesday* V, playing on the disjunctions between sonic identity and visual difference, laments the chasm it is compelled to register between the still world of eternity and the "still whirled" of change, between the World and the world and between the Word and words. Here as elsewhere, Eliot's poetry turns crucially on the ambiguities of "still," a word that simultaneously suggests both continuation and the transcendence of continuation. The intensities of absence are repeatedly inscribed by the very language that seeks to overcome that absence. It is a paradox which cannot but make vividly evident the distance which must be travelled before the "thousand whispers" of the Word's dissolution can reinstate themselves in that reality of which their own sound remains the saving remembrance.

Talk, as has been suggested, is one thing and speech another. "A fool may talk" says Ben Jonson "but a wise man speaks."[5] Michelangelo spoke, while those in the waste land come and go, talking about him.[6] Speech constitutes

---

[5] "Timber: or Discoveries." *Ben Jonson: The Complete Poems*, ed. George Parfitt, Harmondsworth, Penguin Books, 1975, Appendix 1, p. 430.

[6] In a paper read at the University of Western Ontario, Christopher Ricks rightly questioned the assumption that the talk about Michelangelo in *The Love Song of J. Alfred Prufrock* was obviously trivial. It is possible that Eliot had Jonson's distinction between speech and talk in mind, particularly since *Little Gidding* III affirms that "our concern was speech." Moreover, the previous two lines of *Prufrock* refer to a "hundred visions and revisions/Before the taking of a toast and tea." The trivialization here probably governs the succeeding lines and is conducted into them by the soundlink between "taking" and "talking" and the triple alliteration of "taking," "toast" and "tea."

itself around significances. It purifies the dialect of the tribe[7] to urge it to universality from provinciality, but also to free it from distractions finally seen to be made in the image of Babel. Speech impels us to "urge the mind to aftersight and foresight," and the sequence is surely worth noting. The pattern of things is not rendered in language. It is rather the impelling momentum of the endeavor to achieve a language which urges the mind into the pattern of things.

In this way *mythos* and *logos* are joined. The fable is that of the making of the mind, of the recovery and reconstitution of the true self, and of the ancestral journey, skirting the brink of formlessness, making its way to Eden and to Ithaca. Even this brief specification should be sufficient to indicate that the myth of the search for the Word is not simply a narrative arrangement that is used to organize the poem of the mind. Eliot's account of the mind's journey internalizes some familiar elements of heroic poetry. But the internalization is more than an inert application of inherited practices. It is valid, and perhaps movingly valid, as an account of how consciousness forms and discovers itself. It can be described as mythic in the sense that the movement of finding which it charts is offered for participation rather than justification. The œuvre has to disclose itself as the disinterring of a pattern which the reader recognizes as already inscribed in his own mind. The purpose of the text therefore is not to represent the foundational myth directly but to erect a superstructure which even in its substitutions and avoidances is able to summon the myth from the reader's consciousness.

The myth of the search for the Word, of language seeking the destiny of language, has one distinctive satisfaction to appropriate to itself. That satisfaction can perhaps be outlined as the finding of the Word in all the words that have found it. It is a fulfillment able to confer both historical understanding and individual peace. The aftersight and foresight which speech makes possible join us to that her-

---

[7] The phrase has joint origins in Kipling (via Pound) and Mallarmé.

itage of meaning to which the seeking force of the mind has always been directed. To quote Yeats by way of confirmation, all that the imagination "created, or could create" is made "part of the one history and that the Soul's."[8]

The progress in *Four Quartets* from language as betrayal to language as discovery is well-known and is constitutive of other progresses—from the personal to the public, from experience to doctrine, and from the enclosed garden to the historic community. The loss of Eden and the finding of speech chart a movement that is essentially self-reviewing. The end of the poem is the completed symbol that the poem has succeeded in making of itself, and the poem brings about this completion by advancing itself through progressive acts of self-scrutiny. *Four Quartets* is not the only poem to employ this strategy but it may be the only poem in which the strategy is so deeply part of the nature and meaning of the enterprise. In particular, the alternations between the lyric and discursive oblige the poem to examine its own validity, the extent to which its findings may simply be the redeployment of its own discourse, the manoeuvres of self-defence by which it responds reassuringly to its suitably safeguarded gestures of self-appraisal. The investigation can have many results including as in *East Coker*, the poem's symbolic rejection of its own past. More felicitously, it can result in the final joining of the voice of intelligence with the voice of feeling, not in that brilliantly unified responsiveness with which Eliot credited the Metaphysicals, but rather in harmonious complementarity as "the complete consort dancing together," creating between them the patterns of the mind. Eliot's reiterations and evolutions of phrase and imagery, of which inventories could be made easily in a more spacious chapter, also play their part in charting the progress from talk to speech, from the "thousand whispers" of dissolution to the ordering

---

[8] Balachandra Rajan, *W. B. Yeats. A Critical Introduction*, London, Hutchinson, 1965, p. 90.

force of a true grammar of comprehension. The evolutions return to the place, irradiating it sometimes with the experience of the poem and sometimes, more amply, with the history of the œuvre. Speech depends on retrieval, on the macro-poem's gathering self-knowledge. The œuvre must transform itself if it is to be its own *telos*, if its beginning is to be its end. That it does so even in its evolving nuances is the measure of the œuvre's cohesiveness, the penetration of the text by the myth.

An œuvre the *mythos* of which consists of the search for the word must begin on a periphery of removal appropriate to its time and place. It must advance through a distance that can be measured only by its own self-formative progress. Eliot's œuvre does so through a series of language acts each one of which is designed to define a phase in the advancing consciousness, so as to make possible extrication from the phase and thus to render obsolescent the definition the poem achieves. When the phase becomes obsolescent the language of its definition becomes obsolescent also. It is not repeated in the macro-poem. The classical œuvre is generically differentiated. The Eliot œuvre is differentiated by sometimes quite striking distinctions of style and stance, Laforguean in *Prufrock,* Jacobean in *Gerontion,* radically fragmented in *The Waste Land,* numbingly repetitive in *The Hollow Men,* a style that circles on itself on the winding stair of *Ash-Wednesday,* and that opens itself in *Four Quartets* to the undermining of order by the questioning force of events. These differentiations make it possible to say that every poem is a wholly new start, but it is equally valid to say that every poem is an event in a coherent history which ironically or knowingly necessitates its own future. That history consists of the discarding of the terms of illusion, the ascertaining through its absence that the *logos* must exist, the dying into life to attain the threshold of the Word and the realization in the final section of *Ash-Wednesday,* that the precincts of the *logos* can be attained but not inhabited. *Ash-Wednesday* comes to its end in the

257

cry "Suffer me not to be separated," with the white space between that line and the last line of the poem enacting on the page the alienation from which the voice of the poem asks to be protected. The whole movement acts as a preface to *Four Quartets* which opens a consciousness briefly relieved of its exile to the entire cycle of possession and loss and of recovery made meaningful by that loss. The myth of the search for the Word involves a search that is indefinitely self-renewing.

A search that is self-renewing can never attain the ultimate. Eliot is scrupulous in observing this principle. From the word unable to speak a word in *Gerontion*, we pass to the "unheard unspoken" word of *Ash-Wednesday*. There is a token of the word however, a sign made in a higher dream by a silent sister. We move closer to the threshold in *Marina* where speech is to be resigned for the as yet unspoken speech of "The awakened" with "lips parted." In *The Dry Salvages*, the Incarnation is distanced from us as "The hint half-guessed, the gift half-understood." The "here" of the Incarnation can be contrasted with the "there" of the still point in *Burnt Norton* as an indication that an advance has been made; on the other hand, the difference may merely register the distance between a philosophic concept and an historical reality. In the end we approach the garden of our beginnings, at the frontier, as "the last of earth," the "source of the longest river," the climax of the interior journey. Even at this point the intimations of epiphany are "not known" but "heard, half-heard in the stillness," with the stillness itself no more than the imperilled space between two obliterations, two waves of the sea. "We shall not cease from exploration," an affirmation which seems to engender the mind's happiness out of the unfinishable nature of its search, is the right consequence of this irreducible distance from the threshold.

Interpreted thus, Eliot's œuvre seems a highly cohesive accomplishment remarkable in its fidelity to the abstract diagram. It could be taken as evidence that the mind, free from doctrinal guidances and given over to its own momentum, remains responsive to a logic of attainment which its movement through language both achieves and unfolds. The resemblance to the Areopagitican model is striking though the advance, ironically, is through successive failures—it is education through evasion, until evasion is no longer possible. And finality is not promised at the end of time. The speaking of the word and the possessing of the garden, the macro-poem's theoretical points of closure, are approached to be resiled from in *Ash-Wednesday*, relinquished to be retrieved in *Four Quartets* under conditions which make it bleakly clear that the attainment must be unavoidably open to its own denial. In this way Eliot is able to combine an œuvre that is logocentric in more than one sense with an indeterminacy that persists at its heart. The dramatic terminations—death by drowning in *Prufrock*, by disintegration in *Gerontion*, the exotic redemption through Sanskrit in *The Waste Land*, the Lord's Prayer stuttered in *The Hollow Men*, the cry of the communicant at *Ash-Wednesday*'s receding altar—undermine themselves or extend beyond themselves so that what is never quite spoken must once again be half-heard out of the triviality or the rage of events.

In the environment of indeterminacy *The Waste Land* is a crucial landscape. The opening inversion of expectation tells us not that poetry is full of surprises, but that the stuff of consciousness will not cohere. The maimed metrics speak for a maimed world. Thrice in succession the line is identically fractured at its comma and thrice in succession the generative participle is isolated by the comma at the line's last foot, cut off from the world it should nourish and sustain. There is a pause of exhaustion in the fourth line and then the limping movement resumes, this time with the participle varied as a trisyllable. We are in a world of disjointedness, of the mind seeking its roots beneath the debris of its stony rubbish. Such a mind, if it is to establish its grammar of comprehension, must avoid editing the material of experience. It must place that material before itself in its uninterpreted, disconnected givenness. If the evidence does not make possible the deriving of a grammar, the mind can only proceed to acquire more evidence. The encyclopedic interests of *The Waste Land*—the lateral movement across cultures, the movement backwards and forwards through literary history, and the movement up and down the tones of talk that define the social ladder—are thus placed within the nature of the inquiry itself rather than as a mere means of sustaining the poem's magnitude.

The traveller in *The Waste Land* is a higher version of Burbank with his Baedeker. The mind remembering and ransacking, journeying through its allusions and citations, shuffling its broken images as Eliot imagined John Donne to have done,[9] can only endlessly reconnoitre its own surface. On the other hand, the reader, as the fragments accumulate, can see what Tiresias conspicuously fails to announce. If educated by Cleanth Brooks[10] and others, he can reliably discern what the landscape is declaring. When the thunder makes its judgements, the protagonist presumably attains the same degree of enlightenment as the reader and closure is achieved at the point of coincidence.

However it needs only a slight advance from a new critical education, a slightly different weighting of the enveloping irony, for coincidence not to be achieved. The nominal text can remain stubbornly separated from the implied text upon which it is supposed to converge. The thunder's deliverances can be three more of those fragments that the speaker uses to shore up the ruins of a self that remains unable to set its lands in order. If this is not a possibility to which the poem firmly guides us it is also not a possibility it excludes. We must note that the manuscript treats the line "London Bridge is falling down, falling down, falling down," as a separate paragraph, flinging it into prominence through its isolation and causing it to dominate or at least to confront and oppose the preceding "Shall I at

[9] See the previous chapter, "*Areopagitica* and the Images of Truth."

[10] For Brooks's fine study of *The Waste Land* see *Modern Poetry and the Tradition*, Chapel Hill, University of North Carolina Press, 1939, pp. 136-72.

least set my lands in order?" The disintegrative and integrative energies which jointly characterize the poem's climax are thus placed in contest. The foreign-language quotations are not italicized in this version.[11] In a previous version, the line from *The Spanish Tragedy*, "Why then I'le fit you Hieronimo's mad againe" (also not italicized) had been initially interspersed among these quotations.[12] In the version we know, the line on London Bridge and the line on setting one's lands in order are paragraphed together, minimizing the typographical confrontation that originally prevailed between them. The foreign-language quotations are italicized, seeming to identify them helpfully as the fragments which the speaker is taken as intent on preserving. So far, the evolution has been away from indeterminacy. But to complicate the work of those who wish to chart a clear movement of purgation from ambivalence, the line from *The Spanish Tragedy* has been taken out of its position among the fragments. Moreover, it is not italicized as the other fragments now are. The change of position may therefore also be a change of status. The line now precedes the three Sanskrit injunctions and is on the same typographical footing as those injunctions.

It is possible and perhaps desirable to argue that these final changes consummate the movement from indeterminacy. Hieronimo's madness, we might say, is purposive. Its purposiveness can be confirmed by noting how conspiracy lies in the background of *The Hollow Men*. We feign a disguise in order to escape. Alternatively the escape itself, the reality rather than the disguise, may be seen as madness by the world. To all but those who know otherwise, the Sanskrit injunctions, like other broken images, are part of the cultural debris of the waste land, talismans of significance only to the speaker in his madness. To those who know otherwise, those injunctions are the means of setting

---

[11] *The Waste Land: A Facsimile and Transcript of the Original Draft,* ed. Valerie Eliot, London, Faber and Faber, 1971, pp. 88-89.

[12] Pp. 78-81.

the waste land in order. They provide the basis on which a subsequent voice in *Ash-Wednesday* can say: "This is the land. We have our inheritance."[13]

Nevertheless it is simply not clear how much the speaker knows. The typographical insinuations are, we might think, addressed to the reader by the author. The cry of madness, the desperate hope of meaning in that madness, the incomprehensible Sanskrit, and the double futility of fragments "shored against" ruins, dominate the poem dramatically at its close. In the continuum of the œuvre we know what the poem's future is because of other poems which bring about that future. Seen in itself *The Waste Land* can be considered as stubbornly indeterminate, a text capable of accepting many subsequent texts, including the continuing text of its own futility.

Eliot's work in fact relies strongly on the relationship between local indeterminacy and the continuity of that psychic narrative within which the indeterminacy is placed. The yin of the opening motto in *East Coker* is not superseded by the yang of the reciprocal motto with which the poem concludes.[14] The circle composed by the two mottos sustains itself by consuming itself; it must be perpetually redrawn in order to exist. We can find more than one arrangement in Eliot's work of the mirror-stage implied by this reciprocity. In *Little Gidding*, for example, the interderivation of the engaged components is presented as dramatic rather than syntactic. The poet, assuming a "double part" in the dialogue with himself, meets a "familiar compound ghost." Dissociated from himself in order to be reborn as the enunciating self, he confronts an otherness which is his spectral self, "both intimate and unidentifiable." Those who meet are "too strange to each other for misunderstanding." The poet knows himself and yet is "someone other," and the other remains himself, "a face still forming," notwithstanding the transaction of identi-

---

[13] *Ash-Wednesday*, 11.

[14] The final version is the motto of Mary Queen of Scots.

ties. Yeats similarly calls to the "mysterious one" who will be "most like me being indeed my double" and yet "most unlike, being my anti-self." The stage is thus constituted not by the simple interaction of contraries but by the discovery of the self within the complexities of engagement with an otherness it must both incite into being and resist.[15] Thus in *Ash-Wednesday* separation is the otherness of arrival, denying arrival by its awakened presence and yet reconstituting it through its own growth and waning. In the œuvre, the apertures formed by the individual closures can often be the conduit through which the psychic fable propounds and unfolds itself.

In a 1965 essay I had suggested that Eliot's œuvre was situated on the engagement between the spiral of process and the circle of design.[16] The spiral is not of course a macro-metaphor the application of which Eliot's poetry is alone in inviting. Indeed in a recent essay, M. H. Abrams comments that his own book, *Natural Supernaturalism,* is

---

[15] On this matter see Jacques Lacan, "Le stade du miroir comme formateur de la function de Je," *Ecrits,* Paris, Seuil, 1966, pp. 93-100. Edith Kurzweil observes that the "imaginary" in Lacan forms a "Borromean knot" with "the *real* and the symbolic." "Constituted on the basis of the *specular ego* in the *mirror-stage* it is said to subsume a narcissistic relation to the self, although it can exist only in a dual relation with an Other." *The Age of Structuralism: Levi Strauss to Foucault,* New York, Columbia University Press, 1980, p. 147. It must be remembered that according to Lacan, the mirror-stage is connected with an infantile phase in the development of the psyche and that the fall into language creates a self thereafter ineradicably linguistic yet irreversibly separated from that which it seeks to signify. It can be noted that in Eliot's encounter scene a self apart assumes a "double part," and that both the assumed selves cry "What! are *you* here" in an encounter which both participants recognize as fictive ("Although we were not") even while the originating self seeks its identity within that very encounter. The affinities with Yeats's views on the mask are striking. Yeats's further proposition that "The mirror-scaled serpent is multiplicity" (*Ribh denounces Patrick,* in *Collected Poems,* p. 239) again differentiates time from eternity in a mirror image that both claims connection, concedes division, and admits the confusion between primary and secondary reflections.

[16] "The Overwhelming Question," *T. S. Eliot. The Man and His Work,* ed. Allen Tate, New York, Dell Publishing Co., n.d., pp. 364-81.

"iconic of the spiral form which many Romantic thinkers considered the necessary shape of all intellection."[17] The spiral can be thought of as ascending to finality or as yielding repeatedly to that self-interrogation which remains implanted in its shape. Placed half in light and half in darkness, it can circle through making and unmaking so that the scrutiny of the actual repeatedly revalidates and contests the forms of understanding which the mind puts together. If such a movement is integrated within a myth of the search for the word it must characteristically fall short of and turn away from closure. Within Eliot's scheme, as within Spenser's or Milton's, closure remains subject to indefinite postponement even though the orientation towards closure is what gives the mind's work its significance. All shall be well when the fire of energy is made one with the rose of perfect form, when *telos* and origin unite, when yin and yang declare each other instead of contesting each other. But the *when* is not placed within or even at the end of any time frame. As long as it beckons to us in a future that is perhaps projected rather than promised, declaration will be contestation amid that "wilderness of mirrors" from which the mind seeks to deliver itself while knowing its identity to be constituted by the very struggle which defers that deliverance.[18]

[17] *High Romantic Argument*, ed. Lawrence Lipking, Ithaca, Cornell University Press, 1981, p. 91. Quoted by Wayne Booth.

[18] Two articles by William V. Spanos, "Hermeneutics and Memory: Destroying T. S. Eliot's *Four Quartets*," *Genre*, Winter 1978, pp. 523-74 (hereafter referred to as *FQ*) and "Repetition in *The Waste Land*: A Phenomenological De-Struction," *Boundary II*, 1979, pp. 225-85 (hereafter referred to as *WL*) study the question of openness in Eliot's work. Spanos' essays rest on a distinction between Recollection, which is *telos*-dominated and Repetition, which "becomes a dis-closing of what the circle of Recollection, the habitual expectation of closure, seals off, objectifies and forgets: the be-ing of being, its infinite openness and thus its ultimate unnameability" (*FQ*, p. 534). Thus when we "know the place for the first time" as at the conclusion of *Little Gidding*, what comes to be known "is not presence or even absence, but difference, the infinite deferral of presence, which prevents arrival, a return to absolute origins; and which, put positively, makes time man's element and ceaseless exploration in the

As has been shown, Eliot's œuvre is remarkable in the coherence of its design and in its fidelity to the abstract diagram. That very fidelity obliges us to ask whether we are witnessing the execution of a blueprint, whether the documentary of a mind in self-formation can indeed display this extraordinary purity and elegant freedom from

---

element of time his (saving) activity" (*FQ*, p. 563).

In *The Waste Land* Spanos discerns "two analogous journey-quest archetypes," the fertility mythos and the Grail legend, which seem to prefigure the "predicament and quest" of the seeker in Eliot's poem but which "in their *deconstructed state—as traces—resist* appropriation *as* teleological narratives." There is according to Spanos, an emergent pattern which he describes as a "spiral (recurrent-linear) motion in the circular structural surface of the poem." But this pattern is "not textually privileged. Rather it is discovered below the surface of the destroyed logocentric myths as an emergent and primordial but highly ambiguous continuity in the context of real contradictions, real gaps" (*WL*, p. 244).

Spanos' view of the spiral as a dismissal of circularity and a commitment to openness is in contrast to Abrams' Hegelian view of the same form. His two essays break new ground and rightly question the almost axiomatic status of logocentric readings of Eliot's poetry. As my chapter indicates, I share much with Spanos and at one point I seem to discern even more openness than he does. Spanos argues that in *The Waste Land* the "protagonist's 'final perspective' is not a privileged one" (*WL*, p. 251). I argue that there may be no final perspective. Having said this, I must now resume my true position, which is somewhat to the right of Spanos, and note that I give more weight than he does to the logocentric energies of the œuvre. My chapter attempts, in some detail, to show how these energies consistently fall short of arrival, how they consistently halt at the threshold of an always unspoken word. But I also document in, I hope, convincing detail, the depth and momentum of these logocentric energies. They are sufficiently in being fully to engage and to contest (not close) that openness which Spanos sees as the "primordial" continuity in Eliot's work.

Statements that certain forces in a text have been privileged in previous readings almost always imply that equity will be restored and that democracy will prevail in the reading to be offered. What usually takes place is the privileging of other forces. A fully egalitarian reading of a complex literary text may not be possible, and I am not sure that it is axiomatically to be desired. Counter-privileging, on the other hand, is to be resisted and the most effective way of resisting it is to respond with openness to the contest of forces in a text and to the changing line of settlement between them.

waste. Are we contemplating a spontaneous unfolding or an unfolding edited in the name of art? In an earlier book I had incautiously opined that we were looking at a design too subtle and too organic to be planned and that what we were facing was the artifice of reality. The evidence of *The Waste Land* manuscripts and, more methodically, of Lyndall Gordon's *Eliot's Early Years* suggests that this may not be the case.[19] Gordon's endeavour is to establish the continuity between earlier and later Eliot, a natural and perhaps compulsive critical tendency that is powerfully at work in Donne and in Yeats scholarship. But in showing how Eliot's poetry was religious from the beginning and, in particular, how he was engrossed with certain models of sainthood, Gordon does throw into question the "sincerity" of the movement from secular to religious and out of evasion into understanding. It may be difficult to escape the conclusion that we are considering not the artifice of reality but the superior artifice of art, and that the œuvre corresponds to the diagram with scrupulous fidelity mainly because the infidelities have been edited out of it.

This is a disconcerting but not altogether disappointing conclusion. At least we are facing a truly omniscient author who, over the space of thirty years, relentlessly sculptures a macro-poem according to an aesthetic of mind-formation to which he unswervingly adheres. Such a figure is both intimidating and, perhaps fortunately, improbable. We must retreat to the more moderate assumption that though the author may begin by dictating the nature of the macro-poem, the poem as it establishes its identity also claims an autonomy that is the right of that identity. The author must learn to stand away from it, to be in dialogue with it, to allow it the consequences of its own momentum.

Unfortunately we cannot come to rest even with this third step in a series of controlled retreats. The idea of

[19] Lyndall Gordon, *Eliot's Early Years*, New York, Oxford University Press, 1978.

negotiation between an author and his œuvre is certainly one which ought to be pursued in criticism. It is doubtful and it would probably be unfortunate if an œuvre of major dimensions were to unfold without such negotiations. But a plan subject to modification in performance is still a plan. An authorial intention that is responsive to feedback from its actualization still suggests a degree of deliberation which the facts of this particular case may not justify.

Looking at the manuscripts of *The Waste Land* and *Four Quartets* an unsympathetic critic might say that the former work was composed by a committee and that the latter evolved out of an exchange of letters. A sympathetic critic would underline Eliot's sense of responsibility to his colleagues and to his public, his continuing awareness that our concern is speech. In these exchanges the poet is nearly invisible even if he does not quite reduce himself to the ideal status of a fold in language. We may therefore be more accurate when we speak of an authorship rather than an author. It is notable that none of the changes to which this authorship consents reflect any planning of the œuvre or even the consciousness that there is an œuvre to be planned.[20] The decisions are stylistic, almost uniformly concerned with the proper paring and pointing of the language. If *Gerontion* is not made part of *The Waste Land* and if an epigraph from Conrad's *Heart of Darkness* is deferred from *The Waste Land* to *The Hollow Men*, there to be replaced by another epigraph from the same story, the reasons have

[20] For the manuscripts of *Four Quartets* see Helen Gardner, *The Composition of Four Quartets*, Oxford, The Clarendon Press, 1978.

Eliot's references to the importance of the œuvre in distinguishing major from minor accomplishment begin to be prominent only in the thirties. See "John Ford," *Selected Essays*, p. 203; *The Spectator* CXLVII, 1932, pp. 360-61 (on Herbert); "W. B. Yeats," *On Poetry and Poets*, London, Faber and Faber, 1957, pp. 252-62; "What is Minor Poetry," *On Poetry and Poets*, pp. 49-50; "George Herbert," *British Writers and their Work*, ed. J. W. Robinson, Lincoln, University of Nebraska Press, 1964, p. 63; *James Joyce: Sa Vie, Son Œuvre, Son Rayonnement*, ed. Bernard Gheerbrant, Paris, La Hune, 1949, no pagination.

little to do with the regulated unfolding of the macro-poem though critics, including myself, have argued for them in that light. I do not wholly regret having so argued. The text can reasonably be read as what its embedded patterns make it into even though the critic tracing those patterns and according them shaping privileges will seem to resemble Barthes's paranoid reader. If, as the result of the exercise, the critic rather than the authorship emerges not as omniscient, but as the aspiring spokesman of the œuvre's implicit wisdom, that result is not out of keeping with the legitimate hopes of the discipline.[21]

It is difficult to escape the conclusion that accident played a prominent if not a dominant part in the designing of Eliot's macro-poem, that it is not the unedited chronicle of a mind in self-formation nor that edited and purified chronicle which might be the artistic rendering of such a mind. Stylistic decisions can have life-questioning consequences. The entanglements of Jacobean rhetoric in *Gerontion* are potent in conducting us through a world of self-betrayal. The arresting juxtapositions of *The Waste Land*, its insistent paring away of connectives, offer the broken images of the mind seeking itself on the kaleidoscopic surface of its language. The numbing repetitiveness of *The Hollow Men* incarnates a dance of futility which shapes the manner in

---

[21] In "The Frontiers of Criticism" (*On Poetry and Poets*, p. 113), Eliot comments wryly on "the lemon-squeezer school of criticism" and the extortions of meaning it is able to wring from his poetry. But he also affirms that "the meaning is what the poem means to different sensitive readers" and considers dangerous the assumption that a valid interpretation of a poem "is necessarily an account of what the author consciously or unconsciously was trying to do."

In referring to the œuvre's implicit wisdom I do not seek to suggest that the critic should be as invisible as the author, that he should be transparent to a work which then speaks for itself between the two invisibilities. How we read is a matter of our situatedness, but it is also a matter of discerning and answering the otherness of a work whose claim to address that situatedness has already been recognized in our engagement with it.

which the participants comprehend even the nature of deliverance from that dance. Yet these differentiated languages may have been chosen because of the excitement of involvement with their challenges rather than as vehicles for prior understandings about the self and reality. The consequences generated by these languages could have been fitted into the wisdom of the œuvre, directing its movement and helping to shape its sequence of discovery. Style may be the key to comprehension rather than its medium.[22]

If stylistic choices bring the œuvre into being, what are the forces that guide us to its qualified closure? We might imagine that after attaining a threshold in self-formation the œuvre would inscribe itself by the momentum of its own logic. The author would stand aside from the gathering coherence, effaced by the achievement of his language. The true story, or the story as Eliot chooses to tell it, was that *Burnt Norton* evolved from certain leftover lines from *Murder in the Cathedral*. Five years after these surplus lines had been fabricated into a poem, Eliot wrote another poem, *East Coker*, and began to see the prospects for the Quartets as an entity.[23] Even at this point it remained un-

[22] Technique as discovery is one reason *The Waste Land* is both a stylistic manual for the twenties and the delineation of an authentic landscape. The finding power of language has been stressed earlier in this chapter. Such propositions can lead to a view of language as founding rather than finding, or to a more pessimistic view of language as an unbreakable constraint, a barrier that proclaims to us the impossibility of a metalanguage, or to a revelatory disclosure in which the divine bestows upon the human a language of access which it also authenticates. The point is that the drafts show no indication of reflection on the objectives of the finding power.

[23] *New York Times Book Review*, 29 November, 1953. Reprinted in *T. S. Eliot: Four Quartets*, ed. Bernard Bergonzi, London, Macmillan, 1969, p. 24. It is actually *The Family Reunion* rather than *Murder in the Cathedral* to which *Burnt Notion* most strongly attaches itself. Eliot's account of how *The Waste Land* notes came into being ("The Frontiers of Criticism," *On Poetry and Poets*, pp. 109-110) is yet another acknowledgement of the place of accident in his œuvre.

certain whether the number was to be four or three. The arrangement of *Collected Poems 1909-1935* confirms Eliot's statement by its presentation of *Burnt Norton* virtually as a postscript, following upon "Ariel Poems," "Unfinished Poems," "Minor Poems," and choruses from a collective work, *The Rock*. In the quiet of a Gloucestershire house and its formal garden the diminuendo of the œuvre was to take place, not with the eschatological splendours of *The Faerie Queene's* disappearance, but gently disturbing the dust on a bowl of rose-leaves. Circumstances made it otherwise. A macro-poem as intricately put together as any in the language, began and ended amid the design of accidents.

Ezra Pound and
the Logocentric Survival

AFTER *The Faerie Queene*, *The Cantos* is the longest unfinished poem in English. The centuries in between make the long poem more intractable, make it wrestle more strenuously with its fore-conceit and proclaim itself more emphatically as the inquisitor of intention. To study not *The Cantos* but, more restrictively, the unfinished nature of *The Cantos* is an enterprise that deserves a book. A monograph would be confusingly insufficient. A brief chapter such as this at least dismisses that confusion by adequately proclaiming its own inadequacy.

Like Spenser's poem Pound's is unfinished. It too surrounds itself with promises of pattern which it does not renounce but also does not fulfill. Like Byron's poem it is accompanied by different propositions about its nature, though these propositions attach themselves not to inherited genres, but to inherited fables of finding. Spenser's epic appeared before its public in three instalments spaced over nineteen years. Pound's master-work took more than a half-century to unfold, gather, and dissipate itself. History changed while the poem containing history was being written. The mind steering the poem changed in the long course of its Odyssean journey. Like Spenser, Pound is a colleague of both the winged steed and the wandering muses, keeping purposiveness in dialogue with deferral as Calidore does in Spenser's last complete book. Deferral is indeed a notable Poundian strategy, with *periplum* taking the place of Ariostan errancy, with the lack of an "Aquinas

271

map"[1] justifying accretions to the geography of under-
standing and with assurances that the poem's obscurities
will clarify themselves when closure is attained, justifying
indefinite postponements of that closure.[2] Like Spenser,
Pound ends his work with fragments. As with Keats and
Shelley, the poem arrests itself in mid-passage. No other
conclusion seems fitting in a poem which so fully com-
passes all that the mind can span in its deed of life.

Pound's fables of finding are for the most part announced
outside the poem. They have thus the status of authorial
intentions adjusted either to the obstinacies of the text or
to the opportunities offered by its unfolding. The fictions
are the Odyssean repossession of Ithaca, the Dantean as-
cent up the ladder of understanding, the tale of the tribe,
the poem containing history, and the detective story with
Usura as the criminal.[3] All these fictions promise discovery

[1] Letter to Herbert Creekmore of February 1939. *The Letters of Ezra Pound
1907-1941*, ed. D. D. Paige, New York, Harcourt, Brace and World, 1950,
p. 323. See also George Dekker, *Sailing after Knowledge: The Cantos of Ezra
Pound*, London, Routledge and Kegan Paul, 1963, pp. 201-02. It is notable
that periplum, in which the errancy is the result of navigation without
an Aquinas map, is not mentioned until the fifty-ninth Canto. The naming
of deferral is itself deferred.

[2] "Perhaps as the poem goes on I shall be able to make various things
clearer" is Pound's hope in a letter of 8 July, 1922 to Felix E. Schelling
(*Letters*, p. 80). A letter of January 15, 1934 to Sarah Jenkins Cope (pp.
250-51) insists that foreign languages do not make the poem difficult. In
April 1937 Pound writes to John Lackay Brown (*ibid.*, p. 293) that when
he gets to the end the "pattern *ought* to be discoverable" and that his task
is "*finally* to get all the necessary notes into the text itself." The Letter of
February 1939 to Creekmore suggests that any difficulties in the poem
arise from "condensation to maximum extent attainable" rather than from
intentional obscurity. When *The Cantos* are finished all foreign words in
them "will be underlinings not necessary to the sense."

[3] For the Dantean fiction see *Ezra Pound: A Critical Anthology*, ed. J. P.
Sullivan, Harmondsworth, Penguin Books, 1970, pp. 199, 278-79. For
the tale of the tribe see *Guide to Kulchur*, New York, New Directions, 1938,
p. 194. For the poem including history see *Literary Essays*, New York,
New Directions, 1954, p. 86. For the detective story see Pound's 1961
interview with D. G. Bridson (*Ezra Pound: A Critical Anthology*, p. 277).

and closure. The land will be cleansed, the barbarians of the mind will be identified and expelled, the villain will be unmasked and rendered harmless, as the rock-drill drives home the nature of the truth, and the wanderings of the tribe will both define and lead it to its inheritance. History will be seen as a mirror for lawgivers and, as we ascend the ladder of understanding, more and more of the actual will be held in the field of relationship. Other unifications proposed—that *The Cantos* are advice to a prince or (in Pearlman's persuasive adaptation of the Dantean figure) that they constitute a spiral ascent winding its way through the transformations of time—are similarly firm in their promises.[4]

The contesting of closure by forces within the poem that inhibit closure or question its possibility is not unique to Pound and has been the subject of this book from Spenser onwards. The mixed-genre poem has as its potential and even natural consequence the questioning of the poem's pattern by its method. But in Pound the drive to unification is opposed for the first time by a text that is continuously fragmented, the verbal surface of which is a dramatic and prolonged disavowal of the very structures it is supposed to establish. The claims of that surface are indeed so dominant that the promises of pattern must be either driven to the poem's rim or suggested by the author outside the poem's boundaries.

The method of *The Cantos* is of course, the most distinctive achievement of the Pound era. One of its purposes is to suspend placing in time, in order to constitute that simultaneous present of which Pound speaks in *The Spirit of Romance* and of which Eliot speaks some years later in "Tra-

---

For the school-book for princes see Canto LIV. Denis Donoghue (*The Ordinary Universe*, London, Faber and Faber, 1968, p. 292) regards this as the "central concern" of *The Cantos*.

[4] Daniel D. Pearlman, *The Barb of Time*, New York, Oxford University Press, 1969.

dition and the Individual Talent."[5] More significantly for us, the method impedes propulsion to an ending—the narrative propulsion of plot, the didactic propulsion of poetry that has a palpable design upon us, and the logical propulsion of argument. The method promises the minimizing of management. To manage is to petrify, to arrange the givenness of things within the matrix of an interpretation. The author's guidance must therefore be erased from the poem in order to be reborn as the reader's privilege. The facts must be allowed to speak for themselves, to establish their true politics in carefully silent exchanges with each other which the reader must learn to hear and to remember. "All knowledge" Pound tells us "is built up from a rain of factual atoms."[6] Actuality must demonstrate its own will to cohere.

The idealization offered in the last paragraph may seem alluring but it is probably too risky to be practised unreservedly. Moreover, its unregulated practice would result not in a poem but in an outpouring of consciousness. Pound is not lacking in designs upon us, and his pedagogical disposition is strongly brought out in Kenner's interesting comparison of him to Ben Jonson.[7] It is not a deconstructive intelligence which defines *logopeia* as "the dance of the intellect among words."[8] The moral voice is heard often and sometimes heard shrilly in *The Cantos*. Nevertheless the self-assembly of fragments into the Aquinas map of which we have been deprived is more than a large-scale rhetorical device. It is a proper strategy for the disinherited

---

[5] "It is dawn at Jerusalem while midnight hovers above the Pillars of Hercules. All ages are contemporaneous." *The Spirit of Romance*, London, J. M. Dent, 1910, p. 8. T. S. Eliot, "Tradition and the Individual Talent," *Selected Essays*, London, Faber and Faber, 1934, pp. 14-15.

[6] *Guide to Kulchur*, p. 98.

[7] Hugh Kenner, ed., *Seventeenth-Century Poetry: The Schools of Donne and Jonson*, New York, Holt, Rinehart and Winston, 1964, pp. xxix-xxx.

[8] "How to Read," *Literary Essays*, p. 25. Pound considers that Eliot surpasses him in *logopeia* but that he excels Eliot in *melopeia*. "A Visiting Card," *Selected Prose*, New York, New Directions, 1973, p. 321.

consciousness, for the poem of the mind seeking its roots. Even in the seventeenth century, Donne, despite his vigilant reconnaissance of the hill of truth, finally knows it only through its resistance. Pound's reader three centuries later in the history of things falling apart, must voyage across the strange seas of himself, learning the shape of the shoreline empirically as it rises out of the horizon in its suddenness.

There is excitement in a poem delivered from sequential constraints, a poem audaciously heterogeneous, that follows the mind in its charting of itself and yet is not devoured by its own miscellaneity. The fable of the cultural fall is still influential; those in exile from the whole must begin with fragments, and through the accumulation of fragments attain the suppressed language of discourse among them. The forms of understanding must be achieved and not intoned. To bring about this achievement the inherited forms of literature must be approached with suspicion as managerial devices which curb the actual in its creative strangeness, reducing it to the boredom of the predictable.[9] Indeed, Pound's placing of poetry at a threshold at which it emerges from sculpture or music into language indicates the importance of retrieving the unmediated experience before it is made subject to the distortions inherent in conventional language. The ideogram to which Pound was so committed can be thought of as precisely positioned on this threshold, the point at which the visual passes into the linguistic.[10]

[9] The aim of the ideogrammic method, according to Pound, is to move the poem "off the dead and desensitized surface of the reader's mind, onto a part that will register." *Guide to Kulchur*, p. 51. Pound may have profited (though he probably did not) from Shelley's statement (*Defence*, p. 159) that poetry "creates anew the universe, after it has been annihilated in our minds by the recurrence of impressions blunted by reiteration."

[10] In his essay on Vorticism (*Fortnightly Review*, Vol. 96, 1914; reprinted in *A Critical Anthology*, pp. 46-57) Pound distinguishes between lyric poetry, which "seems as if it were just bursting into speech," and imagistic poetry, where painting or sculpture "seems as if it were 'just coming over

The poetry of fragments seeking each other has evident fascinations as a mode of modernity. *The Waste Land* and *The Cantos* share this language. But Eliot's poem defines a landscape in order to pass beyond it. The language act in achieving formulation, also attains the boundary of deliverance. Eliot's point is finally that the fragments will not cohere, that the meaning cannot be found but only bestowed. Pound either has more faith in the secular intelligence or is less disposed to make the religious submission. He remains stubbornly committed to a style Eliot was never again to practise. It is one of the costs of writing a long poem that one must remain true to its beginnings, to the announcements that initiate us into a distinctive language from which thereafter it is disloyal to diverge. Milton's modulation from a baroque hell to Michael's bare edifications is a more difficult transition than is commonly supposed. With Pound, the half-century of composition holds him not only to a way of writing but to a view of how the mind comes to know, of which the way of writing is the vehicle. It is a productive but also a dangerous bondage.

Despite his fragmentary method, Pound's imagination is resolutely holistic. Indeed it can be said that the quality of his imagination maximizes the contest between method and objective. Even at the end of *The Cantos*, as the poet faces the triumph of the fragment, a "rush light" remains, not to illuminate the surrounding darkness, but to "lead back" to the "splendour" of the one.[11] "*A work of art, any*

into speech.' " In an essay on the later Yeats, Pound describes the two sorts of poetry he finds most poetic as the kind which "seems as if sculpture and painting were just forced or forcing itself into words." *Literary Essays*, p. 380. Shelley observes (*A Defence of Poetry*, p. 124) that "every original language near to its source is itself the chaos of a cyclic poem." It is the proximity of primary creativeness to this "chaos" which "threshold" and "crossover" poetics seem concerned to retrieve.

[11] Canto 116. The word "splendour" is used (though not invariably) to translate a neo-Platonic concept (*Enneads* VI.9.4.). It is so used in Stephen Mackenna's translation, which Yeats admired (*Letters*, ed. Allan Wade, London, Macmillan, 1955, p. 715, p. 719; *A Vision*, London, Macmillan,

serious work," Pound insisted in 1935 *"vivifies a man's total perception of relations."*[12] In the crucial essay on Cavalcanti when Pound commends "Mediterranean sanity" (with asides on Hinduism that put in doubt his own acquisition of that sanity) his emphasis is upon the inherence of form, the rose that the "magnet makes in the iron filings," the "plant brain" filled with "a persistent notion of pattern from which only cataclysm or a Burbank can shake it." The intellect in Pound's "radiant world" is not at the tips of the senses as it is in Eliot's potentially synaesthetic Eden. There is a hard boundary between the reading of Spinoza and the smell of an egg cooking. "Thought has its demarcation" and "one thought cuts through another with clean edge," as sky, shore, and sea are distinguished in the Mediterranean clarity.[13] The firm outline and the unmistakable boundary are necessary if the relationship across them is to be drawn with exactness.

The form of the fragment, the rose that exists in the filings, is thus characterised by clean internal outlines, abutments made possible by the erasure of transitions. The

---

1937, p. 20) and which was brought out by Pound's publisher, Faber and Faber. At the end of his translation of Sophocles' *Trachiniae* (London, Neville Spearman, 1956; Norfolk New Directions, 1957) Pound prints the phrase SPLENDOUR/IT ALL COHERES in capitals and adds in a footnote that "This is the key phrase, for which the play exists." For further discussion see Michael Bernstein, *The Tale of the Tribe: Ezra Pound and the Modern Verse Epic*, Princeton, Princeton University Press, 1980, pp. 86-92.

[12] "History and Ignorance," *Selected Prose*, p. 268.

[13] *Literary Essays*, pp. 154-55. See also *Guide to Kulchur*, p. 152. The rose in the steel dust appears at the end of Canto 74, where it is linked to the passage over Lethe into the pain of the world. "So light is the urging, so ordered the dark petals of iron." The pun upon "light" suggests both its reality and its distance, and the ordering of the dark petals the will to form which cannot be annihilated even by that distance.

Although Pound observes significantly that "Eliot would recognize, I imagine, a greater influence of Lanman and Woods, his professors of Sanskrit, than the superficial influence of the French Poets" (*Selected Prose*, p. 319). Hinduism does not figure either prominently or positively in his detection of the principles underlying culture.

277

conventional tissue of connectiveness, which Pound's method eliminates, substitutes abstract for inherent form. We see according to stereotyped configurations and not in accordance with the true coherence of givenness.[14]

The prospects held out by such a poetics can be exhilarating but they involve an act of faith in the fragment, in its stubborn affirmation of a natural citizenship, that may not be justified by the fragment's actual behaviour. Pound can organize his fragments, and the confident movements across time and cultural space can declare the universal in the particular without the need for expository intervention. The facts can seem to bring themselves together, to generate and sustain their own cohesion. It can even be said that the fragment seeks relationship and that when conventional relationships are shorn away, the effect is to engage the reader more fully with the poem by assigning him the responsibility of joining the fragment to its implicit destiny. But the fragment can be rebellious as well as disinherited. Out of its separation it can challenge the very structures it is supposed to seek. Its alienation invests it with autonomy and, even in the politics of poetics, autonomy is half-way to independence.[15]

A further difficulty created by the method is that it assumes a stubbornly logocentric reader, unwavering in his pursuit of the hidden design, who far from being deterred

[14] As Herbert Schneidau observes, "if the texture is made smooth the details cannot stand out sharply." *Ezra Pound: The Image and the Real*, Baton Rouge, Louisiana State University Press, 1969, p. 170. On the other hand as William Chace observes: "By emphasizing the degree to which 'real poetry' consists of precisely shaped 'gists' and piths, and by relying so strongly on Imagistic methods, Pound indirectly deprived himself of a unifying principle that might have framed his crystalline fragments." *The Political Identities of Ezra Pound and T. S. Eliot*, Stanford, Stanford University Press, 1973, p. 37.

[15] In *A Visiting Card* Pound describes the ideogrammic method as the accumulation of concrete examples: "these facts, possibly small, but gristly and resilient, that can't be squashed, that insist upon being taken into consideration," *A Critical Anthology*, p. 193.

by the multitudinous discontinuities of the poem's surface is provoked by those very discontinuities into seeking that which their gathering weight denies. A reader as heroic as this is not inconceivable though he is in amusing contrast to that impervious reader who must have the message of *The Cantos* hammered home by the rock-drill.[16] Nevertheless the obstacles to a holistic reading of *The Cantos* are formidable. They assume not only an indomitable capacity to build connections across the poem's polyglot, spectacularly disjointed surface but also a capacity to assay that surface as a negative, partial, or true exemplification of the principles by which the surface is agitated.[17] The poem then must be constructed, or more specifically, its text must be interleaved, out of a spectrum of readings ranging from the literal to the heavily ironic. Since the poem, by its minimizing of connectives, has largely deprived itself of its capacity to give the reader instructions, the instabilities latent in this requirement are correspondingly magnified. The accumulation of significances thus offers itself to more than one reading strategy and to more than one disposition of stresses and balances even within a single strategy. Among the possibilities the poem does not exclude, that of drifting with its surface, of "giving in" to the poem's flow of consciousness rather than countering that flow with the holistic dedication, may come to seem the most attractive.

Though acknowledgements are now increasingly being made to a poetics of indeterminacy, the form of a poem is still seen by many critics as contingent on its closure. A

[16] The jacket of *Thrones* (New York, New Directions, 1959) states in its advertisement of the previous volume that "the truth must be hammered home by reiteration, with the insistence of a rock-drill." According to Pound *Rock-Drill* was intended to imply the necessary resistance in getting a certain main thesis across—hammering." Interview with Donald Hall, *Paris Review,* no. 28, 1962, p. 49.

[17] Although *The Cantos* requires the participation of the reader to an extraordinary extent, the reader's role seems to be limited to decoding the poem's sub-surface intentionality. A resistant or a sceptical reader is not envisaged.

work which postpones closure by deferral or resists it by divisions within itself must promise it as finality, discover it as origin, or accept it in the Marvellian manner, as the best of different worlds, none of them satisfactory. Thus Walter Jackson Bate in beginning a discussion of *The Fall of Hyperion* observes that the poem is "only a fragment" and that "twentieth-century formalism, with its hunger for intricate neatness, is automatically impatient before the incomplete."[18] Twentieth-century formalism was left some distance behind in the decade after the appearance of Bate's book and certainly no recent essay on *The Fall of Hyperion* has expressed impatience with its fragmentary character. Nevertheless Frank Kermode, whom one might expect to be open to non-closure, is found observing sixteen years after Bate, that "we are all fulfillment men, pleromatists."[19] The ranks of fulfillment men must have been growing thinner even as Kermode made this remark. Fredric Jameson is surely characterizing the current temper more accurately when he writes of "the ideological climate of a contemporary American 'pluralism' with its unexamined valorization of the open." The excitement of indeterminacy is by now part of the new horizon or, better still, of our reluctance to see horizons. Nevertheless it may still be too early to announce the extinction of the breed of pleromatists and to raise as the banner of the decade, Adorno's proposition that "the whole is the false."[20] The fascination of the unfinished may be precisely that it both incites closure and

[18] Walter Jackson Bate, *Keats*, Cambridge, Mass., Harvard University Press, 1964, p. 392.

[19] Frank Kermode, *The Genesis of Secrecy*, Cambridge, Mass., Harvard University Press, 1979, p. 72.

[20] Fredric Jameson, *The Political Unconscious. Narrative as a Socially Symbolic Act*, Ithaca, Cornell University Press, 1981, p. 31. Theodor Adorno, *Minima Moralia*, trans. E. N. Jephcott, London, NLB, 1974, p. 50. "The task of art today is to bring chaos into order" (p. 222) is a more militant rendering of the adversary status claimed by Adorno's book. The book is a counter-text pitting itself against a previously existent text much in the manner of Blake's *Marriage of Heaven and Hell*.

resists it, that to bring it to a conclusion is both desirable, given its commitments, and inappropriate, given its procedures. In saying this we are retrieving the whole truth of Adorno's statement which was not put forward in order to stand alone but rather to live in engagement with the Hegelian statement to which it is the antithesis. We are also characterizing Pound's *Cantos*.

The unfinished stands for many things in the mind. It symbolizes the resistance of the medium, reminding us that the conquests achieved by form are only partial. The actual may consent to fictive management but only within a dialogue in which it remains free to resume its rights. The work of art is a limitation of givenness, conceded in order to be superseded, or to be placed in engagement with other limitations. The unfinished is also a sign of process, its open-endedness an admission of its obsolescence, of the formulation dismissed by that which it makes possible, even as it attains the threshold of definition. The unfinished can be a submission to extinction or a surrender to plenitude. Like the torso, it can suggest but not prescribe the shape of completion, by projecting into that shape the internal relationships already established by its nucleus. It can excite the mind with potentiality while declining to quieten it with closure. An unfinished work insists on its own future.

Pound's poem participates in more than one of these felicities and in its contest between pattern and procedure it vivifies the Spenserian contest between purposiveness and errancy. Pound's voyager, however, is more threatened than Spenser's knight though he, like his predecessor, begins "in the middest," with the flow of givenness and the meaning it discloses or defers. The new voyager charts his course between islands, the floating reminders of what may once have been a continent. As he confronts each island's language he must find the logic of discourse among them, or find perhaps, how the stubborn forms resist the incursions of logic. In 1934 Pound defined the epic as "a poem including history." Elsewhere it was "a poem containing history."[21] The single word that is changed speaks of a work increasingly undermined by its contents, increasingly engaged with the resistance within itself.

The confrontation in Pound is not simply between the holistic commitment and the resolutely fragmentary method. It is also between the interior and the public mode, the meditative and the didactic, the poem of consciousness and the poem containing history. No other poem is partitioned by a line that is firmer or more emphatic, or that is more decisive in proclaiming the need for engagement across its internal frontier. Pound's predilection for the hard boundary ought to strengthen our awareness that his own commitments proceed from different realms. The Odyssean voyager and the Dantean climber of the spiral stairway are both figures of consciousness. The instructor of the prince, the spokesman of the tribe, and the architect of the poem containing history address a collectivity and speak on its behalf. These different renderings of the poem's contest with itself remain present in our apprehension of its overall effect. Too many readings of *The Cantos* situate themselves on one side or another of its internal watershed. It is tempting to withdraw from Pound's politics and to proclaim *The Cantos* as a poem of consciousness. It is equally tempting to argue that the poem's intimidating and partly private erudition is a means of arriving at and authenticating a finally public statement. In each case the area about which we have misgivings is retracted into the area we prefer. The reality is that, as in other poems of contestation including those by Spenser and Milton, *The Cantos* are situated not on either array in this series of engagements, but on the thin line of the engagement itself. It is the fascination of both ranges of possibility and the impropriety of either a choice or a permanent settlement between them that jus-

[21] *Make it New*, London, Faber and Faber, 1934, p. 86. Interview with Donald Hall, *Paris Review*, 1962.

tifies the poem's unfinished status as a sign of its identity rather than of its failings.

To say that no final settlement is attainable is not to say that no settlement is attempted. It is the forms of contestation and the forces of reconciliation that endow an unfinished work with its distinctiveness. In Pound's poetics, "luminous detail" finds its public counterpart in Frobenius' *Kulturmorphologie*.[22] *Paideuma*, which Pound defines as "the mental formation, the inherited habits of thought, the conditionings, aptitudes of a given race or time" occupies territory on both sides of the boundary.[23] The fragment is the natural unit of consciousness but in its unprocessed immediacy it is also the raw material out of which "scientific" propositions about history and society must be built. The emancipation from time and space which characterizes the floating syntax of consciousness also characterizes those constant principles which actual societies can be seen as deviating from or seeking to exemplify. We can object to each of these equivalences and in particular, we should question the givenness of the fragment by pointing out the extent to which it may be sculptured. As a heterocosm it

[22] The importance of Frobenius is heavily urged by Pound, notably in his *Guide to Kulchur*. His statement that all the basic characteristics of a civilization can be discerned in its representative artifacts lends itself to the view that the fragment, properly chosen, implies the whole. Adorno also states that the whole can be true only "if the force of the whole is absorbed into the knowledge of the particular," a requirement he obviously views with some scepticism; *Prisms*, Cambridge, Mass., M.I.T. Press, 1981, p. 62. There is of course, a difference between arguing that particulars subscribe to a structure and arguing that the entire structure can be found reflected in the right particularity.

[23] *Selected Prose*, p. 148. Frobenius, according to Pound, uses the term for "the tangle or complex of the inrooted ideas of any period." *Guide to Kulchur*, p. 57. Pound proposes to use it "for the gristly roots of ideas that are in action." See n. 15, where "gristly and resilient facts" are associated with the "ideogrammic method." The language seems committed both to resisting overall structures and to the proclamation of those structures. We can reply that only the wrong structure is resisted but, as indicated elsewhere, resistance itself can be self-perpetuating.

can be designed to exhibit precisely those relationships the reader is supposed to derive from the uninterpreted evidence. It can predetermine the nature of discovery. However, some element of illusion-making is unavoidable in the artifice of a poem. There must be admiration for the way in which structures are built out of units which seem, at least superficially, anti-structural. They appear to be built, moreover, by natural cohesion rather than as a result of the integument of argument. The contents of consciousness, its unimpeded coalescences, appear to set principles of ordering before us which can be thought of as the laws of both self and society.

Thus *The Cantos* builds connections across the divisions which are so deeply part of it, maximizing the contest between pattern and flow and then undermining its own disjunctions by the integrative trend in its poetics. For those who believe that the poetics of a long poem should be the attempted answer to as well as the posing of its problematics, *The Cantos* represents the kind of sustained risk-taking which ought to accompany major achievement. Nevertheless, a poem that is both divisive and integrative in its procedures faces difficulties it may be unable to resolve or can resolve only by collapsing itself into one part of itself. These difficulties are compounded by the special obduracies which a poem containing history must confront.

Spenser's poem contains history by keeping it at an allegorical distance allowing it only a controlled presence behind the fictive foreground. The intermittent refractions do not call for a theory of history; they suggest rather the extent to which contemporary events can be made to fall within the prismatic capabilities of the poem's world of glass.[24] Milton contains history by prescribing its containment within a providential poem, not subject to necessity or chance. The poem is open by virtue of its continuing adjustment of supernal grace to human sinfulness, but it

[24] *FQ*, III, 2, 19.

is not so open that it ceases to be a poem. It allows its creative power to be contested but it does so in the hope that its basic assumptions will be ratified rather than overthrown. Pound's commitment to immediacy cannot allow him, as with Spenser, the protections of distance, or the tactful insulations of obliquity. It also cannot allow him, as with Milton, the transcendental rectification, the divine rescue of the imperilled aesthetic. As the spokesman of a stubborn secularism Pound must show us the pattern in the evidence, the rose not at the apex of vision but striving to form itself in the iron filings. "We had the experience but missed the meaning" is Eliot's finding on the rim of a bleak world to which there is "no end but addition."[25] The meaning can be only bestowed, not discovered, and the approach to it alters the nature of the experience. For Pound's indomitable secularism the only meaning is that which the voyager wrests from experience, from its shifting seas, and from its yielding of a shoreline that has to be both discovered and remembered.

Pound's poem containing history has to contain it as history. The literary simulation of scientific method, the unmediated presentation of the nuclei of consciousness, the accumulation of facts and the profusion of documents make it difficult to suspend disbelief on the poem's presence. Its economics and politics would matter less if they could be avoided more easily or if they could more confidently be placed among the poem's intellectual fictions, the assumptions that are necessary in order to inhabit its world. Unfortunately the poem's propositions require to be taken literally and to disagree with them may be to dismiss that area of *The Cantos* which cannot be freed from its dependence on those propositions. Once again this necessity drives us into the familiar reading strategy of collapsing the poem into what we consider to be its better part.

[25] *The Dry Salvages*, Section II.

Nevertheless it is not possible to dismiss the poem's public and doctrinal face. To do so is to acknowledge that the work is defeated by the very forces that proclaim its identity. The contention between those forces can be formidable and Pound's own critical prose can be expressive of their powerful disjunctions. "From the time of Queen Anne," he tells us, "the prevailing tone of the better British observers has been one of disgust."[26] Nevertheless "an epic cannot be written against the grain of its time; the prophet or the satirist may hold himself aloof from his time or run counter to it but the writer of epos must voice the general heart."[27] The neo-Platonic *nous* is described with incomparable eloquence as "mind, apart from any man's individual mind—the sea crystalline and enduring—the bright as it were molten glass that envelops us, full of light."[28] Yet the light that surrounds us all is ignored by nearly all of us. A modern Eleusis may be possible "in the wilds of a man's mind only."[29] Across this disjunction floats the defiant cry "Le Paradis n'est pas artificiel" rising from the destitution of the "Pisan Cantos." The city of Dioce can still be built and that news is to be conveyed to the Possum, Eliot, with a bang and not a whimper.[30] This is not quite the stance of the "stunned observer" as William Chace would have it. It is rather a stance that links itself to Yeats's "heroic cry in the midst of despair."[31] It may well be true that in the "Pisan Cantos" Pound fully enters "a world he had for years been building" and that that world is "at once lyrical, decomposed and solipsistic."[32] But it is not the whole world of *The Cantos*. "For forty years" Pound observes with some asperity in 1944, "I have schooled myself not to write the economic history of the U.S. or any

---

[26] *Guide to Kulchur*, p. 284.
[27] *The Spirit of Romance*, p. 216.
[28] *Guide to Kulchur*, p. 44.
[29] *Ibid.*, p. 294.
[30] Canto 74.
[31] *The Letters of W. B. Yeats*, p. 837.
[32] *The Political Identities of Ezra Pound and T. S. Eliot*, p. 105.

other country, but to write an epic poem which begins 'In the Dark Forest,' crosses the Purgatory of human error and ends in the light.''[33] The irony is that in not writing the economic history of the United States Pound has actually rewritten a considerable amount of it. He must integrate this account with a poem of the self's journey, sometimes as a spokesman of the tribe but more often and more dominantly as an exile at its margins. It is for all practical purposes an impossible undertaking, but *The Cantos* finds itself in its sustained endurance of this impossibility.

"It is perfectly obvious," Pound tell us, "that art hangs between chaos on one side and mechanics on the other."[34] *The Cantos* hangs between a public aspect which in its simplicities of causation approaches the mechanistic, and a world which while not chaos can be evoked into order only by being internalized. *The Cantos* navigates towards but does not take refuge in this extreme. If the poem's many intimations of epiphany remain authentic it is because they are not achieved by ascent into the privileged world of the transcendent or by withdrawal into the privileged and protected world of the interior. Pound's "magic moments" proclaim not an ideal but a norm, those primary and persistent rhythms of createdness with which the self and the social order must remain in harmony.[35] Pound's translation of these rhythms into economic and social practices may

[33] "An Introduction to the Economic Nature of the United States." Quoted in *A Critical Anthology*, p. 199. It is notable that Pound speaks of error, not evil, and that he locates error in a purgatory where it can presumably be shed by the aspiration to understanding.

[34] Quoted by T. S. Eliot in "Ezra Pound: His Metric and Poetry." *To Criticize the Critic*, London, Faber and Faber, 1965, p. 171.

[35] Pound's magic moments are not mystic moments. In *Guide to Kulchur* (p. 223) he distinguishes between two kinds of mysticism—one benevolent and the other destructive. In the "Prolegomenon" he writes for *Exile* in the autumn of 1927 (*Selected Prose*, p. 216) he is less charitable: "Many mystics do not even aim at the principle of good; they seek merely establishment of a parasitic relationship with the unknown." As early as 1912 Pound had noted in "The Wisdom of Poetry (*Selected Prose*, p. 361) that the poet in ages of doubt was "the final agnostic."

be more than debatable and after *The Pisan Cantos* even the possibility of a translation may be in doubt. Nevertheless it is translation, not dissociation, which must remain the objective to which human intelligence ought to be dedicated. A poem apprenticed to this necessity has an honourable place among the endeavours of our time.

From a poem containing history one hopes for a theory of history. Spenser does not offer one but his poem, as we have noted, seeks to contain history not by locating it in a structure, but by positioning it in an allegorical hinterland from which it is intermittently brought forward. Even so, its presence in the poem's world questions that world to such an extent as to contribute strongly to the poem's resistance to closure. In *Paradise Lost* the theory that is strenuously advanced is not merely part of the poem's inclusiveness but is essential to the preservation of its claims. Milton's theory of history is in fact its containment, the only means by which the ravaging force of history can be accounted for and held within the dimensions of literature. Even then the poem must invoke the larger security of a providential poem which omniscience designs and omnipotence directs. Pound's Dantean scheme is not so much a theory as an arrangement, a spatial-moral allocation of events. Chronology is rightly ignored so that history can be characterized, so that we can give due attention to its salient features rather than to its successions. "We do *NOT* know the past in chronological sequence. It may be convenient to lay it out anesthetized on the table with dates pasted on here and there, but what we know we know by ripples and spirals, eddying out from us and from our own time."[36] At the same time "Literature that tries to avoid the consideration of first causes remains silly bric-a-brac"[37] and in typical Poundian fashion, the synchronic disposition, superficially proceeding away from causality, must be in

[36] *Guide to Kulchur*, p. 60.
[37] *Selected Prose*, p. 272.

fact all the more decisive in its detection of history's shap-
ing forces. An analysis of causation would seem at first to
offer a prospective theory of history, but Pound's view of
causality is either a matter of his special brand of economics
or a matter of the failure of men to live according to Con-
fucian principles to whose validity history is considered to
testify. "Your generation," Pound writes confidently to Sarah
Jenkins Cope, "has yet to learn how much of life can be
cured by a very simple application of economic sense of
reality."[38] More aggressively, Pound suggests that any
Western work of art can probably be dated, "by reference
to the ethical estimate of usury prevalent at the time of the
work's composition."[39] The effect of the rate of interest on
the manner of painting may not be immediately clear but
Pound is quick to enlighten us: "the greater the component
of tolerance for usury the more blobby and messy the work
of art."[40]

These remarks may serve to remind us that Pound's un-
derstanding of causality can be narrow but a fuller and
more prudently balanced analysis would only push the
question further back. We still have to ask why destructive
choices are so frequently made by societies which seem
capable of choosing otherwise. Kung may write on the bo
leaves that "If a man have not order Within him/He can
not spread order about him,"[41] but we have to learn why
the failure to order the self seems a chronic obduracy rather
than an individual recalcitrance. Even the finding that there
are "two forces in history, one that divides, shatters and

[38] Letter of April 22, 1934. *Letters*, p. 257.

[39] *Selected Prose*, p. 76.

[40] *Ibid.* Pound was apparently impressed by this connection. See *Guide
to Kulchur* p. 27, p. 42, and *Selected Prose*, p. 323. The decrying of blobbiness
and messiness go back to the commitment to clean outline among the
Imagists. However, Yeats as early as 1906 had expressed a preference for
"clean outline" against outlines "blurred with desire and vague regret."
The Variorum Edition of the Poems of W. B. Yeats, ed. Peter Allt and Russell
K. Alspach, London, Macmillan, 1957, p. 849.

[41] Canto 13.

kills, and one that contemplates the unity of the mystery"[42] does not provide us with the basis for a theory of history. It only invites us to arrange events in a series of zones distanced from an ideal centre according to the mixture of the forces. We still have to understand what makes the mixture what it is. It is not simply ignorance which impedes our pursuit of the good, and there has been more than one attempt to define entrapments more powerful than ignorance, either within the self, within the nature of collectivities, or within the impersonal processes by which history can be considered to be driven onward. Pound seeks a poem of the erected wit which makes insufficient allowance for the infected will, or for other forms of compulsion by which we may be tragically dominated.

The lack of a true theory is one more reason for *The Cantos'* remaining unfinished. A theory moves towards argumentative closure, annexing to that closure the facts which support it and the facts to which it can be accommodated. An organization remains open; since it is basically a placing of facts it is not threatened, as a theory is, by the entry of new facts; it is also not advanced towards closure by them. It would be excessive to say that *The Cantos* is an organization of this simplified kind but the additive momentum is apparent in the poem as it is in *Don Juan*[43] and the simulacrum of wholeness which the coalescing fragments are supposed to invoke becomes increasingly subject not to a force of realization but rather to one of deferral. If the holistic energies of the poem urge it to closure, the many contestations of that energy we have outlined urge it to openness, and the discontinuous, resolutely fragmentary procedure remains uniquely powerful in maintaining the rhythms of openness. The crisis the poem undergoes in *The Pisan Cantos* contributes to the strength of resistance to

[42] *A Visiting Card,* London, Peter Russell, 1952, p. 7.

[43] The deleted opening to the second Canto which Pound subsequently reinstates (see note 45) promises a poem strikingly similar to Virginia Woolf's description of *Don Juan.*

closure. Much must be reconsidered and the poem's re-lationship to its own past renegotiated. Moreover *The Pisan Cantos* do not, as is sometimes supposed, endow an interior realm with special and shaping privileges. They merely intensify the contest between interior and public codes, a contest which has always been inherent in the poem but which its holistic commitments are now no longer able to reconcile.[44]

The final reasons for *The Cantos'* remaining unfinished are the implacable logistics of a long poem composed over two generations. The rain of factual atoms from which knowledge is built up becomes a different rain falling from a different sky.[45] Another war is fought to make war im-possible. Mass communications bring the world to our doorstep while the loneliness of the individual intensifies within the global village. The proliferating technologies we have invented erect and proclaim the stereotypes to which we must conform and by which, if necessary, we are to be re-invented. The capacity of the human race for destruc-tiveness multiplies a billionfold. In the contagion of living it becomes harder to think of the *nous* as a conditioning clarity by which all of us are creatively enveloped. It is easier to think of the fragment and its shifting coalescences

---

[44] A concise account of the leading ideas in Pound's view of history is provided by Clark Emery, *Ideas into Action: A Study of Pound's Cantos*, University of Miami Press, 1958, pp. 29-30. The best examination of the unfinished nature of *The Cantos* is provided by Michael Bernstein, *The Tale of the Tribe*, pp. 115-26.

[45] When Pound observes (remembering T. E. Hulme) that "all a man ever *thought* would go onto a half sheet of notepaper. The rest is appli-cation and elaboration" ("A Visiting Card," *Selected Prose*, p. 328) he may seem to be questioning the self-revisionary nature of the long poem. But Pound also says (Canto 74) that philosophy is not for young men because "their generalities cannot be born from a sufficient phalanx of particulars." He is aware of the intractabilities of the long poem: "It can do no harm to stop an hour or so and consider the number of very important chunks of world-literature in which form, major form, is remarkable mainly for its absence." *Literary Essays*, p. 394.

not as the forerunner of a whole that is yet to be, but as that unavoidably intermittent coming together on which, for the time being, the life of the poem may stand. Among these many changes the most crucial may be the change in the man who set his mind to the poem's beginning. He begins in confidence and ends with his errors about him, the drifting wreckage on that drifting sea on which Eliot's voyager finds no end but addition. He grows half a century older in a world more marked by threatening transformations than any through which previous travellers have passed. He is imprisoned, arraigned, and isolated. If he is able to avoid his exile from his own poem it is only by accepting that resistance to wholeness which has characterized the poem from the beginning. That acceptance gives him his tenancy of the now unnegotiable space between the poem's public and interior worlds.

Three among Pound's allusions to Eliot seem to mark out decisive stages in the movement of *The Cantos*. The eighth Canto begins with the line, "These fragments I have shelved (shored) against my ruins." Eliot's word is in parentheses. Pound's word replaces it as if to suggest the real meaning of the statement and to promise that his own poem will move forward from the defeatism, the turning away from the building of the just city, that Eliot's statement is taken to declare. In the first of *The Pisan Cantos*, history has demystified itself to the extent of stripping away its promises, but even against its brutal destitution the announcement of the building of Dioce is made with a bang and not a whimper, with the phrase repeated as if to underline the continuing reality of the claim. Paradise is not fictive, not hallucinatory. It remains in being but the intimations of it are jagged and splintered like the fragments which compose Pound's units of significance, fragments beyond which the poem can no longer advance. This is the way the world ends but in its stubborn survivals it is also the way in which catastrophe cannot end it. In the one hundred and tenth Canto Pound returns to the fragments "shored" from time's wreckage or as the next line puts it, "these fragments shored against ruin." The repeated "shored" suggests that the poet is reaccrediting in dejection the word which his own optimism had once confidently erased. But the omission of the "my" in Eliot's original and in Pound's earlier line raises a crucial indeterminacy, all the more evocative because Pound's phrase is a fragment of a previous text which was itself put forward as a salvaging of fragments. Are the fragments now to be regarded as shored against a ruined self? Or are they shored against a surrounding ruin by being appropriated to that hunger for form within the self, that persisting lucency which remains the prospective ground of their reinstatement? *The Cantos* testifies to the strength of both possibilities. Perhaps it is most adequate to conclude that in saying farewell to a poem which more than any work in history represents its author's persistent deed of life, Pound simply relinquishes the poem to its flow. He had invoked it into order as fully as he could. He gives it back now to what it always was. The final parts of the poem are appropriately titled "Drafts and Fragments," and as George Kearns observes, it "is no longer a poem at all; it is a 'record,' a 'palimpsest,' a 'tangle of works,' 'my notes.' "[46] The palimpsest is used by De Quincey as an image of the mind's inability to obliterate its own history.[47] Despite Derrida's characteristic reservations about its "definitive unfinishedness"[48] the pal-

---

[46] George Kearns, *Guide to Ezra Pound's Selected Cantos*, New Brunswick, Rutgers University Press, 1980, pp. 265-66. It might be noted that Pound in his Foreword to the *Selected Cantos* (London, Faber and Faber, 1967) quotes a deleted beginning to an early draft of the second Canto as "the best introduction" to his poem. That the best introduction should consist of a passage long erased and now reinstated, not in the poem, but in a foreword to it, is a gesture typical of the provisional status Pound sought to attach to his work. Through the many years of the poem's gestation the first thirty Cantos continued to be entitled "A Draft."

[47] "The Palimpsest of the Human Brain," *Suspiria de Profundis*. First published in *Blackwood's Magazine*, March, 1845.

[48] "LIVING ON: Border Lines," *Deconstruction and Criticism*, p. 137.

impsest also serves as an image of erasure, for *The Cantos* as the rewriting of itself, the continuing undoing of knowledge by the endeavour to attain that knowledge. As with Spenser, the poem must be brought to the vanishing point but this time it is made to die away not by the promise of that ultimate coherence which follows the ultimate deferral, but by the withdrawal of the form-making power from its materials. The poem is surrendered not to the encompassing, fully-ordered plenitude of its destiny, but to the unceasing flow which was its origin. The rush light of the last lines is the final dwindling, but a dwindling which remains obstinately connected to that inclusive understanding which it cannot cease to promise. Entering the "acorn of light" is a further example of this microscopy. The individual journey of discovery is dwarfed even in relation to that small seed out of which the huge structure of understanding must grow. The magnitude of the task is emphasized but so is its inevitability, its fitting place in the rhythms of nature and change. Thus the apparent admission of defeat in "I cannot make it cohere" does not suggest that the will to coherence has been a delusion, but rather that it is to be inherited by others whose creative trust will be to exercise it. The will remains part of the nature of things as does the fragmentariness which that will contests. A poem poised on the engagement of these two forces is a proper end to our study of the unfinished.

Afterword

IN MOVING THROUGH examples of the unfinished ranging from Spenser to Pound it is possible to detect a line of continuity. The unfinished is maintained by Spenser as an aesthetic necessity through the engagement between purposiveness and errancy, between closure and the deferral of closure. Deferral can attest to the plenitude of createdness; it can also attest to the intractability of the actual. Finally, it can argue that true closure is the privilege of a supreme fiction to which lesser fictions must consent to remain open. The extraordinary opening encounter of *The Faerie Queene* in which not simply Error, but Error and all its progeny, are exterminated or exterminate themselves in one brief battle with the Redcrosse knight places the end of the poem in its delusive beginning. The over-conclusiveness obliges us to question every subsequent finality and so to acclimatize ourselves over the long course of Spenser's romance to a poetry which, though not relinquishing finality, nevertheless places it beyond the poem's horizon.

Deferral saves us from relinquishment, and if the just city cannot be built in history, it can be built out of history or notwithstanding history, prefigured in the minds of the elect. Pound, who is no lover of Milton, is drawn to this possibility but it is Milton who, in the line of succession from Spenser, converts the Spenserian engagement of genres into the literary basis of his theory of history. "History may be servitude. History may be freedom"[1] Eliot observes with what may seem irreproachable platitudinousness. For

---

[1] *Little Gidding*, III.

295

Milton the question mark implicit in the observation stands over the openness of the future, a future which the divine poem must contain. In Browne's Calvinist poetics the divine poem has already been written; it exists inviolably in its fore-conceit.

> . . . that terrible terme, *Predestination*, which hath troubled so many weake heads to conceive, and the wisest to explaine, is in respect to God no prescious determination of our estates to come, but a definitive blast of his will already fulfilled, and at the instant that he first decreed it; for to his eternitie which is indivisible, and altogether, the last Trumpe is already sounded, the reprobates in the flame and the blessed in Abraham's bosome.[2]

In Milton's more uncertain universe the divine poem is similarly not subject to necessity or chance (VII, 172-73), to that "hasard" from which the symbolist poem sought to protect itself, including, in the end, the hazards of misreading.[3] Nevertheless, remaining free from hazard, it must successfully enclose the hazard of human freedom. It must truly be a poem containing history without prejudice to its maintenance as a poem. The language of the poem is written by its human actors. The outcome of that language, its relationship to what it finally signifies, remains withheld

---

[2] *Religio Medici* 1, II. Text cited from *Sir Thomas Browne: The Major Works*, ed. C. A. Patrides, Harmondsworth, Penguin Books, 1977, pp. 72-73.

Glanvill's account of the providential poem provides for a more benign relationship of containment to content.

> There is an exact *Geometrical Justice* that runs through the Universe and is interwoven in the *contexture* of things. . . . It supposeth him [God] from everlasting ages to have *foreseen* all *future* occurrences and so wonderfully to have seen and constituted the great *machina* of the *World*, that the *infinite* variety of *motions* therein should effect nothing but what is his *eternal wisdom* he had considered *fit* and *decorous*. *Lux Orientalis*, 1662, pp. 97-98.

[3] See Wylie Sypher, *Literature and Technology*, New York, Random House (Vintage Books), 1971, pp. 20-28 for "hasard" and the symbolist poem.

from those actors, to be announced at the end of time, or by controlled disclosures in time which open themselves but only partly, to the nature of the ending.

Byron's *Don Juan*, the hardest to place of all the poems studied, negotiates the contest of genres by drawing attention to the comedy of that contest. While making commitments to purposiveness and errancy, the poem makes them in a mocking confusion of claims about itself which in the end precludes the dominance of any claim. Byron reminds us that we live in a world which is not particularly poetic and which remains accessible to poetry only because a poetic voice talks continuously in it and declines to be silenced. We could say that *Don Juan* takes its stand on the fragment, that it is a calculated anti-Bildungsroman in which a person is what survives or what is put together by the episodes through which that person fortuitously passes. Life is a chronicle, not a history. Its meaning lies only in the mind's commentary on those random events which have composed it and from which it has rescued itself. Byron's indifference to wholeness can be read as a decisive step away from the Spenserian deferral of wholeness by a poem which can only be harmonized beyond time, or the Miltonic enclosure by wholeness of a poem increasingly threatened by its contents. We could say more if even this much were not pretentious according to the decorum of Byron's poem.

The Triumph of Life bases itself on the primacy of the fragment with an intensity not subject to the moderations of comedy. The light that does not enlighten, the bewilderment of givenness, the limited disclosure with its truncated finality, its vivid authenticity and its sheer resistance to interpretation, suggest that there may be no answer but to live in engagement with what we cannot change and do not know. Since the disclosure is so deeply divided within itself, none of the strategies for controlling itself which it offers can overcome its undecidability. Any strategy must be seen as a partisan recommendation on one side or another of that undecidability.

Keats can enter his subscriptions to the grand march of intellect, to Apollonian management, and to the undeviating advance of passion and endeavour. But the poetry of the second *Hyperion* situates itself on the exactions of a process of change that is transformational rather than revisionary, that erases rather than reconsiders its own past. The givenness of deprivation is the here and now of the fragment. The whole that justifies the part, or more correctly, the end that justifies the erasure of all that has led up to it, is not denied but also cannot be extrapolated from the characteristics of that phase of attainment which the fragment represents. The cost of transformational change is real. The consequence is on a horizon, yet to be incarnated, known only by the price that has been paid to make it possible. Like the work of his other Romantic colleagues, Keats's two poems seem to be marked by a disengagement of the fragment from the whole, by an indifference to the strategies of deferral or retrieval which reconcile the overall design to local intractability and by a commitment to undecidability as a vehicle of understanding rather than as a range of disturbances by which understanding is undermined.

Against this history Eliot and Pound appear as literary conservatives. Eliot indeed is almost neo-classical in his meticulously sculptured poetry of retrieval, in his devotion to the Areopagitican model, exemplified not as the progressive finding of truth, but rather as the progressive exhaustion of error. Since his search begins on a suitably distant periphery, Eliot's concern is with the notations of absence, but the purpose of the notations is not to mourn a departed force of integration (as Donne does with Elizabeth Drury) but rather to establish that a departure has taken place. Because of this departure the evidence cannot be made to cohere without the intervention of something beyond the evidence. Eliot's treatment of the spiral of process as the translation into time of the circle of design not only testifies to the absent whole but enables that whole to be continuously enacted by the very nature of the endeavour to reach it. "The detail of the pattern is movement" and the fragment, fully known and finally placed, no longer "caught in the form of limitation,"[4] will make evident its finding of itself in the completion which it has always invited. This is the characterization the work invites and achieves; it does not exclude another characterization inherent in the ambiguous figure of the spiral which can be seen as eluding the circle even as it translates it. We seek finality, but the ways in which finality offers itself to our seeking remain subject to the eroding force of the river within us. That the river is within us and the sea all about us is a fact whose depths are admitted by Eliot's poetry even while it strives to overcome that admission by a hunger for pattern which runs fully as deep in its nature.

Pound can be regarded as more resolutely experimental than Eliot or as the prisoner of a single experiment, a mind committed to the fascination of Eliot's *Waste Land* phase. *The Waste Land* is a deeply indeterminate document and not simply because there are at least two ways of reading its ending, each at least as plausible as the other; it is also indeterminate because it defines a state of consciousness capable of accepting any text, including that text of radical scepticism which proclaims the impossibility of a text. A mind dedicated to developing the *Waste Land* method could move into a poetry of profound undecidability. It is of course a nice critical exercise to determine how close to chaos undecidability can proceed if it is to retain poetic status.

Pound's fragments are more denuded of connectives than Eliot's and possibly more resistant to decipherment. Nevertheless the accumulation of fragments that is *The Cantos* insists on as well as contests an overall reading. "I gather

[4] *Burnt Norton,* V.

the limbs of Osiris" is the title of an early grouping of Pound's prose,[5] a title that recalls, perhaps unintentionally, the Areopagitican model of truth-attainment. "I cannot make it cohere" is a cry which would not have its impact if it did not come after fifty years and more than one hundred and ten cantos in which the will to achieve coherence has been tirelessly exercised. Pound's passion for finding the rose in the steel dust makes the fragment significant and the detail luminous only in so far as they lead us to the whole. The difference between Pound and Eliot is that Pound does not conduct us to a brink where we can admit the necessity of a transcendental rescue. That the principles of experience lie latent in experience and are accessible to the search for knowledge are articles of faith which Pound does not abjure. But the faith is radically questioned by a method which seems unerringly chosen to provide the maximum possible resistance to its objective. The poem's interior dissensions are strengthened by its persisting confrontation of the lyric and the didactic, the personal and the public— a confrontation which mirrors and modernizes the contest of genres in Spenser and Milton. These many engagements which the poem can neither eliminate nor arbitrate constitute its indeterminacy and give that indeterminacy its literary justification.

In a notable recent book, Marjorie Perloff detects a tradition of undecidability that descends from Rimbaud to such writers as Pound, Stein, Ashbery, and Beckett, and that is in contrast to the high modernism of writers such as Eliot.[6] As this book indicates, the roots of undecidability go back considerably further. We have undecidability in the engagement of genres in Spenser and Milton and in the larger contentions that engagement invokes. In Shelley's last poem the undecidability is in the nature of the

[5] *Selected Prose*, p. 21.

[6] *The Poetics of Indeterminacy: Rimbaud to Cage*, Princeton, Princeton University Press, 1981.

given and in its resistance to interpretation. In Keats the undecidability lies in the interim nature of the fragment, its openness to supersession by that for which it prepares but cannot foresee. It is true that Perloff is specifically concerned with undecidability embedded in the fabric of discourse, but such undecidability is a natural evolutionary movement of the history this book has sought to outline.

Definitions of undecidability can vary, but one plausible definition would treat a poem as undecidable when it is equally accessible to contesting codes. On this basis, several of the poems studied in this book must be regarded as undecidable. A more extreme kind of undecidability is implied by Barthes when he tells us that the "interrupted flow of the new poetic language initiates a discontinuous Nature which is revealed only piecemeal . . . modern poetry is a poetry of the object. In it, Nature becomes a fragmented space, made of objects solitary and terrible, because the links between them are only potential. Nobody chooses them for a privileged meaning." We can conclude though Barthes does not say this, that because these "potential links" are multifarious and thus accessible to several codes, they remain fragile and shifting, imperilled even in their coalescences. In classical writing, on the other hand, "words are abstracted as much as possible in the interest of relationships." A word "is hardly the sign of a thing, but rather the means of conveying a connection."[7] Binary engagements as has been shown in this book, dispute this connection to the extent of obliging it to be submitted to deferral. Nevertheless, deferral initially remains dominated by the promise of a single code beyond time. The subsequent diminution of this promise is the natural consequence of the passing of a world-view in which the single code is transcendentally guaranteed. Although the secularization of the sacred and the internalizing of the heroic

[7] *Writing Degree Zero*, trans. Annette Lavers and Colin Smith, New York, Hill and Wang, 1977, pp. 49-50.

are able, uneasily, to reaffirm this promise, they can do so only within the vulnerabilities of fictions which, being self-generated, are open at all points to self-interrogation. The historical momentum of the movement we have charted is therefore towards intensified undecidability. *The Triumph of Life* serves to illustrate this intensification since, paradoxically, it is equally accessible to several codes by being equally resistant to all of them. Pound's place in this continuum is problematical. The contest he sets up between the whole and the fragment is the most fundamental version possible of the classic forms of contestation studied earlier in this book. But the submission of the contest to deferral—that which classically separates the unfinished from the defeated—rests on the proposition, by now questionable, that the single code is the deep language of the fragment. Notwithstanding its determined drive to unification the poem must remain a strong example of Barthes' geography of the discontinuous—islands of actualization separated by the huge spaces of multivalent potentiality.

The unfinished is resistance to closure carried to the extent of denying closure. There are less extreme forms of resistance which the opening essay on Marvell has sought to outline. An œuvre which like Eliot's is developmentally continuous in its unfolding of a psychic narrative can re-open that which has apparently concluded. In a poetry of stances such as that practised by Donne and Yeats the decisive closure a stance invites may have to be placed in relationship to other stances elsewhere in the œuvre. Closure is often brought about by exclusion and a poem thus closed can take various attitudes to its potential interrogation by that which it excludes.[8] A text may solicit a counter-

---

[8] The most fundamental interplay of stances is between reality seen as "a single being" and reality seen as a "congeries of beings," perceptions which must, according to Yeats, "alternate in our emotion and in history." Reconciliation of these two perceptions is not possible since "human reason" is "subject always to one or the other." The mind here does not seem to be situated on the line of engagement between contending prin-

text within the œuvre but also from the reader. Indeed, the reader's response can continue a poem that is formally closed and can even be guided in doing so by forces within the poem's containment. Such arrangements, or invitations, become more effective with poems circulated in manuscript to a restricted and identifiable audience. Some of Donne's poems may invite such tactics, and the hyperbole that constitutes the little room that is an everywhere may be vulnerable precisely when it is most resounding. The security of the room may well be questioned by the inflation needed to protect it.[9]

The unfinished poems studied in this book resist closure or give themselves to openness, often through patterns of contestation, generic and substantial, which move forward on the poem's own momentum to a point where they can no longer be resolved. To make the poem other than self-defeating, closure can be assigned to an enveloping form which legitimizes the poem's openness by placing that openness in the closed field of the providential work. The coincidence of beginning and end, of origin and objective, can be characteristics governing movement in this field so that deferral becomes not a statement of frustration but the admission of a more complex containment in which the

---

ciples. It draws the line by its alternating occupancy of, or vacillation between, those principles. It is obliged to assume a stance to declare itself; but its declaration must remain open to the counter-stance constituted by what it is required to exclude. "Could these two impulses, one as much a part of the truth as the other, be reconciled, or if one or the other could prevail, all life would cease." "Pages from a Diary Written in Nineteen Hundred and Thirty," *Explorations*, London, Macmillan, 1962, p. 305. It should be noted that the earlier Yeats is able to make more Coleridgean statements on balance and reconciliation. See, e.g., "Poetry and Tradition," *Essays and Introductions*, p. 255.

[9] In Herbert, the extension beyond closure arises from a labyrinthine main text's being overthrown in the last lines of the poem by a sub-text whose decisive simplicity authenticates it as the true text. The reader must then reconsider the overthrown text and its generation of its own subversion after the poem has nominally ended. "Affliction 1," "The Pearl," "The Collar," and "Redemption" are examples of this tactic.

poem can participate only by relinquishing its own claim to closure.[10] The abandonment of this model does not eradicate the needs to which it testifies. Instead, the abandonment opens the way to the recognition of other macro-, meta-, and infra-structures—the poem of consciousness, the otherness of unconsciousness and the absent structure of the political unconscious—to which the responsibility for closure can be assigned.[11] Enveloping form can be replaced by emergent form or by a causative form, the evidence for which is found to lie not in the poem's integrative effort, but in the very rifts and discontinuities which gather in subversion of that effort.

Both in surrenders to the divine poem and in penetrations of secular alternatives such as those we have cited— the attempts to posit or interrogate Demogorgon's nature— the underlying impetus is the valorizing of closure. It seems inevitable that this valorization should be contested by a counter-valorization of openness, particularly when the institutional forces of closure and containment are seen as threatening rather than reassuring over the range of our economic and social relationships.[12] The text as repression,

---

[10] It might be noted that in Gnostic myth, Wisdom is the first pleromatist and that the creation *cum* fall is the result of eagerness to learn the secrets of the pleroma. Yet Wisdom is also the last pleromatist instructing us in that transcendence of creation which brings about its absorption in the pleroma. The analogy with that kind of literary work which both betrays and retrieves its own intention need not be laboured.

[11] It should be evident from the subsequent paragraphs of this Afterword that in making this statement I am by no means dismissing the possibility of a political unconscious.

[12] Jameson's pointing (with justification) to the unexamined valorization of openness (*The Political Unconscious*, p. 31) obliges us to point to the hitherto equally unexamined valorization of closure. With the two claims contesting each other, a different and important viewpoint is offered to us for the appraisal of many major works. We may express this hope without prejudice to the background recognition that the contest itself remains open to study as a critical fiction that may be historically dependent. Historical relativism does not necessarily dismiss the fictions it places. Moreover, it is not clear that a historical study can be conducted from a vantage point exempt from the relativity it professes to detect.

the text as a cover-up which investigative reporting lays bare, the endeavour to understand as exposed to betrayal by its elected language are, among other things, refractions in critical theory of situations by now too familiar to be underlined.

In pointing to these relationships the attempt (at this stage) is not to suggest a sociology of literary forms, or of the critical fictions which govern our reading of these forms. The relationship of a fiction to shaping forces which it both disguises and recognizes can be much more complex than straightforward parallelism and can depend heavily on tactics of compensation and evasion identifiable only by discriminating study of the fiction's pattern of admissions and disclosures. The endeavour in this book is limited to indicating what the new critical fictions make available and to arguing that the habitual prestige accorded to closure has inhibited consideration of the varieties of openness. With the removal of these inhibitions it becomes possible to see the dissensions in a text as opportunities rather than frustrations—not as defeating the logocentric claim but as requiring that claim to accept negotiation with forces of interrogation and resistance which it is no longer possible not to recognize. The result may not be settlement but it will be continuation—the continuation of a debate in which the forces engaged can define and evolve themselves only through their engagement with each other.

Barbara Herrnstein Smith's fine and instructive book is obviously among the provocations for this study. I do not intend to contest her work to the extent of maintaining that there is no such thing as closure. It should be apparent, however, that resistance to closure is a persistent fact in literature and may be nearly as persistent as closure itself.[13]

---

[13] *Poetic Closure*, Chicago, University of Chicago Press, 1968. See especially "Coda: Beyond Closure," pp. 260-71. The view offered is that up to the present, "anti-closure" has been "repeatedly seen as an impulse, not a reality" (p. 261). The understandings offered by my book are also in contrast to the following remarks by M. M. Bakhtin: "There is no place in the epic world for any openendedness, indecision, indeterminacy.

I shall refrain from arguing that resistance to closure lies in the nature of language, which is obliged to dismantle what it formulates, or in the nature of consciousness, which is obliged to undermine what it constitutes. This book does not seek to make ultimate statements though it may provide the material for such statements.

Nevertheless, to speak of the form of the unfinished is to make certain claims, or to request acknowledgment of forces in the work that constitute order as much as they or other forces deny it. The view taken is that the work has borders, that it is not subject to uncontrolled dissemination or to dissolution in its intertextuality, and that it is able to demand some measure of answerability from the tissue of texts that might conceivably be its reader. Language is not the blind fury that unfailingly slits the thin-spun life of the work. The constitution of the work is a constitution that is dialogic and not a decomposition brought about by a range of undecidables which binary arrangements must either evade or suppress. The poems we have studied address their own subversions and though they clearly cannot overcome those subversions they remain in debate with that which they cannot unify. They are given form by the styling and drama of that debate.

It can be objected that the drama is all too predictable, substituting binary for unitary organization and thus subscribing to an allegedly enlightened conservatism that regressively seeks to preserve new critical appearances by accommodating them to their less radical subversions. The

---

There are no loopholes in it through which we glimpse the future; it suffices unto itself, neither supposing any continuation nor requiring it." *The Dialogic Imagination*, Austin and London, University of Texas Press, 1981, p. 16. It can be argued that the epic is only an early phase of the long poem; however, Bakhtin's opposition is not between the epic and the post-epical but between poetic discourse and the discourse of the novel (p. 286). In contrast, the evidence of this book suggests that the long poem may be fundamentally dialogic, a debate conducted round its own dissensions, and that such a debate is made more difficult to avoid by the inclusiveness which is the long poem's historical characteristic.

word "objected" has been used in the hope that some readers will take exception to its employment. We might reply that a binary disposition set up to question the unitary possibility is only technically to be described as binary. The terms of this particular dialectic include such prospects as the bottomless chess-game and the endless play of signifiers.[14] For our purposes it may even be symptomatic that the language used in these figures restrains the very indeterminacy the figures seek to formulate. There cannot be a poetics, even of the unfinished, to which the search for organization is not admitted. Once admitted, that search cannot be defeated since the defeat would not succeed in erasing purposiveness. It would merely invert the purpose for which the search was allowed. Instead of the assimilation of all actuality to a fully inclusive consciousness (as foreseen by Spenser and Milton) we would have the surrender of consciousness or its humiliated withdrawal from an actuality so dense that it not merely resists but repudiates interpretation. The intermediate area between these assimilations is the area occupied by what Adorno chose

[14] Endless play is a long-familiar idea in Hindu thought. It points to the exuberance of a creative energy, unconstrained by human attributions of purpose, responsible only to its own ongoing. The dehumanization said to be implicit in such understandings has been rebuked in Western thought and cited to establish the superior involvements of Western humanism; the alleged dehumanization is only a function of a scale of perception increasingly verified by every scientific advance. The consequence of endless play in a truly infinite cosmos is not at this point the minimizing of the human but the overdue questioning of homocentric arrogance.

We can speculate that the cosmic play is subtractive, the retirement of the uncircumscribed, the arch-mind contemplating or performing its own absence before itself. A minority interpretation of *Paradise Lost* VII, 168-73 supports this reading of the creation though not of an endless creation. Alternatively, we can speculate that the problematics of the play and therefore its aesthetic pleasures lie not in contemplating absence, but in maximizing presence within the forms of manifestation. On either understanding, play in the literary field would claim a significant relationship with cosmic play. In Derrida's understanding, on the other hand, play seems the ongoing admission of the inability to claim such a relationship.

to call Negative Dialectics—an area of contestation without prophecy or promises but not deprived of limited consolidations.[15] Understanding is fissured and the presence of the fissure is the safeguard of understanding rather than its betrayal. The meetings which take place across that fissure should be based upon or succeed in constituting a dialectic of difference rather than negation. At the same time there are restrictions placed upon openness—restrictions which maintain the possibility of form—because openness is to be thought of not simply as the result of a contest between equal and divergent forces but more fundamentally, as one of the contestants.

The previous chapters also seek to situate themselves on the ongoing encounter between a creating self and the developing otherness of a work which increasingly claims its autonomy from that self. Both forces in the engagement are changed by the engagement; neither can be absorbed by the other if the engagement is to continue. Although we can look at the engagement as a study in fruitless inter-subversion it seems at least as profitable to consider it as re-positioning within the fictive enclosure those acts of negotiation, resistance, and dialogue which characterize any deep encounter of the self with the world. The difference is that the collective self can be seen as increasingly threatened by its creation, as called upon to remake itself in the image of the social and technological forms which are its offspring. The poem, on the other hand, can be seen as threatened by its creator and as gallantly asserting its natural inchoateness against the tyranny of its logocentric parent. Yet even when the fictive valorizations reverse or redistribute those recognized in the real world, the nature of their engagement clearly remains responsive to forces outside as well as within the language theatre. The continuity of this engagement supports the previous chapters: it is a

[15] Theodor W. Adorno, *Negative Dialectics*, translated by E. B. Ashton, London, Routledge and Kegan Paul, 1973.

continuity they attempt to uncover in certain specific works in the succession of literature.

At some point in that succession it is apparent that the fragment must free itself from relationship to the whole, that it must develop a poetics of independence.[16] Disinheritance, exile, citizenship, retrieval, reinstatement, annexation to a final cause which closes the circle by the reconstitution of origin are all terms of literary politics which bespeak the fragment's colonial status, its dream of identity within the imperial perimeter. In moving towards the fragment's self-reliance, its right to significance without incorporation, it is, surprisingly, the Romantics who point the way rather than the main voices of the Pound era. In writing thus of a way I do not necessarily suggest that the way is desirable. A map is drawn, there are literary possibilities, and literature moves into those possibilities. It is the nature of creativeness to populate empty spaces. But the manner in which the possibilities are occupied and, perhaps more significantly, the language of occupation, reflect forces beyond the literary enclosure. This is not a time when collectivities offer fulfillment. It becomes steadily harder to discern the basis for creative membership of any whole political, economic, or administrative, with which we are likely to be confronted. As we face the proliferating stereotypes within which we are exhorted to find our future, Adorno's proposition that the whole is the false can seem

---

[16] According to Gilles Deleuze and Felix Guattari "We no longer believe in the myth of the existence of fragments that, like pieces of an antique statue, are merely waiting for the last one to be turned up, so that they may all be glued back together to create a unity that is precisely the same as the original unity. We no longer believe in a primordial totality that once existed, or in a final totality that awaits us at some given date . . . ," *Anti-Oedipus: Capitalism and Schizophrenia*, trans. Robert Hurley, Mark Seem, and Helen R. Lane, New York, Viking Press, 1977, p. 42. Unlike the authors, I do not argue for the triumph of the fragment. My point is only that if the forces of fragmentation are to contest fully those of systematization they must eventually do so on the basis of an independent, not a derived aesthetic.

considerably more than a means of engagement with Hegel. The primacy of the fragment, its givenness, its irreducibility, and its resistance to the manipulation that follows on decipherment are not propositions inappropriate to such a world.

Postscript

Rig-Veda X, 129

TRANSLATED BY CHANDRA RAJAN

om

Non-being was not, nor Being in the beginning;
The world was not, nor the heavens beyond;
What was covered? Where? What contained it?
And was there only water? mysterious, unfathomed?

Death was not, nor Immortality;
Of Night and Day there was no knowing,
No breath of air; by Itself the One breathed;
Other than It, indeed nothing whatever was.

Darkness was, by darkness concealed in the beginning;
Unformed water this whole Universe;
What lay hidden in the Void, impelled
By its own glow of consciousness, mightily,
Became manifest the One.

Desire, Creative Will, at first arose in the One,
The primeval seed it was of Consciousness.
The seers with wisdom, searching within,
Found the bond of Being in Non-Being.

Stretched across was this ray of light,
Was there truly a Below? truly, was there an Above?
Forces of Creation were there and majesty of Power,
Potentialities below, the Will above.

POSTSCRIPT

Who truly knows, who here can tell?
Where it was born, whence came this Creation?
After this outpouring only, appeared the Shining Ones;
Who then can know whence it arose!

This flow of Creation, how it arose,
Whether it was ordered or was not,
He, its Ruler, in the outermost space,
He alone knows, unless—He knows it not.

Index

313

Library of Congress Cataloging in Publication Data

Rajan, Balachandra.
The form of the unfinished.

Bibliography: p.
Includes index.
1. English poetry—History and criticism.
2. Unfinished books.   3. Poetics.   4. English
language—Versification. I. Title.
PR509.U53R3 1985   821'.009   84-42900
ISBN 0-691-06637-X (alk. paper)